WHILE WASHINGTON BURNED
THE BATTLE FOR FORT ERIE 1814

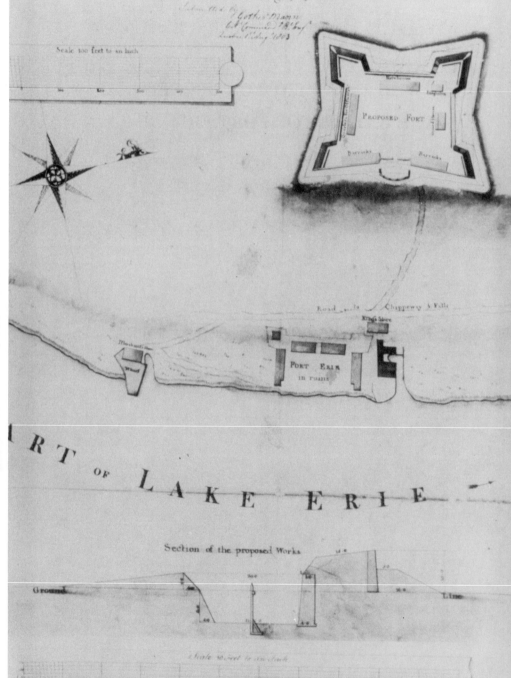

PLAN of the SITUATION of FORT ERIE

with the New Works & Buildings proposed *Vide Report of this Date*

Submitted by Gother Mann
Lt Col Commandg R. Engrs
Quebec 14 Aug 1803

Scale 100 feet to an inch

PROPOSED FORT

Barracks   Barracks

Road to the Chippewy & Falls

King's Store

FORT ERIE
in ruins

Wharf

PART OF LAKE ERIE

Section of the proposed Works

Ground   Line

Scale 10 feet to an inch

WHILE WASHINGTON BURNED
THE BATTLE FOR FORT ERIE 1814

The Nautical & Aviation Publishing Company of America
Baltimore, Maryland

Library of Congress Card Number: 92-50541

ISBN: 1-877853-18-6

Printed in the United States of America

Library of Congress Cataloging-in-Publication Data

Whitehorne, Joseph, 1943-
    While Washington Burned: The Battle for Fort Erie 1814 /by Joseph Whitehorne.

      p.   cm.
    Includes bibliographical references and index.
ISBN 1-877853-18-6
1. Fort Erie (Ont.)—history—Siege, 1814.
I. Title.
E356.E5W45 1992

973.5'2—dc20

Table of Contents

Preface   vii

Chapter 1—Overview and Background   1

Chapter 2—Plans and Operations   15

Chapter 3—Invasion and Retreat   27

Chapter 4— Siege I, In The Bag   41

Chapter 5—Siege II, Successful Defense   59

Chapter 6—Siege III, The Sortie   69

Chapter 7—Finale   83

L'Envoi   95

Annexes   99

Bibliography   195

Notes   209

Index   224

Preface

The War of 1812 between the United States and Great Britain is virtually an enigma to many Americans and also has been subjugated in British scholarship to the larger issues of the global conflicts of the Napoleonic era. It is somewhat better understood in Canada, where it is seen as the first of a series of experiences ultimately defining the Dominion as a separate nation. And yet, in many ways, the war also instilled a similar sense of identity for the United States. Prior to 1812, most Americans had remained focussed on European affairs. The United States was essentially an inferior adjunct of the Atlantic world, deeply concerned about preserving its republican form of government in a hostile monarchical environment. By the end of the war, Americans felt a new sense of confidence about their style of democracy and its ability to survive under stress. Many at the time called the two-year conflict a Second War of Independence. Having proven that the country could stand up to Britain and survive, the leadership in Washington was able to discard its fixation on Europe and turn to the development and exploitation of the interior of North America. U.S. arms had been sufficiently successful to fend off any British efforts to limit this continental growth. Thus, in this context, the War of 1812 was not a failure. Rather, it was the final act of the movement begun in 1775 that gave American citizens their sense of uniqueness and independence.

U.S. military events in the early phases of the war hardly could be objects of national pride. As the new republic blundered into war, it suffered several humiliating incidents, climaxing with the burning of Washington in 1814. Consequently, 20th Century Americans may be prone to view the war as something of an irrelevant fiasco, rather than as the psychological liberator its contemporaries considered it as well as a major influence on subsequent U.S. military tactics and policy.

Throughout the war, the bulk of the opposing forces deployed against each other at places along a huge front extending from Maine to Lake Superior. The points of strongest contact were along the St. Lawrence and Niagara rivers. The Niagara area, in particular, was a flash point, because of the forces' proximity to one another and its importance to controlling the Great Lakes communications routes. Both belligerents deployed their largest forces into the two river valleys, where they presumed that decisive military aims could be achieved. The British and Canadians believed they were fighting for the continued royal control of Canada. The Americans, on the other hand, after first coveting Canada, realized that ultimately they were defending against the seizure of U.S. territory and the imposition of British control in the Great Lakes—St. Lawrence regions. Today, while the images of Washington burning and the victory at New Orleans remain vivid, few can recall the events where most military activity occurred during the war. Nearly one-half of all casualties were reported in the Niagara Region, and one-quarter of all wartime deaths occurred there during the 1814 operations. The battles of Washington and New Orleans both involved hastily organized militia forces. And while militia men were active in the north, as well, the successes experienced there were achieved for the most part by well trained regulars and state volunteers. This fact explains the post-war disdain for militia amongst military thinkers and the growing conviction that national defense was dependent upon a standing army of regulars, supplemented by volunteers trained by regulars. Thus, it may be that the fighting along the northern borders—especially with regard to the events of the summer of 1814 along the Niagara River—gave birth to the modern regular army. Not only were the battles fought at Niagara sources of inspiration and pride, but also, they served as the training grounds for the generation of men who would lead the armies that would engage, eventually, in the Civil War. Many of the administrative and logistical lessons of the 1814 Niagara operations endured in some form into the 20th Century, as exemplified by the medical evacuation system.

The military errors committed at all operational levels further provided lessons, of things to avoid, in later conflicts. President James Madison, to his credit, resisted imposing unconstitutional measures in the emergency. However, he proved to be a weak commander-in- chief and not a good judge of the top men he selected for civilian and military positions. Both his secretaries of war proved inadequate. John Armstrong, appointed to replace the senile William Eustis in February 1813, was stubborn and meddled to excess in military matters best left to local commanders. The country was divided into nine, and later ten, geographical military districts, with each competing for resources. The War Department rarely compelled a district to cooperate with any other. The British, on the other hand, enjoyed a much more centralized system. Governor General Sir George Prevost held civil and military authority over all of British North America. He empowered his deputies in Upper and Lower Canada (modern Ontario and Quebec) with similar authority. Thus, strategies and resource allocations could be made efficiently and responsively, in part offsetting potentially greater American strengths—a capability demonstrated dramatically along the Niagara Frontier in 1814.

With family roots deep in the State of New York and in the American military, I always have been curious about the War of 1812. While most attention, particularly at the high school and college level, focuses on the causes of the war, very little has been devoted to the war's operations except possibly to passing comment about the burning of Washington or about Andrew Jackson's triumph at New Orleans. At an early age, I can recall my grandfather, an old soldier himself, remarking that the Battles of Chippawa and Lundy's Lane permanently altered the U.S. Army's self-image. These comments and the surviving letters of an ancestor who served on the Niagara frontier made me aware that there was more to learn about the war. While assigned as staff historian to the Secretary of the Army, it was my privilege to learn in part how much more.

In April 1987, workers discovered human remains on a construction site at Fort Erie, Ontario, Canada. The land on which they were found had been pasture prior to the 1940s; then occupied by a few small summer cottages. Progress caught up with the site in the 1980s and it was rezoned for numerous year-round residences. Fort Erie is located at the mouth of the Niagara River, opposite the city of Buffalo, New York. The rezoned building lots are on the shore, with a view of the city's skyline. The site in question was about 800 yards from restored Old Fort Erie, now a regional park. Both places were areas bitterly fought over in mid and late 1814, during the final campaigns of the War of 1812.

The discovery halted construction as local authorities tried to determine the status of the remains. Provincial officials viewed the site and determined that a full archaeological effort was necessary to learn the dimensions of the burial grounds and to establish the origins of its occupants. The city of Fort Erie hired a private archaeological firm from Toronto, which began a project that ultimately became a major international endeavor. The discovery of U.S. military artifacts among the remains prompted my assignment as historian to support the effort. My research provided new insight into medical and military operations of the 1812-14 period, as well as a much deeper personal understanding of the war.

While conducting my research, I learned that very little of the substantial amount of literature on the war dealt with any work resembling operational studies. Numerous general histories have been written over the years as have many specialized articles. Nearly all of them tantalized my curiosity more by what they did not say as by what they described. Supporting the archaeological project increased my interest in how the U.S. Army of 1812-14 functioned and how it operated under the stress of a campaign. The uniqueness of the Fort Erie operation, climaxing as it does in the only formal siege of the war, makes the subject additionally noteworthy.

This study is intended to add insight to a significant episode in U.S. history.

I am grateful to the many friends, colleagues, and librarians who have assisted me in the research and preparation of this work. The archival sources cited in the bibliography provide an indication of the number of people who have helped make this work possible. I would especially like to thank Michael Musick of the U.S. National Archives, Washington, D. C., for his help and interest. His familiarity with the Archives' holdings greatly shortened what could have been a life- long task. I also appreciate the support and help given me by Patrick Wilder of the Sackett's Harbor and Fort Ontario, New York State Historic Sites. Also, for his generous sharing of research, documents, and insights, I owe a special thank you to Donald E. Graves of the Historical Section of the Canadian Ministry of Defence, Ottawa. This work could not have been possible without him. Finally, I would like to express my deep appreciation for the superb typing support and computer work done by my long-suffering and tolerant wife, Ellen. The credit is yours, the errors are mine.

Joseph W. A. Whitehorne
Cedarville, Virginia
May 1991

Chapter 1

OVERVIEW AND BACKGROUND

The hostilities that erupted between the United States and Great Britain in June 1812 stemmed from a series of tensions that had built up over several years as a result of Napoleon's struggle for supremacy in Europe and Britain's struggle against him. U.S. maritime interests were caught between the equally offensive policies of the two belligerents. The Royal Navy assumed a dominant position to enforce Britain's policies, hence it became the focus of much American ire. Affronts to American sovereignty, such as the impressment of suspected British deserters from U.S. flag ships brought howls of rage from many political leaders. Tensions had risen to a high pitch in 1807, after HMS *Leopard* fired on and detained the USS *Chesapeake* off the coast of Virginia.

The image of a treacherous Great Britain persisted in the western part of the United States because of continued British reluctance to end support for former Indian allies now living in the Great Lakes region. The British wished to keep the natives as friendly as possible in case allies would be needed in the future to counter the population disparity between Canada and the United States. Every act of Indian hostility was attributed by the Americans to British treachery rather than judged on its own merits. Western politicians felt that war with England would end the Indian threat in the Old Northwest. Perhaps more importantly, it seemed to provide a golden opportunity to pluck the Canadas from the Crown and add vast amounts of land to the New Republic. President James Madison's administration was unable to control these pressures, ironically declaring war on 18 June at about the same time British

Orders in Council promised to end most of the abuses that were upsetting so many Americans.[1]

The U.S. military was not ready for war. The Navy was efficient but small. After several preliminary successes, it was suppressed by the Royal Navy, which then proceeded to blockade the U.S. coast. Significant naval action shifted thereafter to the Great Lakes. The U.S. Army was woefully inadequate in size and mobilization planning, and thus was forced to rely on newly raised regulars and levies of untrained volunteers and militiamen. British America was most vulnerable at Montreal, and its capture would cause all positions further inland to wither. Unfortunately for the Americans, the largest source of the most willing volunteers was the midwestern region. Consequently, the United States launched the first major campaign of 1812 against Fort Malden, opposite Detroit. Led by an elderly veteran of the Revolution, William Hull, the U.S. forces were handled quickly by British General Isaac Brock, who captured Detroit, as well as Hull's army, in August 1812. A few months later, on 13 October, Brock turned back an American probe against Queenston on the Niagara River, losing his life in the battle.

This initial engagement set the pattern of the war along the border. The Americans received little strategic direction or coordination from the War Department, while their forces continued to nibble timidly along the edges of British America. In November 1813, a potentially promising thrust up the St. Lawrence Valley toward Montreal was turned back at Crysler's Farm and Chateaugay. Earlier in the year, U.S. Forces experienced modest success capturing Fort George on the Niagara Frontier on 27 May, only to be thwarted by disasters at Stoney Creek and at Beaver Dams. The one salutary effect of this poor military performance was that the unsuccessful old veterans initially in charge soon were replaced by younger, abler, and more vigorous men. By 1814, the fighting would be harder and the American forces more efficient as a result, despite War Department directives that remained inadequate to the end. A great deal of the hardest fighting would be carried out on the Niagara Frontier, with much of the action hinging on Fort Erie.

On 3 July 1814, a force of about 4,000 Americans, under the command of Major General Jacob Brown, crossed the Niagara River from points near Buffalo and quickly captured the British fort and garrison at Fort Erie, Upper Canada. This move marked the opening of the most hotly contested campaign of the War of 1812. About 1,800 Americans and 2,400 British were killed or wounded during the next four months in a series of battles which would remain prominent in the U.S. military memory for generations. The campaign ranged the length of the Niagara frontier, with battles at Chippawa and Lundy's Lane and numerous skirmishes. Despite some tactical success, the Americans were forced back into Fort Erie by the end of July, fighting an arduous siege throughout August and September that was characterized by heavy casualties on both sides. The U.S. forces lingered at Fort Erie through October, finally abandoning the fort in early November, which ended the Niagara region's bloodiest campaign.

Fort Erie had been a military site since 1764, when the Senecas deeded the land to the Crown and Captain John Montresor built a small fort there to protect the ferry site from Black Rock and the road west along the Lake Erie shore to Detroit. It was the first permanent British fort built in what is now Ontario. In addition to guarding communications, the fort also was the debarking point for Lake Erie waterborne travellers. In the early years, it served as a depot for troops transiting to the western garrisons in the aftermath of Pontiac's rebellion, and continued to function more as a secure depot than as a fort because it had little capability to interdict the route or to offer a stout defense, if attacked.[2]

The fort remained very much an administrative backwater even during the American Revolution, when the bulk of the region's military activity focused on Fort Niagara to the north. The British retained control of the area after the war pursuant to a controversy over the terms of the 1783 Peace of Paris treaty. During this period, the Fort Erie garrison commander, Captain Thomas Powell, operated a trading post across the river at Buffalo Creek in conjunction with Cornelius Winney, one of the few Americans in the area. Powell later made efforts to bring in a group of Americans to run a saw mill at Scajaquada Creek north of Black Rock, the site of the ferry crossing. British authorities discouraged luring Americans into the area, and Powell was reprimanded for his lack of judgement. It was British policy, instead to attract as many of the displaced Iroquois tribesmen into the area as possible to help block white settlement.[3] For this reason, the British established the large Buffalo Creek Reserve in 1780.

All this changed as a result of the terms of the 1794 Jay Treaty, which required that the British forces surrender the American forts they were holding. Thus, on 11 July 1796, Captain Roger H. Sheaffe turned over Fort Niagara to U.S. troops, and British troops moved to establish themselves at Fort George and points along the west bank of the Niagara. Once more the river marked the line between two hostile powers, and underscored the need to strengthen the Fort Erie position, among others. New construction in 1779 and again in 1791 slightly shifted the fort's location which, because of its proximity to the lake shore, continued to sustain unsatisfactory levels of winter damage. Consequently, construction began in 1803 on a stronger fort of stone, situated on higher ground further inland from the earlier locations. The eastern side of the fort, with barracks built into the stone walls, was completed by 1807, and an earthen bastion in front of the east gate was added by 1810. However, little substantial work was done after 1807 on the western ap-

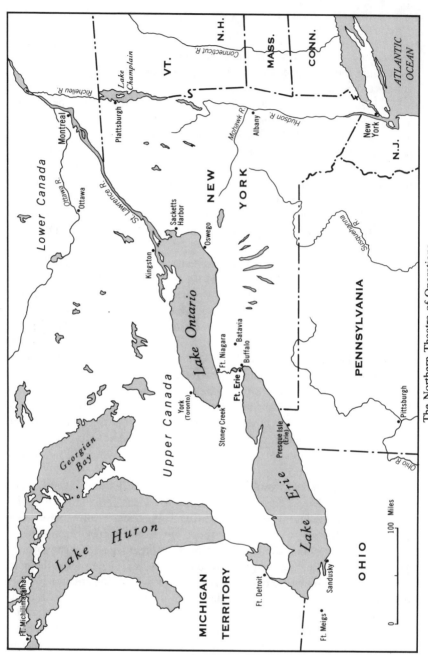

The Northern Theatre of Operations

proaches to the fort. In 1812, after the declaration of war, this defect was remedied, partially, with earthworks and a detached palisade.[4]

British authorities at Fort Erie learned of the declaration of war several days before their American counterparts. Seizing this advantage, a force from Fort Erie intercepted and captured on 27 June the salt-carrying sloop *Commencement*, owned by her captain, Peter H. Coit of Black Rock. The fort also resumed its role as an important communications link, as well as blocked the egress of U.S. ships held at Black Rock and at a small naval shipyard along Scajaquada Creek. To support this latter mission, the British established three earthwork batteries at key points along the river to the north of the fort.[5]

The buildup of U.S. land forces along the Niagara took several months before it became a threat. Consequently, Major General Isaac Brock, the British commander in Upper Canada, was able to move the bulk of his small force westward to deal with the U.S. threat at Detroit, and then return in time to confront the slowly growing American force in the Niagara area. New York Militia general Stephen Van Rensselaer had added a force of nearly 2,000 militiamen and 1,000 regulars in Lewiston to his command of 1,400 regulars at Fort Niagara and 2,200 troops at Buffalo. A mixed force of British regulars and militia manned strong points along the west bank of the river. Brock requested Indian agent Major John Norton to bring 600 of his Iroquois charges to reinforce the defensive forces along the Niagara. They roved from Fort Erie to Fort George, wherever the threat of invasion seemed greatest, and conducted patrols on both sides of the river to learn about American activities. The British judged the most likely crossing points as being somewhere along the seven miles between Queenston and Fort Niagara, or in the Black Rock—Fort Erie area.[6]

Events occurred in rapid succession beginning early in October 1812. A small army brig, the *Detroit*, had been captured at the fall of Detroit itself and was used along with another captured ship, the *Caledonia*, to transport U.S. prisoners of war eastward. Upon landing, the Americans were marched along the west bank of the Niagara to Fort George in view of their comrades on the opposite shore. From there, they would embark for Kingston and, eventually, Montreal. The ships were moored off Fort Erie under the protection of its guns. Their presence was noted by Lieutenant Jesse D. Elliot, the officer commanding the U.S. naval yard on Scajaquada Creek.[7]

Lieutenant Elliot formed a mixed force of soldiers and sailors to capture the British ships. The raiders left the American shore at 0300 on 9 October and swiftly commandeered the surprised vessels. Their captors allowed the ships to drift northward in the current. Sailing Master Thomas Watts assisted by army Captain Nathan Towson and the men of his artillery detachment managed to get the *Caledonia* to Black Rock, where the U.S. battery stationed there provided cover. Elliot was not so lucky with his prize. British batteries

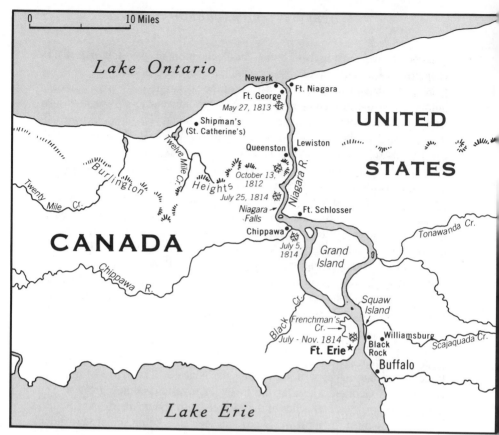

The Niagara Frontier

established north of Fort Erie opened fire on the *Detroit*, while the current swept her along until she grounded on Squaw Island. A detachment from the British 49th Regiment rowed over and briefly recaptured her. However, the unit was forced to abandon the ship when U.S. Lieutenant Colonel Winfield Scott sent a larger force to evict the British. The Americans then destroyed the *Detroit*, burning her to the water line. The more fortunate *Caledonia* survived to become the first ship in the U.S. Lake Erie fleet.[8]

Meanwhile, General Van Rensselaer slowly began engaging the British with his militiamen and regulars. His strained relations with Brigadier General Alexander Smyth, the senior regular soldier in the Niagara region, however, seriously impaired any hopes of success. General Smyth commanded the troops in the Buffalo area and vigorously objected to his militia counterpart's plan to stage a crossing with all available forces at Queenston. Instead, Smyth advocated an assault in the Fort Erie area. Van Rensselaer correctly objected to this scheme, because Fort Erie was one of the major points of British strength. In the end, Smyth's arrogance and the generals' mutual antipathy prevented Van Rensselaer from enlisting the troops at Fort Niagara or Buffalo during his planned assault.[9]

A first attempt to cross the river on 11 October was thwarted by bad weather. A second try on 13 October met with greater success. Queenston Heights was defended by an artillery battery and three companies of the 49th Regiment as well as some Lincoln militiamen. Other British guns defended the river bank north to Fort George, whose 500-man garrison was poised to support any threatened part of the line. The Americans landed on a dark, rainy morning against sharp resistance. Eventually, a party led by Captain John Wool captured the British battery on the Heights. General Brock had rushed from Fort George and was killed trying to rally a force to recapture it, as was his deputy, Lieutenant Colonel John McDonald, in a later try. The successful 600-man U.S. first wave, now led by Lieutenant Colonel Winfield Scott, was not reinforced by the reluctant New York Militia still on the U.S. shore. Thus, when the Fort George garrison under Colonel Roger Sheaffe counterattacked, the Americans were surrounded and forced to surrender. The U.S. disaster resulted in the transfer of command from Van Rensselaer to Smyth, but not before the hapless New Yorker and Colonel Sheaffe had agreed to a brief truce, which lasted until 19 November.[10]

The bombastic General Smyth earnestly demonstrated his ineptitude. After peppering his troops with a series of boastful proclamations, he launched a hesitant probe against Fort Erie, much as the careful Colonel Sheaffe had expected he would. Two columns of boats set out from Black Rock in the early morning darkness of 28 November. These were intended as the vanguard for a larger invasion. One column under Colonel William Winder headed for the battery positions opposite Black Rock. The other column under Lieutenant

Colonel Charles G. Boerstler aimed to capture the bridge at Frenchman's Creek, which would isolate Fort Erie from British reinforcements coming from Chippawa. Colonel Boerstler's unit was fired upon by a force under Lieutenant Colonel Cecil Bisshopp and turned back when two of its boats sustained damage from artillery fire. Colonel Winder's column enjoyed somewhat greater success, surprising the militia at the ferry site and capturing a nearby battery and barracks. U.S. troops turned away a militia force assisted by a detachment from the 49th Regiment led by Lieutenant Thomas Lamont, but not before capturing many of its personnel, including the wounded lieutenant. The main body of Winder's force then withdrew to its landing site with the prisoners. However, a group of soldiers and sailors led by Captain William King, 15th Infantry, continued toward Fort Erie. This group, in turn, was overwhelmed by defenders from the fort, who also forced the remainder of Winder's column to withdraw.[11]

Meanwhile, General Smyth's main body had arrived by boat from Buffalo at Black Rock, where it was disembarked and given its dinner. Smyth sent a message to Colonel Bisshopp demanding Fort Erie's surrender. Bisshopp, secure in the knowledge that the remainder of the 49th and Major Norton's Indians were en route from Chippawa, rejected Smyth's peculiar demand. The main American force then marched back to Buffalo with nothing to show for its efforts. Smyth made one more abortive attempt to cross the river early on the cold morning of 1 December. However, at daylight, he recalled his waiting men from their boats positioned along the U.S. shore, and the disgruntled troops lost all semblance of discipline. Soon thereafter Smyth fought a duel with New York Militia Brigadier General Peter B. Porter, who had rightfully criticized his leadership. General Porter was a New York State politician and businessman who had been long associated with the development of the Niagara frontier. Entering Congress in 1809, he was an ardent advocate of internal improvements and a leading member of the War Hawk group where he spoke for the annexation of Canada. He entered military service in 1812 as New York Quartermaster General and was serving as a volunteer under Smyth's command. The following summer, Porter assumed command of a brigade of militia, volunteers, and native troops, which he led successfully until the end of the war.[12] Smyth was relieved a short time later and faded into well-merited obscurity. This incident ended operations for 1812, and both sides settled into quarters for the long Niagara winter.[13]

The area remained quiet until February 1813, when the British called up the militia around Fort Erie to resist a predicted U.S. attack across the Niagara ice, which failed to materialize. In March, Major Norton and his Indians were recalled from their winter quarters around Brantford when reports from U.S. deserters intimated an imminent U.S. attack upon the fort and its adjacent batteries. Defensive preparations were completed by the 17th, but the U.S.

attack that day consisted of only a six-hour artillery bombardment, which caused few casualties. Norton observed that the 500-man garrison suffered little, but that the British counter fire was equally ineffective.[14]

The situation along the frontier changed radically on 27 May, when U.S. Forces launched a successful attack on Fort George. Under the general supervision of Major General Henry Dearborn, Captain Oliver H. Perry and Colonel Scott executed a skillful amphibious landing. The Americans assaulted the lakeshore north of the fort and pressed the defenders through the village of Newark, with the help of gunfire from the fleet and from Fort Niagara. British Brigadier General John Vincent skillfully preserved most of the defending force with a well-managed withdrawal to the south and west. The British situation might have proven more critical had not the senior U.S. officer on the ground, Major General Morgan Lewis, called off Scott's aggressive advance after Fort George itself had been taken. As a result, General Vincent was able to gather the bulk of his force at Beaver Dams and continue his withdrawal in the direction of Burlington Heights.[15]

General Vincent subsequently ordered the remainder of his forces along the Niagara shore to pull back, as well. Thus, units at Queenston, Chippawa, and Fort Erie all surrendered their holds. The withdrawal in the Fort Erie area was covered by fire from the thinly manned Fort Erie batteries, supported by the Lincoln Militia, which demolished as much of the fort as they could in the process. The destruction included the warehouses and dwellings belonging to Stamford merchant Hugh Alexander, which he had built adjacent to the fort. The 9th U.S. Infantry, commanded by Lieutenant Colonel James P. Preston, crossed the river from Black Rock to occupy the smoldering ruins. They remained at the Fort until 9 June, when they returned to the U.S. shore, destroying what little was left before their departure. Preston's brief occupation allowed the U.S. ships trapped at Black Rock and at Scajaquada Creek to join the U.S. Lake Erie fleet. The departure of the Americans left the fort unoccupied until the British returned on 12 December 1813.[16]

The Americans' squandered their initial advantage in a series of inept westward thrusts, each resulting in disaster. The first American probe was defeated at Stoney Creek in a 5 June evening engagement, during which American Generals Wilder and Chandler were captured. This meeting encouraged the British to move closer to Fort George. An American counterthrust was brilliantly handled at Beaver Dams on 24 June, resulting in a large part of the U.S. force again falling into British hands. These actions cornered the invaders in the general vicinity of Fort George. Further action devolved to a series of raids and counterraids, wherein civilian property was the main target. During this period an unsavory group of New York Militia Cavalry, known as the "40 thieves," led by Buffalonian Cyrenius Chapin harassed the countryside. Another force, the Canadian Volunteers, authorized by General Dearborn, consisted of Canadian turncoats who carried out various scouting and military police duties, settling many a personal score along the way.[17] The Volunteers were led by a resident of Newark, the former Upper Canada politician Joseph Willcocks.

The British continued to keep the Americans contained and off balance, orchestrating a series of raids across the Niagara and against the Fort George perimeter. A party of Lincoln Militia, led by Lieutenant Colonel Thomas Clark, successfully attacked Fort Schlosser on 5 July and made off with quantities of stores. A few days later, on 11 July, Colonel Bisshopp led a mixed force of 240 regulars and militiamen against the U.S. Navy Yard on Scajaquada Creek. The British succeeded in destroying the dockyards and buildings while again carrying off quantities of stores. A counterattack of New York Militia and Senecas from the Buffalo Creek Reservation, all led by General Porter, vigorously turned back the British troops. Bisshopp, long a mainstay of the British command, was mortally wounded, dying five days later at Lundy's Lane. This assult marked the first time native Americans supported U.S. forces in the Niagara area. It would not be the last.[18]

The U.S. garrisons at Forts George and Niagara were gradually reduced over the autumn, as reinforcements were sent from there to support operations along the St. Lawrence River. By December 1813, the number of U.S. defenders had been reduced to a few hundred demoralized men under the inexperienced and equally demoralized militia general, George McClure. The American situation encouraged British Colonel John Murray to deploy the 8th Regiment and some militia and Indians to the 40 Mile Creek to check the U.S. raiders. When General McClure learned one of his outposts had made contact with this force, he panicked. Although the British were 20 miles away, he decided to abandon Fort George and all positions on the west bank of the Niagara. On 10 December, in the course of the evacuation, McClure had Colonel Willcocks and his men torch the village of Newark with little warning. The order destroyed 80 buildings and rendered about 400 people homeless during a blizzard.[19]

The British retaliated quickly under the leadership of Lieutenant General Gordon Drummond, the newly arrived senior officer in Upper Canada. General Drummond was a moderately experienced soldier, who had entered the British Army in 1789 as an ensign in the Royal Scots. He was promoted rapidly, earning by 1794 the rank of lieutenant colonel and commanding the 8th Regiment in the Low Countries. Drummond later led his regiment on campaigns in the West Indies, Minorca, and Egypt. From 1805 to 1807, he served as a major general, division commander, again in the West Indies. In 1806, he was posted to Canada, where he was assigned as deputy to Governor General Sir George Prevost. Drummond eventually assumed the duties of the senior crown military and civil official in Upper Canada, replacing the lamented Isaac Brocks' successor. He proved himself an active, involved leader.[20]

General Drummond quickly approved a plan proposed by Colonel Murray. On the snowy night of 18 December, Murray led a force across the Niagara River in boats hauled overland from Burlington. By 0500 the next morning, his men had captured Fort Niagara with relatively few British casualties. Brigadier General Phineas Riall crossed from Queenston as soon as the fort was secured with 500 men from the 1st and 42d Regiments and 500 natives. Before Riall recrossed the river, Lewiston and every settlement between Fort Niagara and Tonawanda Creek had been burned. General Drummond then moved his headquarters to Chippawa and resumed his plans to neutralize the U.S. shore.[21]

The attack left American defenses in chaos and General McClure discredited. His replacement, militia Brigadier General Amos Hall, did not assume overall command until 26 December. General Hall had less than 2,000 militia to defend the Black Rock—Buffalo area, many of them more worried about their families than they were about making a valiant defense. The British struck again on the night of 28-29 December. General Riall landed two miles north of Black Rock, with about 600 regulars and 150 native troops. Hall confronted them with his full force, advancing along Guide Board Road (modern North Street) until Hall's men were stopped and mostly scattered by the better disciplined British. The redcoats captured the bridge across Scajaquada Creek as well as a nearby battery (the "Sailors' Battery"). Nearly 900 British reinforcements crossed from Fort Erie, reoccupied since 12 December, to Black Rock under the protection of guns re-established on the old battery positions. New York Militiaman Chapin and a few die-hards manned an artillery piece at what is now Shelton Square, engaging the British as they advanced down what is now Niagara Avenue. Chapin, although concerned about his record of raiding, surrendered along with his crew when their gun dismounted from its own recoil. By this time the American defenders had lost all cohesion and the area was at the mercy of the British. Buffalo and Black Rock were torched on 31 December and 1 January, and the British withdrew to the river's west bank, retaining only Fort Niagara on the U.S. side. Western New York was in a panic. Newark had been avenged in spades.[22]

A much shaken force of New York militiamen slowly filtered back and took up positions around Fort Niagara and along the U.S. river bank. Under their dubious protection, the devastated village of Buffalo began to make a remarkable revival. By May 1814, it boasted three taverns, four stores, 12 shops, 23 houses and 30 to 40 other commercial and farm structures. It also served as a center for thriving lumber and brickmaking businesses, which would make valuable contributions to future military operations. Rebuilding proceeded at

Fort Erie with equal vigor. The fort was restored sufficiently to house more than 200 men, while at least three heavy guns were placed within its limits. By early summer 1814, Fort Erie was considered fully capable of defending itself and surely would be an early target of any American offensive, if a sufficient force could be gathered.[23]

Chapter 2

PLANS AND OPERATIONS

The main U.S. forces in the 9th Military District, which comprised Vermont and the area of New York state above Newburgh, had shifted eastward in late 1813 to support Major General James Wilkinson's inept operations along the St. Lawrence River. Following the defeats at Crysler's Farm and Chateaugay in November, the U.S. Army established itself near French Mills (now Fort Covington), where it remained idle in inhospitable, wintry camps from 13 November to February 1814. The effects of General Drummond's raid along the Niagara River eventually caused Secretary of War Armstrong to direct a deployment in defensive positions all along the frontier. His orders once more shifted American forces away from a strong effort in the St. Lawrence area.[1]

Accordingly, Major General Jacob Brown moved on 13 February with 2,000 men to Sacketts Harbor to augment its defenses. The remainder of the command's force marched to the Plattsburgh area, where General Wilkinson soon after led it on the abortive 30 March operations against La Colle Mill. Wilkinson finally was relieved on 24 March and replaced by Major General George Izard. Izard was not, however, placed in command of all the troops in the 9th Military District. Secretary Armstrong preferred instead to coordinate the activities of Generals Brown and Izard himself. As a consequence, the so-called Left (Brown's) and Right (Izard's) divisions of the district operated almost independently of one another.[2]

In the meantime, General Brown, positioned at Sacketts Harbor, received an order from Secretary Armstrong on 28 February to attack Kingston. Brown had migrated to Jefferson County, New York, as a young man where he had risen to prominence as an entrepreneur, farmer, and land speculator. He was a state militia brigadier general in 1812, distinguishing himself in several engagements. His defense of Sacketts Harbor in May 1813 earned him an appointment in the regular army and promotion to major general in January 1814. Brown was an aggressive, engaging leader, but he could also be stubborn and had a limited sense for technical and strategic matters.[3]

Armstrong's order was cautiously worded and included a second directive, authorizing Brown to send substantial forces to the Niagara area if that course seemed more feasible. Although Secretary Armstrong was focussed on Kingston, his directives were so confusing that Brown and his naval counterpart at the harbor, Commodore Isaac Chauncey, selected the Niagara alternative. Commodore Chauncey did not believe the Navy was strong enough to support an attack on Kingston. Thus, what the oblique Armstrong had intended as a screen to mask his main intent was on the way to becoming the 9th District's main effort for 1814.[4]

Soon, General Brown had 2,000 troops on the road heading west. He had gotten no further than Batavia on 21 March when discussions with his second-in-command, Brigadier General Edmund P. Gaines, began to give him second thoughts. General Gaines correctly interpreted the Secretary's Niagara inclosure to the Kingston attack orders and suggested that his commander's actions might not be what the War Department had intended. Brown hurried back to Sacketts Harbor to discuss the orders with Commodore Chauncey once more. The session with the cautious sailor again convinced Brown that he had the option to shift his strength to the Niagara. Brown understood that any move against Kingston required support from the Navy, which Chauncey would not guarantee, thus Niagara seemed to him the only possible alternative. Accordingly he allowed the troop movements to continue. Secretary Armstrong, somewhat nonplussed at the turn of events, yielded to Brown's actions, saying he was mistaken but perhaps "Good consequences are sometimes the result of mistakes.[5]

The marching column was joined near Buffalo on 24 March by newly appointed Brigadier General Winfield Scott. Scott had left Fort George the previous October for duty in the St. Lawrence operations. After a brief stay in Washington, he spent the first months of 1814 in Albany, coordinating supplies and militia call-ups in support of the forthcoming campaign. Brown knew Scott was technically better qualified than he was. Consequently, he had no qualms about leaving the troops in Buffalo under Scott's control when he returned to Sacketts Harbor on 20 April. Both Brown and Armstrong wanted to assure the harbor's safety, and requested another militia draft to reinforce its 1,500 man garrison.[6]

Despite this activity, the War Department still had not articulated an overall strategy for the 1814 campaign season. Secretary Armstrong presented to the president on 30 April a concept based on the assumption that control of Lake Ontario in 1814 would be beyond U.S. capabilities. Consequently, the best he hoped for was to use Lake Erie, which the United States did control, thanks to Captain Perry's victory the previous year, to secure Detroit and, possibly, to gain control of a portion of the Niagara Peninsula. If the U.S. Navy by chance was able to assert itself on Lake Ontario, the troops in the Niagara area then could be used against Kingston. The successful 6 May British raid on Oswego underscored again the ineffectiveness of the Navy, as far as Armstrong was concerned. It seemed to him that the alternate represented by the U.S. force at Buffalo would be the better choice. Armstrong envisioned that seizing the Niagara area would lead to the capture of York, cutting off the British hinterland while rendering Kingston vulnerable to assaults from east and west.[7]

The discussion of these plans coincided with the collapse of the fighting in France and with the advent of the British capability to reinforce substantially their forces in Canada. Although Secretary Armstrong was aware of these changing circumstances, he was unable to secure a speedy decision. President Madison's cabinet failed to react until 7 June. The approved plan directed the U.S. effort not only against the Niagara area, but also toward the far Northwest, despite Armstrong's protest. The president and Secretary of the Navy William E. Jones had added a scheme to operate against the British posts on Lake Huron, Forts Michilimackinac and St. Joseph. This latter concept diverted nearly 1,000 troops under Colonel George Croghan with their shipping away from Buffalo and reduced General Brown's capability to deploy and support his force.[8]

Curiously, the plan also implied U.S. Navy control over Lake Ontario could be achieved after all so that General Brown's operations would be assured of success. In fact, the strategic success of the whole operation depended on Navy cooperation. Based on his directives from Washington, Brown assumed Commodore Chauncey understood his role. Unfortunately, the requirement was never made clear to the naval commander. Brown wrote Chauncey on 21 June requesting the fleet's presence at the mouth of the Niagara by 10 July. He also requested that Chauncey transport the 1st Rifle Regiment from Sacketts Harbor at that time as reinforcements. These developments seemed contradictory to earlier expectations and clearly put a burden on Chauncey to produce at an earlier date. In fact, the commodore did not appear until 4 August, long after he could have made a decisive contribution.[9]

It was further assumed by the American planners that General Brown would be able to gather a sufficient number of troops to secure both sides of the Niagara and to capture Burlington and York. The optimum figure was 5,000 regulars and 3,000 militiamen and volunteers. As it was, he never was able to assemble more than 3,500 men from both categories in his command. An expected influx of recruits at Buffalo never materialized in part because of Colonel Croghan's requirements further west. Thus General Scott trained what he called "skeletons" of regiments, while a few reinforcements trickled in.[10]

General Brown returned from Sacketts Harbor on 7 June to monitor the final preparations proceeding under the able General Scott. Rather than keeping his force idle, Armstrong suggested to Brown that he use it to capture Fort Erie as an easy morale raiser. Brown assumed that this suggestion was a green light to launch his campaign, as well as an indication that the Navy would do its part. Brown counted on a fairly quick link with the U.S. Navy on Lake Ontario. He recognized that he otherwise could not sustain his force for a prolonged campaign, as Buffalo was too remote and insufficient ground transport was available. Brown favored crossing the Niagara at Fort Erie to open the campaign, because at that point he could be assured of quickly moving sufficient forces and heavy equipment, despite the relative scarcity of boats. He intended to follow the Niagara north to Queenston Heights, then move against either Fort George or Burlington, as the situation allowed. Secretary Armstrong favored making the first move against Fort Erie for the more prosaic reason that it promised an easy victory.[11]

British planners were equally busy and perhaps, more coherent in the spring of 1814. Napoleon's surrender in April led the government in London to inform Governor General Sir George Prevost that it planned to reinforce his command as quickly as possible. The British campaign plan, however, was not completed until early June, and Prevost was not aware of it fully until July. The overriding strategic objectives were to protect Canada as effectively as possible and to achieve control over key U.S. land areas so as to enhance the British position at any future peace conference. Specifically, in the north, plans were made to control Northern Maine, the Detroit area, Lake Champlain, and the area around Fort Niagara. Elsewhere, preparations began to attack Washington and the Chesapeake area and to close the mouth of the Mississippi River at New Orleans.[12]

The British sent more than 10,000 fresh troops to Canada. A first wave of 3,127 delivered in July was followed by four brigades totaling 14 regiments. These brigades came from the Duke of Wellington's experienced victors over Napoleon. Units arriving in the first wave included the Royal Scots (1st Regiment), the 90th Regiment coming from duty in the West Indies, and the 6th and 82d Regiments from France. These deployments allowed the gradual westward shift of British manpower to confront General Brown's Niagara buildup. Local British strategy entailed retaining naval dominance of Lake

Ontario, while achieving a sufficient land force in the Niagara area to deal with Brown. General Drummond placed his forces between York and Fort Niagara, with most of his strength deployed at points along the river frontier. His strategy called for adequate garrisons to be maintained at Forts Niagara and George, while other forces on the peninsula were placed so they could deploy as a mobile defense against U.S. attacks. By the end of June, Drummond had shifted the 103d Regiment from Kingston to Burlington while also deploying the Glengarry Light Infantry from Burlington to York as additonal back-up. The Glengarries were a fencible regiment raised in 1812 from amongst immigrant highland Scots in Canada. Many of the regiment's members were veterans of previous military service and almost all were Catholics. First led by the famous Colonel George "Red" MacDonnell, the unit was regarded as a well-trained and highly effective.[13]

The task of keeping enough British troops concentrated to face General Brown's main force while carrying out other defense responsibilities was formidable, as indicated by a series of successful U.S. raids along the Lake Erie shore. For example, attacks launched on 14 May at Port Dover and again on 19 May at Port Talbot by the Erie, Pennsylvania, garrison caused considerable damage. The American attackers seemed to be able to move at will throughout the area, destroying property and carrying off persons suspected of aiding the British war effort.[14]

The 8th (King's) Regiment was garrisoned at Fort Erie and along the Niagara shore throughout the spring until June 1814 when high numbers of sick and deserters necessitated a withdrawal to York for rest. By then, most of the men who remained in the garrison came from the recently deployed 100th Regiment. General Drummond assigned the command of the frontier district to Brigadier General Phineas Riall, a brave, choleric Anglo-Irishman with limited combat experience. General Riall had obtained a commission at age 19 in the 92d Regiment in 1794 and rose rapidly in grade to brevet lieutenant colonel in 1800. He led brigade-sized units in the West Indies in 1809-10 on several expeditions against French held islands. Riall was made a major general in June 1813 and was assigned to Canada that September.[15]

General Riall held 600 men of the 41st Regiment at Fort Niagara, while elements of the Royal Scots (1st) Regiment defended Fort George. That regiment and troops from the 100th held strong points along the river southward to Fort Erie. An especially important site was at Chippawa. Each strong point also had men from the Lincoln Militia assigned to it. A detachment from the 19th Light Dragoons and two troops of provincial dragoons roved the entire front as did groups of Major Norton's Indians. By the end of June, General Drummond had about 2,800 officers and men at the Niagara front with another 1,800 staged close by to the west. The British seemed reasonably well-prepared to deal with the growing American threat.[16]

This threat came from a force made formidable, in large measure, by the efforts of General Scott. While General Brown tended to the defense of Sacketts Harbor from 20 April to 7 June, Scott's vigorous training programs transformed the troops in Buffalo into the best force the United States fielded during the war. Scott's achievement shaped the nature and character of the little army that crossed the Niagara and later came under siege at Fort Erie.

As late as 1814, no standard training period for recruits, nor any policy for unit training existed, largely because of a lack of initiative on the part of many senior commanders. More serious was the absence of any standard drill manuals. Those which were available, William Duane's *Handbook for Infantry* (1813) and Alexander Smyth's *Regulations for the Field Exercises...of the Infantry* (1813), both based on French manuals, were confusing and incomplete. The 9th Military District tried to compensate for this deficiency by declaring Steuben's *Bluebook*, first published in 1778, as the standard. The works of Smyth and Steuben proved valuable in standardizing camp activities. However, General Scott preferred using the original French system "cribbed" by Duane and Smyth and available in translation, *Rules and Regulations for the Field Exercises of the French Infantry* (1803). In his memoirs, Scott says he trained first his officers, then had them train the men. (This point is questionable since no orders creating officers' squads, can be found and considering that his subordinates would have been exposed to the drill system in some form from Duane and Smyth.)[17]

General Scott initiated on 22 April an increasingly vigorous training program as soon as the troops had settled into camp in the Flint Hill area north of Buffalo.[18] The program would last the full ten weeks before the troops deployed. Scott required daily battalion and company drills—personally conducting some, and each Sunday he conducted a full field inspection of the entire force. Scott's success in training depended on having a solid base of human talent. The troops he began with were relatively well-trained already, and their officers were sympathetic to Scott's goals. The quality of the troops may be reflected in the fact that General Brown took all three of his inspectors general—the staff officers charged with training oversight, among other things—with him to Sacketts Harbor. The move surely reflected the views of Brown and Scott that the training weakness really lay in Brown's command.[19]

The hard work greatly improved the overall quality of leadership as well. Experienced officers, such as the newly arrived Major Thomas Jesup, 25th Infantry, needed little urging to drill their men for extended periods. Major Jesup was himself well-qualified and kept his men hard at it for many seven- to ten-hour days. He later recalled, "The consequence was that when we took the field in July, every corps maneuvered in action, and under the enemy's artillery, with the accuracy of parade."[20]

By early May, the entire duty day was devoted to drill. Regimental commanders were expected to supervise a minimum of four hours of squad and platoon drill each morning. Emphasis was placed on mass movements and developing, instinctively, the desired pace and cadence.[21] Scott made it clear that he expected everyone to participate in the drills, regardless of special duties or commitments, such as those of quartermaster and paymaster.

An inspection on 8 May by one of the assistant division inspectors general, Major Azor Orne who had just returned from the Harbor, indicated improvements in the regiments' capabilities. Individual weapons were found in excellent condition, and the men slowly were being issued haversacks as General Scott had directed in early April. The big problem, especially in the 9th and 11th infantry regiments, was the condition of the men's clothing.[22] The situation was so bad that Scott announced to the troops on 8 May that he was making every exertion'' to procure sufficient cloth to have uniforms made for all the men who needed them. He encouraged the units to make up in drill and discipline what they lacked in appearance.

Supply procedures continued to be tightened throughout May and June. Units were directed to use the system outlined in Smyth's regulations as a guide for marking and numbering clothing and unit equipment. Scott desired the system to be standard throughout the division. At the end of May, he was compelled to prohibit the use of hospital tents in headquarters and guard details. Surgeons' requirements for medicines, hospital furniture, and surgical equipment also were monitored to assure that necessities were being met. The inspectors general had discovered that the doctors had been reporting what was on hand to the apothecary general, but not stating their needs.

By early June, the drill schedule had become even more demanding and increasingly sophisticated. The men received added instruction in the firing motions using three ranks, and the drilling schedule was expanded further. At reveille, sunrise, the troops were expected to turn out under arms to perform squad and company drill for about two hours until breakfast. Following a short break, drill continued until dinner at about 1200. Then at 1500, the entire division fell out for battalion drill which lasted until 1900. The men then ate supper and enjoyed free time until lights out at 2100. General Scott, alone, determined if weather conditions merited any amendments to this schedule. Volunteer units were subjected to the same regimen after they had joined the command.

On about 20 June, General Scott organized his brigade into standard size units for these afternoon training drills. Ten uniform companies were formed from the 11th Infantry (four companies), and the 9th and 25th Infantries (three companies each). Once gathered in their regimental areas, the companies were mustered into a drill battalion, organized by the date of rank of their captains, regardless of regiment. This composite battalion then was wheeled into columns of companies, the companies made roughly equal in size, and then divided into two platoons each. Scott and the field officers then took turns, hour after hour, drilling this nearly perfectly sized regiment. The officers gained considerably more experience conducting such large unit drill. The men, in turn, became accustomed to taking orders from officers outside their own units. These developments proved most valuable in the forthcoming campaign. Scott was pleased with the progress made, commenting, "They began to perceive why they had been made to fag so long at the drill of the soldier, the company, and the battalion. Confidence, the dawn of victory, inspired the whole line."[23]

Each infantry company had been required on 29 May to designate one of its better privates as a pioneer. In addition, each regiment named a corporal to be in charge of these privates whenever they were away from their companies. Those selected were exempted from their companies' extra duties so they could train. General orders specified that they would carry "proper tools," such as saws, spades, and axes. These were "handsomely cased" in leather and carried in leather slings over the shoulder. The pioneers wore a linen apron, which extended from neck to knee. At regimental drills, the corporals positioned themselves with the regimental staff while the privates stood to the center rear of their companies. When General Brown's force became besieged in Fort Erie in August and September, the improvements in the fortifications were made by infantry work parties under the direction of these pioneer soldiers, supervised by the few engineer officers. Their authority extended over any soldiers assigned to them, regardless of regimental affiliation.

As the training continued, General Scott and his fellow brigadier, General Eleazer W. Ripley, continued to press the regimental leaders to enforce division policies, frequently insisting on full participation at drills and on the officers' presence at reveille. Scott intuitively connected the health of the men with the sanitation of the camp. Smyth's regulations were cited again as a guide for properly policing the encampments. The men were required to bathe three times a week, "in the lake, not in the creek," and tents were expected to be struck the first fair day after every rain. Special stress was placed on the quality and cleanliness of food preparation. An officer was required to inspect the food before every meal, and even salted meats were expected to be cooked.

Equipment issue was accelerated by the last week of June, with most units receiving everything necessary. Orphan units were attached to one of the regiments to ensure they received adequate supplies. For example, when the companies of the 22d Infantry under Captain Sampson L. King arrived on 30 June, they were attached to the 9th Infantry where Major Henry Leavenworth supervised the new units' proper supply and equipping. By 3 July, the companies were at the same levels as earlier arriving units, with no serious shortages. These incoming units posed a major supply problem for General Scott's quartermaster, Captain John G. Camp. Colonel James Fenton of the 5th Pennsylvania Volunteers, for instance, wrote ahead from Erie, Pennsylvania, to warn Scott that the quality and sufficiency of his men's firearms and flints were inadequate for a campaign. Fenton wanted Scott to know that the Pennsylvanians would have to draw additional weapons, and announced further that his regiment had no rations contractor and, consequently, would have to impose itself on the resources available at Buffalo. Fenton's 3 May letter, incidentally, was Scott's first notion that the 5th Pennsylvania was being assigned to Brown's Division.[24]

The clothing promised earlier by General Scott arrived on 23 June. The uniforms were made of grey cloth, because of a shortage of the standard blue color. Final requisitions were based on a series of intensive inspections conducted by the division inspectors general.[25] All personnel regardless of rank turned out in as complete a uniform as possible to include the new knapsacks. These were expected to contain one shirt, one pair of summer pantaloons, one pair of shoes, one pair of socks or stockings, one fatigue frock, one pair of trousers and one blanket. A hairbrush and handkerchief were the only authorized optional items. The inspectors noted the deficiencies on the turn out, provided requirements to the quartermaster, and directed the units to requisition what they needed.

The troops were issued woolen "round-abouts," with sleeves, to wear in the summer heat in lieu of the heavier woolen coats. Companies that already had been issued new uniform coats were told to box and return them, each marked with the owner's name, as soon as the round-abouts were available. All other clothing items not authorized similarly were to be boxed and stored. Every man was required to have a haversack containing three days' bread and meat, and the officers were encouraged to conform. The last items issued to the men before they crossed the Niagara to Fort Erie were gun slings and worm screws. Clearly, General Brown's force was as close to the ideal in training, discipline, and equipment as any organization fielded by the United States during the war. The men carried and wore in practice what in other units amounted to only theory.[26]

The condition of the militiamen accompanying the force understandably was not the same. The 5th Pennsylvania Volunteers, already mentioned, were in the best shape. This unit had been on active service since March, at Erie, Pennsylvania, where elements participated in several of the raids on Canadian targets mentioned previously. During its stay in the Erie garrison, the men were fully equipped and clothed. Everyone except the field officers drew the regular army enlisted soldier's uniform. The field officers continued to wear their state militia uniforms.[27] The Pennsylvanians were disciplined and toughened further by their road march along the lake shore from Erie to Buffalo,

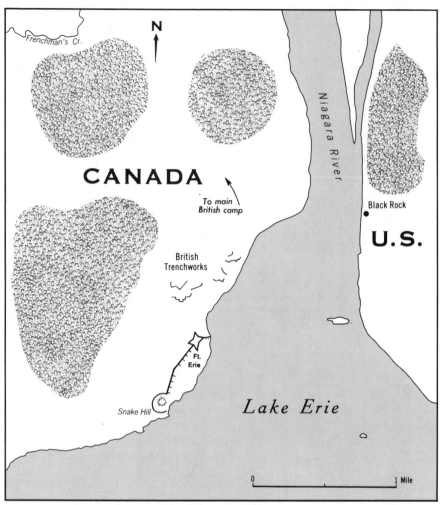

Fort Erie and environs

where they were fully integrated into General Scott's training program. By the time the unit's rear guard reached Buffalo by boat on 22 June, the growing militia portion of General Brown's force had been augmented by as many as 250 Indians, mostly Iroquois—a number that would reach about 500 by the time operations began. The Indians dressed as they pleased, most going into battle painted and with minimum clothing.[28]

The New York militiamen called up for the campaign were much slower in reporting. A portion of General Hall's Division already had been serving rotating tours along the Niagara Frontier since the burning of Buffalo. Hence interest in additional dangerous duty was quite low, which accounted for the poor response to Governor Daniel D. Tompkins' call on 3 May for militia. Efforts to deloy the militia were impeded further by a lack of equipment. Stocks had been depleted at the state armories by earlier call-ups and the previous winter's disaster and had not been replenished because of controversy over financial responsibilities between New York State and the federal government.

The commander of the militia brigade, General Porter, had hoped to stage 1,000 men under arms at the rendezvous point at Canandaigua by 20 May. The men drifted in, but not the equipment. Consequently, Porter was forced to leave his infantry at Batavia under the command of Colonel Philetus Swift while they awaited supplies throughout June. As the time for the invasion approached, Porter hurried ahead to Buffalo with about 150 mounted men, where he took command of the Pennsylvanians and the Indians already on hand. The New York militiamen operating along the Niagara Frontier continued, under Porter's loose control, to conduct security and support missions on the American side of the river.[29] The hours of "fagging," which the men had endured were about to be tested, as General Brown took Secretary Armstrong's supposed green light and prepared to send U.S. forces once more across the Niagara in search of a victory.

Chapter 3

INVASION AND RETREAT

The American forces were alerted for an imminent move on the afternoon of 2 July. General Brown's orders for the day specified the concept of operations and also directed that private property and civilian welfare in Upper Canada should be respected. Under Brown's plan, Scott's Brigade, with the artillery under Major Jacob Hindman would land 1.5 miles north of (or below) the fort, while, General Ripley's Brigade would land 1.5 miles southwest (or above) the fort. The beachheads were located beyond the range of Fort Erie's guns. Elements of the New York Militia would continue to guard the east bank of the Niagara, while General Porter's Brigade of Pennsylvania Volunteers and native troops would cross the river as soon as feasible. The U.S. schooners *Tigress* and *Porcupine*, under Lieutenant Edmund P. Kennedy, would assist in moving troops and then provide fire support.[1]

General Ripley immediately expressed reservations about the plan, revealing for the first time a lack of enthusiasm for the campaign. Ripley's uncertainty should have alerted General Brown to find a more ardent subordinate, even at this early stage of the campaign. Ripley, born in 1782 to a New England theology professor, began his public career in the Massachusetts State legislature in 1807-1809. He was commissioned a lieutenant colonel in 1812 in the 21st Infantry, which he commanded, trained, and led into battle at York, Fort George, and Crysler's Farm. Promoted to brigadier general in April 1814,

Ripley led his brigade throughout the Niagara operations of that year. He was an accomplished drill master and regimental leader, but Brown believed he had "a greater share of physical than moral courage."[2]

General Ripley had been assigned two gun boats and two smaller craft in which to transport his entire command. The gun boats' draft required that they stand off shore while the troops were ferried to the landing point, 50 at a time in each of the smaller boats. Ripley earlier had observed British activities on the western shore, which convinced him that he might be landing at a well-defended site. Concerned over a possible vulnerability to the first landing waves, he urged General Brown to call off the operation. Brown rejected Ripley's argument, stating the landings would go as planned. Ripley proffered his resignation which Brown refused, ordering the General to carry out his part of the plan. Events would prove Ripley's fears groundless. However, the incident heightened General Brown's suspicions regarding Ripley's zeal and leadership, impairing their relationship and negatively effecting the conduct of future operations. Brown's militia background, perhaps, prevented him from firing a respected senior regular officer, regardless of the provocation.[3]

General Scott's Brigade departed on schedule in the darkness of 3 July, landing between 0200 and 0300. The zealous and aggressive Scott, already the veteran of an amphibious assault, was one of the first to leap out of his boat and wade to shore, setting the example for his men who would follow. Unfortunately, the big general plunged into a sinkhole, cape, chapeaux, sword, and all. Alert sailors pulled the soaking general from his plight before he drowned. His situation undoubtedly relieved some tensions, but by then everyone knew his prickly ego well enough not to laugh aloud. Scott's men were safely ashore before they were fired upon by a British picket, which withdrew immediately. Major Jesup's 25th Infantry advanced closer to the fort, while the landing boats returned immediately to shuttle more men and equipment. At first light, a small group of native troops arrived and moved west of the fort to screen the approaches.[4]

Major Jesup's advance indicated that General Ripley's force had not as yet landed. Jesup sent Lieutenant Stanton Sholes to inform General Brown of that fact, while the 25th pressed the British outposts into Fort Erie itself. When the first of Ripley's men did land, Brown placed them under the command of his adjutant general, Colonel Charles K. Gardner, and proceeded to attack the fort with the troops on hand. The native scouts positioned themselves so they would link Ripley's landing site with the remainder of the force. Lieutenant Sholes returned to Jesup, accompanied by the force's engineer officers, the able Lieutenant Colonal William McRee and Major Eleazer D. Wood. The officers informed the infantry commander of Brown's revised plan and supervised the preparation of battery positions for two 18 pounder guns, while the men of the 25th edged closer to the fort. At daybreak, the British fired two or three rounds from their cannon, injuring four soldiers from Jesup's regiment. Jesup was authorized by Brown to parlay for Fort Erie's surrender with its commander, Major Thomas Buck of the 8th Regiment. During the two hours grace given Major Buck for a decision, the Americans finished positioning their battery. Finally, at about 1700, the British major agreed to surrender his garrison. The redcoats marched out and stacked arms. The 137 regulars in Buck's command, mostly men from the 100th Regiment and Royal Artillery, were shuttled as prisoners of war to the American shore. The estimated 30 Lincoln militiamen were paroled.[5]

General Riall first heard of the American landing at 0800. He immediately ordered five companies of the Royal Scots, under Lieutenant Colonel John Gordon, south from Fort George to Chippawa to reinforce that position. He then ordered the 8th Regiment, resting at York, to move to Chippawa immediately to augment 800 regulars and 300 militiamen. At Chippawa, Lieutenant Colonel Thomas Pearson had moved south with the light companies of the 100th Regiment, some militiamen, and a few native troops. Colonel Pearson, in turn, sent word to Fort Niagara for Major Norton to hurry south with nearly 300 warriors, who had gathered earlier for just such a contingency.

Colonel Pearson's combined force probed as far south as Frenchman's Creek. His scouts encountered the Americans in strength on a ridge north of Fort Erie, adjacent to the ferry landing. These were men from Ripley's Brigade, who had finally crossed the river and were ready to contribute to the operation. General Brown ordered General Scott's Brigade to confront the British probe. On the morning of 4 July, the American vanguard skirmished northward against light, but continued opposition, 16 miles to the Chippawa (Welland) River. Pearson's forces had delayed the Americans, but were forced back to their original positions at Chippawa. Reinforced early on 4 July by the Royal Scots and the 19th Light Dragoons, they suffered four men and eight horses wounded. The U.S. advance was not completed until midday of 4 July, because of Pearson's opposition and the need to restore the bridges destroyed by the retreating British. Part of the British force pulled back to the heights west of the falls in response to a rumor that the Fort Erie landings might be a diversion for a converging attack across Grand Island from the east and Point Abino from the southwest.[6]

The remainder of the American force followed behind General Scott, with General Brown, Hindman's artillery, and Ripley's brigade closing into the Street's Creek area held by Scott at 2300 on 4 July. Fort Erie was placed under the command of Lieutenant Patrick McDonough after the main force left. His men immediately started work on improving the western defenses of the fort, replacing earlier British construction with new earthen walls and digging a deep exterior ditch.[7]

General Riall had expected Fort Erie to resist much longer than it did. His initial moves had been based on the need to mount a relief effort for a besieged garrison. Surprised to learn U.S. forces were reaching the Chippawa area as soon as they were, he decided to hold at the Chippawa position established by Colonel Pearson. Its main feature was the Chippawa (Welland) River, a deep, 150-yard-wide, fast-flowing stream that ran from the west into the Niagara, forming a line directly across the American advance. The shore road bridged the river close to its confluence with the Niagara. Riall directed that the bridge, as well as several houses masking artillery fields of fire, be destroyed, leading his officers to presume that he intended to remain on the defensive until he was reinforced substantially.[8]

General Scott had approached the British line in his 4 July advance but judged it too strong to breach with his momentum and had pulled back to the south side of Street's Creek, where he established his camp around Samuel Street's farm, "The Grove." This was the point at which he was joined later by the rest of General Brown's force. A flat cultivated area stretched about one mile between the forces behind their respective streams. A grove of trees divided the field, and both stream banks were lined with brush and trees. The open area extended about three- quarters-of-a-mile to the west, where it ended in a dense pine forest. The American position was vulnerable to infiltration from this forest, while the other foliage impaired observation for both forces.[9]

General Porter's Brigade of Pennsylvanians and native troops was the last unit to reach the scene. Its men began crossing at the Black Rock ferry during the night of 4 July. The first across bedded down where they could, but those arriving later got little rest before marching north the next morning. (Two companies of Pennsylvanians had remained in Buffalo performing security missions.) General Brown travelled south to meet the brigade and rode the last three miles with Porter, explaining the situation and outlining a plan for his men to screen the woods to the west. The unit reached the American position by about noon and the men were allowed a brief rest and a light meal, if desired, before going into action.[10]

Skirmishes had erupted throughout 4 July between opposing pickets then increased in intensity on the morning of the 5th. General Riall was unaware of the fall of Fort Erie and presumed he was facing only a part of the American force. He directed his scouts to explore the enemy line. A few of Major Norton's men reconnoitered the U.S. positions and discerned that their wooded western flank was vulnerable to harassment at the least. Information from civilians convinced Norton and Riall that much of the U.S. force was still to the south, so Riall ordered Norton to move his entire force south of the Creek and to create as much trouble as possible for the Americans. Unfortunately for Riall, the scouts seriously underestimated the size of the U.S. force. Thus, with the arrival of the 8th Regiment, the British general decided by about midday that he had enough strength to attack as soon as the destroyed bridge across the Chippawa could be restored.[11]

General Riall ordered the militia and Norton's natives to move with the support of the flank companies through the woods to a point where they could enfilade the U.S. positions with a heavy fire. He planned to go on the offensive at about 1400, but the British movement to attack did not begin until about 1600. The British natives and militia pressed into the western woods as soon as Riall's main body began to cross the Chippawa. They had covered about half the distance to the American lines when they began to encounter enemy skirmishers. These were General Porter's Pennsylvanians and natives carrying out the scheme to clear the woods that General Brown presented to Porter earlier in the day. Things then began to happen very fast. While Porter's men pressed the British skirmishers to the north and west, Brown detected the dust kicked up by the British main body. He immediately recalled the American pickets and ordered General Scott to deploy his brigade across Street's Creek onto the open plain. Scott's men who had enjoyed a delayed Independence Day dinner, were completing a period of drill and thus were in hand to begin an immediate movement.[12]

At about 1630, General Porter's men encountered the light companies supporting the British skirmishers and then brushed against General Riall's main force. Porter took the only action possible, directing a mad dash back to the safety of the main American position. A foot race ensued, in which several of the Pennsylvanians were captured including Lieutenant Colonel Robert Bull, who was later killed by his native captors. While that drama was unfolding, General Scott's men were deploying into the open area. Captain Towson's Battery, consisting of three 12-pounders, followed across and set up along the shore just north of the mouth of Street's Creek. The battery successfully neutralized the fire from a British counterpart which had moved south of the Chippawa. Scott's Brigade deployed under British fire with the 22d Infantry closest to the Niagara shore and the 9th and 11th further west, respectively. Major Jesup's 25th Infantry was at the Brigade's western most point. Reportedly, the coolness with which the well-trained troops deployed prompted Riall to declare, "Those are regulars, by God." Whatever he actually said, his force was soon in trouble. The Royal Scots and the 100th Regiment advanced into increasing deadly fire from infantry and artillery. In addition to Towson's battery, three more guns from the Biddle and Ritchie batteries were firing from across Street's Creek.[13]

General Scott advanced his line, periodically halting it to volley. Major Jesup's men on the U.S. left flank advanced independently to within 120 paces of the 100th Regiment on the British right (west). The 100th Regiment's commander, Lieutenant Colonel George Hay, the Marquis of Tweeddale, recalled, "I never saw more than their heads when they fired upon us." He soon went down with a severe leg wound, and his colleague, Colonel Pearson of the Royal Scots, was shot in the mouth. Jesup's men brushed aside the light British forces in the woods and wheeled around to flank Tweeddale's men. The rest of Scott's Brigade had closed to within 80 yards of their enemy when their commander ordered a charge, coinciding with similar action from Jesup. The main body was inspired by Major John McNeil of the 11th Infantry, who urged his men to show they could use "cold iron" when challenged. The 8th Regiment, somewhat outdistanced by the advance of Riall's other two regiments, was able to cover their withdrawal from the unexpectedly proficient Americans.[14]

General Brown had directed Ripley's Brigade forward to help Scott when the severity of the fight became apparent. Brown tried to position it just to the left of General Scott, but its movement angled too far to the right to allow a successful envelopment of the withdrawing British. General Ripley's men apparently exchanged fire with some of Major Norton's natives, who then withdrew with the rest of Riall's forces. By 1800, the British forces had extricated themselves and were reestablished on the north bank of the Chippawa, once again destroying the bridge. They had been ineffectively harried by Captain Harris's company of Dragoons, originally sent across Street's Creek to support Porter. The frantic efforts of the last redcoats to withdraw across the Chippawa inspired General Brown to consider an immediate assault. He was dissuaded from doing so by his engineer officers after they had surveyed the strong British position in the approaching twilight.[15]

The two forces spent the next two days recovering from their violent clash. It was apparent that both sides were in for a different, harder campaign than hitherto had been seen in the war. On the U.S. side, the debilitating attrition had begun, which ultimately would erode much of General Brown's offensive capability. The creaking American replacement system could not keep pace with the demands that would be placed on it. As the victors controlling the battlefield, the Americans collected and buried the dead and evacuated the injured by boat to the U.S. shore. A funeral service was conducted by the Left Division chaplain, the Reverend David Jones, a veteran of the Battle of Fallen Timbers.[16]

Meanwhile, U.S. scouts began looking for a way to flank the British positions, discovering a little-used track leading to the junction of Lyon's Creek with the Chippawa. American engineers immediately began to improve it. The road was ready on 7 July. Scott's Brigade demonstrated along the Chippawa line to hold Riall's main force while Generals Ripley and Porter used the road to move against Riall's western flank. General Riall had anticipated this strategy and already had withdrawn some of his heavy equipment. After the Royal Scots light companies reported on the morning of the 7th that they could not prevent the Americans from crossing, Riall ordered a withdrawal to Queenston and then to Fort George. Several heavy guns were dumped into the Chippawa, but none of the buildings or earthworks were demolished. Once at Fort George, Riall ordered all troops unessential to garrison it and Fort Niagara, to join Colonel Hercules and his 103d Regiment near Burlington, where waited about 1,000 Lincoln militiamen and several hundred warriors newly gathered by Major Norton. The entire force camped along 40 Mile Creek. Lieutenant General Drummond also ordered the Upper Canada Incorporated Militia from Kingston to Fort George. The 89th Regiment and the flank companies of the 104th Regiment were sent to York. Governor General Prevost further sent the 6th, 82d and the 90th Regiments newly arrived at Montreal to Drummond.[17]

The Americans quickly pursued, taking over the Queenston Heights position by 10 July and scouting even further northward. On the move, a store opened at Stamford by Hugh Alexander—who had been burned out at Fort Erie in 1813—was pillaged and a large stock of recently arrived goods was lost. The incident seemed to reflect a decline in discipline among many U.S. units in the battle's aftermath. Captain Gordon's Company of Pennsylvanians refused to go beyond the Chippawa River, and its members tried to persuade others to do likewise. General Brown ordered Gordon to return his men to Fort Erie to work on the fortifications. Despite this incident, Brown still considered the militia generally sound.[18] By 11 July, General Scott had resumed a program of drills and inspections; every day at 1600, men not on an operational mission were required to stand full equipment inspections. Shaves and haircuts were expected, and Scott insisted that unit officers enforce his standards of cleanliness and appearance or be cited for failure to exercise proper supervision.[19]

The ferocity of the Chippawa fight and the return to discipline seemed to drain the enthusiasm of many native troops. On the British side, Generals Riall and Drummond had not been pleased with their warriors' performance at the battle. Apparently, this disapproval and Riall's withdrawal to Fort George convinced many tribesmen to leave. By 8 July, Major Norton reported he had only 20 warriors in his command. Then, while the British were encamped at 40 Mile Creek, two U.S. natives escorted a captured British chief into camp, with a proposal from the U.S. leader, Red Jacket, that the warriors on both sides pursue a neutral role. Most of the western tribesmen agreed and left for home. The U.S. warriors began leaving General Brown's camp soon thereafter. By 23 July, only 50 Stockbridge natives under Captains Robert Fleming and Abner W. Hendricks remained to assist the U.S. campaign. For the British, Norton was able to persuade substantial numbers to return and serve as scouts and comprise light forces until the fighting ended.[20]

General Brown, meanwhile, faced bigger problems than retaining his native irregulars. The presence of the British troops in the forts at the mouth of the Niagara River deterred him from advancing west toward General Riall at 40 Mile Creek—a move that would have left his rear echelon threatened by the garrisons. Brown had written Commodore Chauncey before the invasion, asking that the Navy rendezvous, with reinforcements, at the river's mouth. When the fleet failed to show by 13 July, Brown wrote Chauncey an anguished letter, pleading with him to come quickly to assist in capturing Fort George. Brown's forces needed the Navy's heavy guns to ensure a successful siege.[21]

The situation proffered other serious implications as well. Although General Brown had moved supply headquarters from Batavia to Buffalo, he and his men were still at the end of a very fragile chain. The main supply depot for western New York which stored supplies arriving from Albany until their shipment either to Buffalo or to Sacketts Harbor, remained at the point where Ridge Road crosses the Genesee River. Brown depended on ground transport to haul enough supplies overland from the depot to keep up with the Left Division's rate of consumption. Already lacking sufficient transport and without the fleet to open a water route, the success of the entire campaign suddenly was in jeopardy.[22]

Banking on the Navy's arrival, Brown decided to send large combat patrols to the vicinity of Fort George rather than take on General Riall's mobile force. During one patrol on 12 July, New York Militia Brigadier General John Swift was killed in a confusing engagement with a British picket from the 8th Regiment. General Porter led an even larger force toward Fort George on 15 July, consisting of the Canadian Volunteers, three companies of his New Yorkers, some native troops and Captain John Ritchie's Artillery. The force would enable Major Eleazer D. Wood, one of the engineers, to reconnoiter approaches to the fort. The alert British outposts engaged Porter's men as well, capturing five and wounding two others.[23]

These patrols conveyed Brown's intentions to General Riall, who tightened his grip around the area under U.S. control. Awaiting reinforcements from General Drummond and under orders not to risk his own force, Riall pressed his units into positions between 20 Mile and 12 Mile creeks. Major Norton's warriors, the newly arrived Glengarries and the Lincoln Militia patrolled as far east as St. Davids, between Queenston and the fort. Other units raided points along the U.S. communications line. On 9 July, one of Norton's groups attacked a picket outside Fort Erie, killing two men and capturing six.[24]

On 20 July, General Brown advanced his entire force to the Fort George area, where it operated for two days before withdrawing to the Heights. Brown had learned in a 23 July letter from General Gaines that the Navy would be unable to supply the heavy ordnance he required. Commodore Chauncey stated further that he did not believe the fleet was strong enough to interdict the flow of British reinforcements arriving from Kingston. Consequently, Brown directed a withdrawal from positions before Fort George and on Queenston Heights to the Chippawa River. The Americans delayed at Queenston Heights long enough to send their sick and wounded across the river to Lewiston before reaching the Chippawa on 24 July.

During the American withdrawal, one of Major Norton's parties captured a U.S. artillery deserter who unveiled the U.S. move. Norton sent a mounted warrior to inform General Riall, while he led the remainder of his scouts to discover the new U.S. positions. Soon joined by a party of militia and British officers, the patrol continued south until it blundered into American pickets and sustained some casualties. The encounter established the location of the main American force in the old Chippawa camp grounds and prompted Riall to advance 1,000 men, under Colonel Pearson, to regain contact.[25]

General Brown obviously was preparing for a change of circumstances. He directed the shipment of as much heavy artillery as possible from locations in western New York. Four 12-pounders with solid, shrapnel, and canister rounds and 25 barrels of gunpowder were shipped from Batavia. Nearly all of the ammunition, rifles, and sabers in stock at Fort Schlosser on the east bank of the Niagara were delivered, along with the fort's only ten-pound mortar. Five 18-pounders located at Oswego and 600 solid shot sent there from Sacketts Harbor were also shipped. This heterogenous collection later became part of the heavy defenses of Fort Erie and Black Rock.[26]

Once he decided to pull back from Queenston Heights, General Brown required all the units "to be rendered light as possible," ordering officers' personal baggage returned to Buffalo, along with "subjects for general hospital." The men and the baggage crossed the river at Fort Schlosser. Brown also ordered all women attached to the army to return to Buffalo, where they would be reassigned to the hospital. At that time two women were serving as hospital matrons and one as laundress in each regiment. Surgeons from the 9th and 23d infantries convinced General Brown to modify this part of his order, which allowed a matron and a laundress to remain with each regimental hospital. All other surplus persons and material were shipped across the river under the supervision of Major William A. Trimble, 19th Infantry.[27]

The reinforced British, now under the overall command of General Drummond, quickly pressed forward. While a column led by Colonel Hercules Scott of the 103d advanced from the direction of Burlington Heights, a second under General Riall marched from Fort George. Colonel Pearson's advance force was set up on a hilltop almost parallel with the falls along a road running from east to west called Lundy's Lane. General Drummond brought the 89th Regiment from York to Fort George on the morning of 25 July. He ordered Lieutenant Colonel John G. P. Tucker with 500 men of the 1st and 41st regiments along with some Indian troops from Fort Niagara, to proceed along the east bank of the river in order to threaten the U.S. depots at Youngstown and Lewiston. At the same time, Lieutenant Colonel Joseph W. Morrison's

89th Regiment moved along the west bank to reinforce Riall. Riall, in turn, brought up four guns and the rest of his 1,500-man force to support Pearson.[28]

Hearing of Tucker's feint from Colonel Philetus Swift's New York Militia stationed in the area, General Brown assumed that Tucker's force was the main British effort. Fearing for the safety of an important depot and hospital at Fort Schlosser, he dispatched General Scott and his brigade from Chippawa on the afternoon of 25 July to counter that threat. By coincidence, the British columns on the west side of the Niagara were approaching the same point from the opposite direction. The meeting produced a bitter engagement starting about 1800 at Bridgewater Mills, or Lundy's Lane, as it is known today.[29]

General Scott's Brigade marched confidently northward along Portage Road, noting a few scattered British scouts as it progressed. When the aggressive brigadier sighted the main British position at 1700, he deployed his men in a line, then held them in position, perhaps realizing for the first time that he had encountered a very large force. "Dread seemed to forbid his advance, and shame to restrain his flight," observed one British officer. The British cannon fire became so galling that Scott had no recourse but to try an advance. Seeing this, General Riall began to pull out Pearson's men from their Lundy's Lane positions. But, the withdrawal was stopped when General Drummond galloped onto the scene ahead of his reinforcements. The timely arrival of the Queenston force with additional artillery and a rocket detachment meant that Scott was attacking a force nearly double his numbers.[30]

The Americans advanced at 1800 with the 9th, 11th, and 12d Infantries on line, focussing on the British guns located on the hilltop. The 25th Infantry moved along the British flank, directing an enfilade. Using Captain Thomas S. Seymour's company to keep a tenuous link with General Scott, Major Jesup of the 25th engaged several small groups before setting up a blocking position at the Lundy's Lane—Portage Road intersection. The confusion in the woods and growing darkness made fighting intense. General Riall, severely wounded in the arm, wandered into the American's position and was captured by Captain Daniel Ketchum's Company. Though wounded, Riall had enough presence of mind to comment on the appropriateness of his captor's name.[31]

General Scott's assault bent backward the British flank, but did not silence the British guns. His pleas for help were met and the Ripley and Porter brigades arrived about 2100. By that time, Scott's force had been reduced to about 600 men. General Ripley ordered Colonel James T. Miller with his 21st Infantry to seize the guns while the 23d Infantry attacked the British left and Porter's Brigade engaged the enemy right. The British were being reinforced by Colonel Scott's 103d Regiment and Colonel Drummond's 104th Regiment Flank Companies while Ripley was deploying. The American attack in the intense confusion proved successful, and the guns were captured, however, the presence of new British troops prevented any American exploitation. The

British launched several unsuccessful counterattacks to try to recapture the lost guns, with the opposing lines exchanging volleys in the darkness within 10 to 15 yards of each other before the British broke contact sometime after midnight. The Americans also pulled off the hill at General Brown's direction, leaving all but one of the captured guns, because they lacked harness for the gun horses. In the course of the fight, General Drummond had been wounded painfully in the neck and Generals Scott and Brown had been hit so severely that they had to be evacuated. The casualties on both sides exceeded 1,500 men, with U.S. forces losing particularly high numbers of senior officers.[32]

The American casualties from Lundy's Lane were sent to Chippawa and then on 26 July travelled by boat to Tonawanda then to Buffalo. Militiamen served as boatmen. Those wounded who expired on the night of the 26th were buried at Tonawanda. Medical facilities were taxed heavily handling the casualties brought in after the battle. One surgeon said mortality would have been considerably higher were it not for the care given the men by the wives and other camp followers attached to the hospitals during the crisis. Left in possession of the battlefield, the British were forced to dispose of the slain. Several large pyres were built and most of the Americans' remains were incinerated; only a few were buried.[33]

Prior to his evacuation at 0100, General Brown had told the surviving senior officer, Brigadier General Ripley, to withdraw the troops to the Chippawa campground. He wanted the men to regroup there, then return to the battlefield in daylight. At the same time, the wounded who could be found were to be evacuated. Ripley later marched all the men he could gather to Lundy's Lane at about 0900 the next morning. He found the British in possession of the battlefield and decided to fall back toward Fort Erie.[34] Ripley correctly assessed his force to be in no condition to resume the fight. He had been able to collect only about 1,500 exhausted men. Major Henry Leavenworth of the 9th Infantry had only 64 men while Scott's entire brigade could muster fewer than 600. The 11th Infantry could count only about 125 men. The case of Lieutenant Samuel Tappan's Company, 23d Infantry, was typical: Forty-five men had gone into battle, but on the morning of 26 July only nine men were on hand. Another 19 men straggled in over the next few days, while 17 were identified as killed or wounded. This attrition, especially the loss of key leaders, severely impaired the cohesion and effectiveness of the units that had survived.[35]

The ultimate tragedy was that General Brown's shock-induced instructions transformed the U.S. tactical victory into a strategic British victory—a victory made more significant considering the United States' inability to sustain an adequate personnel replacement system. On the other hand, General Drummond's violent experience at Lundy's Lane, caused him to exercise extreme caution in subsequent dealings with the Americans. This cautious approach eventually would give the U.S. forces the time they needed to get Fort Erie into a defensible condition. General Brown insisted from his hospital bed that the fort be retained as a bridgehead, despite the increasingly discredited Ripley's advice to the contrary.

Chapter 4

SIEGE I, IN THE BAG

General Ripley led his battered forces back to the Black Rock ferry site on the afternoon of 26 July. The next day, he continued the withdrawal into Fort Erie. General Drummond missed some opportunities at this phase of the campaign. If he had pursued the Americans promptly and attacked them in the first confusing days, he might have been able to overwhelm the Fort Erie garrison before it could get organized. British scouts did probe southward early in the dawn chill on the 26th. They collected a few stragglers and encountered some enemy dead, then saw Ripley's desultory advance. The Americans halted 1.5 miles south of the previous day's battlefield, burned a saw mill, then headed back once more, evacuated their camps along the Chippawa, and moved south. Despite this information, the British pulled back to Queenston Heights that afternoon.[1]

The next afternoon, General Drummond advanced his men to a point mid-way between Niagara Falls and Chippawa. On 28 July, the British light forces crossed the river using any platform that could float, because the Americans had destroyed the bridge again. The Dragoons took a back road to approach Fort Erie from the west, while Major Norton's scouts moved along the river road. The first Americans encountered a mile south of the river comprised a truce party, bearing letters for General Drummond. Major Norton held them, and the two groups chatted about the recent battle until their business was completed. General Brown was enquiring about the status of his mortally wounded aide, Captain Ambrose Austin, and offering to exchange him for Drummond's aide, Captain Robert K. Loring, who was an American prisoner. Later the scouts, along with the Glengarries and the Dragoons, hovered opposite Strawberry Island and watched the Americans for another two days until Drummond's main force joined them. Drummond had moved the 89th Regiment to Fort Niagara to assure that his rear was secure in the face of possible U.S. Navy activity. He further wanted to verify that reinforcements were on the way.[2]

All this delay had given the Americans under General Ripley sufficient time to gather themselves and to convert Fort Erie into a formidable position. Ripley had continued the withdrawal into Fort Erie on the 27th. The U.S. forces under Lieutenant McDonough had done some work on the original facility while the fighting was going on to the north. Most of this work, however, had been limited to repairing to the old fort itself with little thought to developing the surrounding area. This strategy changed with the arrival of Ripley and his troops.[3] Battery positions were laid out between 28 and 31 July and work begun under the supervision of Lieutenant David B. Douglass, along with the help of unit pioneers. Douglass' own company built a small battery to the right of the original fort, while he oversaw the efforts of several hundred men at Snake Hill. Unit fatigue parties worked in eight-hour shifts around the clock on the ditches and breastworks, linking the old fort with the flanking batteries. The old fort quickly became a segment of a larger system of parapets and traverses, all edged by a wide ditch and abatis.[4]

The fortified area encompassed about 30 acres. The so called "Douglass Battery" located on the fort's north (or right) side, was connected to the old fort with a seven-foot-high parapet bounded by the exterior ditch. To the west (or left) of the fort, a longer parapet with a double ditch ran about 800 yards nearly parallel to Lake Erie's shore. It terminated at Snake Hill. This was a low sand mound that was built up by about 25 feet. The stockade on the west side of the old fort itself was replaced by bastioned earthworks. A British patrol on 30 July attacked the U.S. outpost at the ferry crossing opposite Black Rock, seizing some of the boats that the Americans were guarding.[5] This activity contributed added urgency to the American efforts. On 2 August, the Douglass Battery was sufficiently complete to secure its guns in position. Snake Hill received part of its armament the next day, and responsibility for its further development passed to the battery commander, Captain Towson. Its location on Snake Hill may be plotted with reasonable accuracy by combining the information provided in the papers of Lieutenant Douglass with other contemporary maps and modern terrain analysis. Douglass described the parapet as extending westerly 299 yards from old Fort Erie, where it angled southerly, and continued 342 yards at which point, it ran 76 yards further

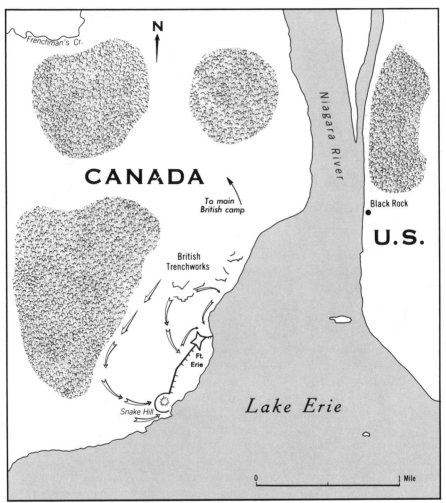

Fort Erie and environs
Drummond's attack, August 15th

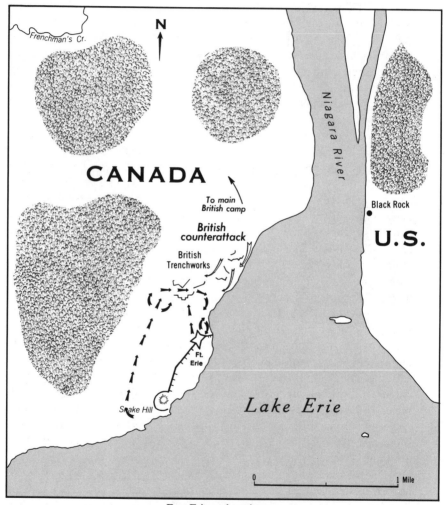

Fort Erie and environs
Brown's sortie, September 17th

around Towson's Battery to the shore. The battery was on Snake Hill. The scale map he provided allows the angles he cited to be calculated, thus permitting some precision. It is believed that Snake Hill is the area on Lakeshore Road in the vicinity of its intersection with Albert Road.[6]

The British main body arrived on 2 August on the heights opposite Black Rock. Camps eventually were set up about two miles above the fort (in the vicinity of the modern-day racetrack), and General Drummond considered whether to take the place by siege. Before that, however, Drummond attempted to flush the Americans out of the fort by taking the war to the U.S. shore. He ordered Lieutenant Colonel John G.P. Tucker to cross the river with a force consisting of six companies of the 41st Regiment, the Light Company of the 89th and the two 104th Flank Companies. Alerted on 2 August for a move that night, the force was expected to seize the Scajaquada Creek Navy Yard, capture or neutralize its guns, then destroy depots in Buffalo and Black Rock while committing as much other mayhem as possible.[7]

Colonel Tucker led his force in nine boats across the river at about 2400 on 2 August. Unfortunately for Tucker, his movement had been observed by Major Lodowick Morgan and his men from the 1st Rifle Regiment, who were guarding the area. The Americans tore up the boards of the bridge across the Scajaquada and entrenched themselves behind some hastily constructed barricades. Tucker's men advanced without making any efforts to secure the area and at 0400, blundered into the smaller force of the American defenders. Major Morgan's men delivered a withering fire in the darkness, pinning down most of the British force and deterring several gallant efforts to rush the useless bridge. The British withdrew slightly into some woods and attempted to lay down a base of fire. At least 13 more boatloads of men reinforced Tucker's force, after which they tried to flank Morgan's position. Morgan detached 60 men from his force of 240, under Lieutenants James H. Ryan, Thomas L. Smith, and William Armstrong, to block this threat successfully. After two and one half hours of punishment and with 44 casualties, Colonel Tucker withdrew, leaving a small covering force on Squaw Island until his main body regained the far shore. Major Morgan reported two killed and ten wounded.[8]

General Drummond observed the latter part of the action from the opposite shore and was upset at what he felt was the bungling of an opportunity to draw the Americans out of their beachhead or to force them into a battle. Drummond reasoned that the U.S. defenders on the eastern shore now would be fully alerted, and that he did not have the capability for a full-scale counter-invasion. This left him with no other option than to embark on a siege of Fort Erie. Major Norton's scouts had skirmished with the American pickets on the west bank to divert attention from Tucker's group at Scajaquada. Several of his natives were killed, but the encounter increased his familiarity with the outer defenses around the fort.[9]

General Drummond sent the 41st Regiment to Fort George, replacing it with the newly arrived DeWatteville Regiment. This unit, composed of Swiss mercenaries with the addition of some men from other parts of Europe, had been raised in 1801 and had seen considerable action against French forces in Italy, Spain, and Portugal before being assigned to Canada in 1813. The regiment's commander, Louis DeWatteville, was made a local major general, hence the unit was led by Lieutenant Colonel Victor Fischer. The unit, which had seen action at Oswego the previous May, reached Fort George on 29 July and was transferred to Fort Erie by 8 August.[10]

British engineers on the night of 5 August began building battery positions north of the fort on the river's edge. The enfilading capability of these positions would prompt the Americans to build large traverses throughout their area. At the same time, animal parks and hospital tents were emplaced in what Lieutenant Douglass called the "most secluded places." Large numbers of soldiers participated in the work parties to sustain this effort. The incessant labor proved very trying to the men on both sides.[11]

The Americans continued to develop their fortifications throughout the siege. The engineers dealt directly with the quartermaster in Buffalo, Captain John B. Hogan, to get needed supplies. Large orders, such as requests for 400 shovels or 200 axes became routine for harried supply officers. A junior quartermaster officer was engaged full time at Fort Erie just keeping track of outgoing construction materials. By the end of August this officer also supervised the eight yoke of oxen that had been sent to perform heavy hauling at the request of the senior engineer, Lieutenant Colonel William MacRee. By that time, the American positions had been developed thoroughly. A total of 27 guns lined the works. Overhead cover had been emplaced for all the artillery positions, and Snake Hill had been formed into a fully enclosed redoubt. Most of the troops were housed in tents throughout the siege, but these soon became shredded by British shell fragments. When General Brown resumed command on 2 September, he increased effort to provide shelter for the troops. Quantities of "two- or three-foot" plank were delivered. By 13 September, all loose boards in the Buffalo area had been transferred, and General Brown was demanding another 10,000 feet.[12]

The U.S. forces were able to sustain the large presence at Fort Erie because they nearly controlled the water route from Buffalo. Several ships from the Lake Erie Squadron arrived from the west in late July with 1,000 troops under Brigadier General Duncan McArthur. But, Secretary Armstrong's fears for the safety of Detroit in early August led him to order McArthur to return with a portion of his force. Most of the ships were retained, however, to secure the water route and to provide firepower on Fort Erie's water flank. (Two of these ships would be lost to a brilliant British raid on 12 August, but the loss would have little effect on the movement of goods and men between Buffalo and the fort.) On 1 August, Captain Hogan reported he had 13 boats of all types on hand. Four of these were under repair, and another two were set aside for the exclusive use of the ordnance department and the rations contractor. Thirty light bateaux, each capable of hauling 30 men, were under construction while all the oars necessary were on hand already.[13]

These small craft operated between Black Rock and the fort or from Sandytown to the fort. Sandytown was an area at the foot of Porter Avenue, now eroded away, which was later marked by the entrance of the Erie Canal into Black Rock Harbor. The site was directly east of of the fort, across the water to Buffalo. The first British battery set up opposite Black Rock could, in part, interdict the water route between Black Rock and the fort. At least one boatman lost his arm to British fire while ferrying reinforcements to Fort Erie. Since the Americans depended on daily contact with the Buffalo area depots for provisions, resupply and the transfer of personnel, a great deal of movement occurred at night, with boats crossing and recrossing in the darkness. The Americans established a battery (located west of modern Niagara Street at the foot of Gull Street) under Lieutenant Colonel George McFeely at Black Rock to suppress the British fire on U.S. shipping and to harass the opposite shore. Daytime crossings were made more often from Sandytown to a point near Snake Hill. After 15 August, many private individuals crossed to this area to sell produce to the troops. General Brown allowed this trade so as to improve his men's consumption of fresh vegetables.[14]

With regard to the issue of medical support and the condition of the command, regimental surgeons had reported relatively little illness or disease during the training period prior to the invasion. Smallpox and "intermittent fevers," described by Doctor Amasa Troubridge of the 21st Infantry, posed a modest health problem during May and June. Such patients were referred to his hospital at Flint Hill. The influx of reinforcements and militiamen in late June brought about an increase in the incidence of typhus. Doctor Joseph Mann reported that "intermittent, acute rheumatism" became a major complaint during the campaign, caused, no doubt, by the men's prolonged exposure to the elements. The arrival of more militia in September marked an increase in diarrhea and what Doctor Mann called "idiopathic dysentery." Certificates of disability issued after the war indicate that many survivors of the Fort Erie siege suffered serious physical problems, such as hernias and severe hemorrhoids that made any labor impossible as well as the virulent, long-term diarrhea cited by Doctor Mann. The compensation awarded to troops for debilitating rheumatism contracted while on fatigue duties at the fort also support Doctor Mann's observations.[15]

The men were pushed to their physical and emotional limits in the course of the siege, performing heavy labor for extended periods under dangerous conditions. Although rarely without food, the men's diet provided little nutritional benefits. The men's basic ration consisted of salt pork and hard bread. Spirits, vinegar, salt, and soap were available occasionally, but supplies of soap and vinegar proved particularly difficult to obtain.[16]

The rations were issued directly to units by contractors on the signature of unit commanders. The inspectors general assured that prisoners of war were fed properly, while surgeons signed for rations in their hospitals.[17] The hospital ration differed substantially from that given to the troops in their regiments. Hospitals were authorized to procure a variety of vegetables and dairy products apart from the basic ration. Further, the surgeons were allowed to draw only those component parts of the rations they needed. They could sell their surpluses and use the money earned to procure additional specialty items.[18]

Cooking was often done by civilians. In several cases, the quartermaster hired local women or the wives of soldiers to cook for a group. This was especially the case for fatigue parties or groups of teamsters or carpenters, which were not as well structured as the line units.[19] The items purchased from civilian entrepreneurs who dared to visit the fort included butter, onions, and potatoes and a few prepared items, such as pies and cooked meat. The prices charged for these items, as expected, were exorbitant. Consequently, the continued scarcity of foods to ward off scurvy in the soldiers' diet was an increasing concern. Finally, on 25 August, the commanding general directed the quartermaster, Captain Hogan, to procure potatoes at any price "to save my men from the ravages of sickness which is (sic) making rapid approaches toward paralyzing my strength." This marginal diet was sometimes made worse when bad weather impeded the flow of goods, creating temporary scarcities. It may be deduced from these circumstances that the men were not well-fed, were subjected to hard physical labor, were afforded little sleep, and were under considerable tension from the British bombardment.[20]

Before the invasion, General Scott had periodically visited all the various regimental hospitals, warning the physicians that the campaign would bring busy times for them.[21] His predictions were all too accurate. These field hospitals were supported by an existing hospital system. By 1814, general hospitals already were established in Burlington, Vermont, Plattsburgh, Malone, and Greenbush, New York. The threat to facilities at Fort Schlosser convinced General Brown in late July to erect a permanent general hospital at Williamsville, about 12 miles east of Buffalo. Williamsville was the headquarters of the 5th Brigade of the New York Militia. It had been used by the Army ever since General Smyth had established winter quarters there in 1812. At that time, log barracks were built along the south side of the village's main street between Ellicott Creek and Garrison Road. These barracks were converted into temporary medical facilities in October 1813. Patients from Lewiston were transported by boat to Fort Schlosser, then overland. Those capable

A View of Lake Erie and Fort Erie from Buffalo Creek, 1810 by E. Walsh. (Public Archives of Canada)

The Storming of the Northeast Bastion by Lieutenant Colonel William Drummond's Column, 15 August 1814. Engraving for the United States Magazine, *1841 by E.C. Watmough. (Chicago Historical Society)*

Colonel Josiah Snelling (1782-1828) Inspector General of Brown's Left Division. He monitored training, the status of supplies, troop health and the care of prisoners of war. (Minnesota Historical Society)

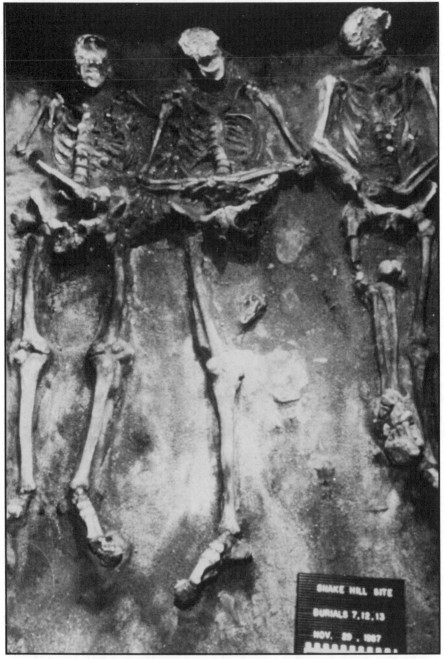

Remains of three U.S. soldiers discovered along with 25 others in 1987 at Snake Hill.
(Photo, Sergeant Jay Llewelyn, USAF, Armed Forces Institute of Pathology)

1814 scene showing a surgeon and light artillery sergeant in the foreground and a captain, musician and light artillerymen in the background. (USA Center of Military History)

of the trip then were sent to convalesce at the Greenbush hospital, near Albany. The Buffalo area hospital was commanded by Doctor James Mann and Surgeon's Mate Joshua B. Whiteridge.[22]

The site for the new hospital was selected on 29 July on the recommendation of the senior surgeon, Doctor Ezekiah Bull. Thus, 90 acres and the stables of Raphael Cook's farm were leased for the construction of a general hospital. Ironically, the contract specified "no burying place in the premises." Despite this, a well-kept series of mass graves along Aero Drive remain as the last vestiges of this hospital. These further provide evidence that having a burying ground adjacent to a medical facility was an accepted practice. The Williamsville cemetery contains the remains of both U.S. and British personnel. The British remains are in their own grave on one edge of the plot. The segregation of enemy and friendly dead seems to have been a tacit, if not official, practice on both sides. The Williamsville facility was designated a general hospital in August, and Surgeon's Mate Joseph Lovell was assigned to its command. He was succeeded in 1815 by Doctor William Thomas.[23]

As soon as General Brown decided to concentrate patients at Williamsville, a vigorous building project was begun. At first, a large tent city was erected as indicated by the use of 3,000 board feet of timber for flooring 100 hospital tents and 12 loads of hay for bed ticking. Each tent could hold 16 to 18 men. In early September, General Brown, once more in command, embarked on his extensive effort to shelter the troops at Fort Erie. Additional amounts of timber were sent across the Niagara to make tent flooring. Likewise, canvas was delivered for use by the besieged troops. Brown directed that the wounded be moved into permanent buildings so that every tent possible would be available for troops in the field. Captain John Larkin was named supervisory quartermaster for the construction of the Williamsville Hospital. He brought in skilled workmen from as far away as Rochester and Utica. Huge quantities of locally produced brick were purchased in Buffalo and hauled to Williamsville to help construct the hospital barracks. Subsequent purchases of glass and shingles to complete the buildings substantiate the permanent nature of the structures. Patients, among them Generals Scott and Riall, began being moved to the Williamsville site on 30 July.[24]

An additional general hospital was opened at Buffalo in July to accommodate the surge of wounded from the Battle of Chippawa. This was located at Sandytown 400 yards from Buffalo Creek. The wounded were brought to the site by boat, then carried by litter the last few hundred yards. By 1 August, it held nearly 1,100 patients. The British raid on 3 August a few miles north at Scajaquada Creek demonstrated the hospital's vulnerability. Consequently, as many men as possible were removed to the growing Williamsville facility. Doctor Bull with Surgeon's Mates Thomas and Lovell supervised the Williamsville facility. Surgeon's Mate William E. Horner remained at Buffalo caring for the small numbers of patients who could not be moved. Thereafter, the Buffalo Hospital served as the clearing center for casualties from Fort Erie, sending patients to Williamsville as quickly as it could. Those who died there were buried in an adjacent graveyard, identified only years later when human remains were discovered.[25]

Several smaller regimental hospitals in the Buffalo and Black Rock areas had come in with their units. Despite their regimental affiliation, they supported all troops sent to their area. Buildings were leased to house these facilities. In addition, rooms in private houses were rented for the use of convalescent officers. Beginning in late October, the sick and wounded at Williamsville who could travel were sent in a series of convoys to the hospital at Greenbush. Beginning on 8 November, everyone possible was moved to Williamsville. Most officers and about 80 critical patients remained in private houses around Buffalo. The unprecedented casualty rate experienced throughout the campaign combined with that at Plattsburgh and elsewhere to place heavy demands on the medical supply system. Apothecary General Francis LeBaron at Albany advised his superiors in Philadelphia that the Williamsville Hospital "devoured" reserve stocks "like cormorants," so that by November nothing was left on hand.[26]

The siege of Fort Erie promised even more business for the medical system. Active patrolling began almost as soon as the opponents regained contact on 2 August. The day after the Scajaquada skirmish, the British command group reconnoitered the U.S. positions. It was apparent that the Americans were improving their position at a feverish rate. They had built abatis at approaches out of the woods leading into the open clearing around the fort and its supporting earthworks, in addition to making substantial improvements to the fort itself. Resigned to the likelihood of siege, General Drummond ordered a full advance to the area and directed that battery positions be prepared. The task of supervising this effort went to a junior engineer officer, Lieutenant George Phillpotts. The lieutenant was greatly hampered by the lack of equipment, later recalling that he had "entrenching tools for 120 men, 20 axes, 200 sand bags."[27]

The British labor parties began work on 5 August using fascines covered by brush to screen themselves from sniper fire from the fort and flanking artillery fire from the U.S. battery at Black Rock. U.S. artillery fire proved so endangering that while work continued on Battery Number One, the British also began constructing traverses for permanent protection. By 9 August, they completed a single-gun battery on the lake shore to fire on shipping and to contend with the Black Rock Battery. By 11 August, Battery One was ready to receive its guns. A trenchline was extended inland from it toward the next possible gun position. In addition, picket breastworks with abatis were built forward of the battery, while a strong trenchline also was constructed to the rear.[28]

Meanwhile, Brigadier General Edward L. Gaines, believed by the convalescing General Brown to be more aggressive than General Ripley, assumed command on 5 August. Gaines was a product of the southern frontier who entered the Army in 1797. He had served in various engineering and administrative jobs until the war, but thereafter proved himself to be an aggressive regimental commander. Apparently, Brown had made his decision even before the Lundy's Lane fighting. Gaines received a letter from Brown ordering him to "repair immediately to Chippaway" on 20 July. Ripley loyally resumed command of his own brigade with responsibility for the defense of the Snake Hill area.[29]

The tempo of combat patrols and skirmishing already appeared vicious. When the battery construction began, Major Norton's men moved right and forward of the position to screen the workers. Their movement alerted the U.S. pickets who were sheltering behind their own abatis and inaugurated a brisk exchange of fire which became the daily pattern thereafter. A sharp skirmish ensued on 6 August, as the British defended the battery site. General Gaines later reported the incident as an effort to involve the British in a general engagement before the siege lines hardened. Both sides engaged in considerable skirmishing across no-mans-land, especially in the direction of the dangling British west flank. The U.S. First Rifles, skilled at such engagements, were ordered across the river on 4 August. They attacked the battery on the 6th and again on the 10th and 12th, only to withdraw each time after a hard fight. During the fight of 12 August, Major Morgan, the hero of the Scajaquada fight, was killed. The British unmasked Battery One that same day, clearing the trees from its front, thus prompting the American attack.[30]

Battery One had been located at a spot on the shore about 1,000 yards from the fort. It contained a long 24-pounder, two brass 24-pounders, one 24-pounder carronade and an eight-inch mortar, all of which had been laboriously hauled from Fort George. The battery opened fire on 13 August, inaugurating the weeks of pounding the Americans were to receive. Fortunately for the U.S. fortifications, the fire proved only marginally effective. Inexperienced engineers had positioned the battery too far back from Fort Erie for its missiles to cause much damage.[31]

The harassment of Battery One by U.S. naval gunfire was sharply curtailed by a daring British operation, similar to the American exploit of 1812 discussed in Chapter One. The U.S. ships *Ohio*, *Porcupine* and *Somers*—each with a crew of about 30 men, and all under the command of Lieutenant Augustus Conklin—had been deployed on Fort Erie's water flank. The ships were to provide additional fire support and security for the small boats plying back and forth between the shores. Seventy-five British seamen, led by Commander Alexander Dobbs, carried a gig 20 miles from Queenston to French-man's Creek. Helped by the Lincoln Militia from there, they carried the gig and five bateaux eight more miles overland through the forest to a point on Lake Erie west of the fort. On the night of 12 August, Dobbs and his men floated into the Niagara, surprising the American sailors who presumed until too late the boats were friendly. After capturing *Somers* and *Ohio* in a brief struggle, the ships were floated northward and anchored off the mouth of the Chippawa River, where they provided protection for that site, which was serving as General Drummond's intermediate supply base.[32]

The U.S. Ontario fleet, which had arrived finally off the mouth of the Niagara River on 4 August, no longer could assist General Brown's original concept of operations. However, Commodore Isaac Chauncey was able to establish a sufficiently tight blockade to cause growing logistical and personnel strength problems for the British. With the U.S. Navy loose, for example, most British reinforcements were forced to endure the hard 16- to 20-day march from Kingston around Lake Ontario, rather than risk the two-day water crossing. The situation implied a critical reduction in the flow of supplies, which ultimately could weaken the besieging forces. The presence of the U.S. fleet combined with an inability to interdict the American water routes to Buffalo sufficiently to starve out the U.S. garrison pressed General Drummond to attack Fort Erie rather than to rely on the slow strangulation characteristic of a typical siege. His decision was further reinforced by his false assumption that the U.S. garrison of nearly 3,000 men numbered less than 1,500 men.[33]

The British general developed a complicated plan entailing a three-column converging night attack. One column, led by Lieutenant Colonel Fischer of the DeWattevilles, would move several miles west and attack Snake Hill. A second column under Colonel Hercules Scott of the 103d Regiment would move along the river bank from Battery One and attack Battery Douglass. The third column, led by Lieutenant Colonel William Drummond of the 104th Regiment (a distant relative of General Drummond, would attack Fort Erie itself. Lieutenant Colonel Tucker would command a reserve positioned in the existing piquet line. The piquets themselves, led by Lieutenant Colonel Robert Nicholl, were expected to make a distracting demonstration midway along the British line near Buck's Road. General Drummond's command post would be adjacent to Battery One.[34]

Colonel Fischer was assigned his own regiment, the 8th Regiment, the light companies of the 89th and 100th Regiments, some artillerymen, and a few dragoons. General Drummond's orders did not reflect an especially high opin-ion of Fischer's men. The column was to depart early enough to cover its route through the forest in daylight so none of the men would have the opportunity to desert. The officers were expected to conduct periodic roll calls for the same purpose. Drummond further ordered that the men remove the flints from their muskets to prevent an accidental discharge, which would reveal their movement and remove the element of surprise. The other column commanders were not as burdened with such guidance. Colonel Drummond was to lead the flank companies of the 104th and 41st Regiments and some artillerymen, as well as 140 sailors and Royal Marines. Colonel Scott led his own regiment, the 103d. The attack was set for 0200 on 15 August.[35]

Meanwhile, the Americans reinforced their line with men and guns. To the north (or right side), the Douglass Battery was supported by a force under the general supervision of Lieutenant Colonel MacRee, the chief engineer. Starting at the lake's edge, about 100 dismounted New York cavalrymen, led by Captain Claudius V. Boughton, held positions. Next in line were the 50 men of Douglass' Company manning a six-pounder and a 12-pounder. To Douglass' left, Captain Edmund Foster commanded the remaining 165 men of the 9th Infantry. Between the 9th Infantry and the fort, Captain Micajah Harding of New York had 120 men from the New York Militia and the 5th Pennsylvania. Lieutenant Colonel Thomas Aspinwall led reserve elements of the 11th and 22d Infantry regiments, situated at a point roughly equidistant from the fort and from the Douglass Battery.[36]

Fort Erie itself was defended by two companies of 118 men from the 19th Infantry and by about 60 artillerymen under the command of Captain Alexander J. Williams. The artillery in the fort consisted of a 24-pounder, an 18-pounder, and a 12-pounder. The American line stretched about 800 yards southward to the lake shore near Snake Hill. Captain John J. Fontaine's Battery of two six-pounders was adjacent to the fort itself. 250 yards further south along the breastworks was Captain Thomas Biddle's Battery of three six-pounders. A combined force of companies from the 1st and 4th Rifle regiments, under the command of Captain Benjamin Birdsall, manned the line from the Fontaine Battery southward to a point where it joined with Swift's New York Militia Regiment and the 5th Pennsylvania. These units, under the command of Brigadier General Peter B. Porter, in turn linked with Brigadier General Ripley's Brigade at Snake Hill.[37]

The focus of the Snake Hill defenses was Captain Towson's Battery of six six-pounder guns. To the extreme left, Major Eleazer D. Wood commanded four companies of the 21st Infantry, 250 men. Two other companies from the 21st commanded by Captains Benjamin Ropes and Morrill Marston were positioned in reserve behind the battery to protect it from any attacks coming from the direction of the shore. Three companies from the 23d and Captain John T. Chunn's company from the 17th Infantry were placed between the battery and the militia. By 13 August the units were reasonably well entrenched, and the entire line was protected by the abatis.[38]

Chapter 5

SIEGE II, SUCCESSFUL DEFENSE

Increasingly heavy British artillery fire commenced with a shower of hot shot and explosive shells at first light on 13 August. U.S. positions at Fort Erie and Black Rock returned brisk fire but many rounds sailed harmlessly over their intended target. Fire from the *Porcupine*, using grape instead of solid shot, did some harm, but the ship was chased away with hot shot. The barrage continued through the night. Rocket fire began on 14 August, and the barrage lasted through the day. At about 1600, a lucky shot from the eight-inch mortar hit a small U.S. magazine, making a spectacular explosion. The Americans were standing a retreat ceremony at the time, and General Gaines directed the men to give three cheers and struck up the bands to show that no real harm had been done. He sensed, however, that an attack probably was imminent.[1]

Despite the American bravado, the explosion persuaded the British that they had inflicted more damage than they actually had. The fire slackened at about 0030 on 15 August and ceased entirely about an hour later. This alerted the U.S. garrison to the imminent possibility of an assault. Generals Gaines and Ripley put their men on full alert. At about 0200, General Ripley was riding with his aide, Captain Samuel Harris, toward Snake Hill when the British attack commenced. The assault, lasting about 20 minutes, provided an incredible display of defensive fire power, which made the night as bright as day.[2]

Colonel Fischer's column had departed at about 1600 to assume its attack position before darkness. A light twilight rain accompanied the British column for the first part of its passage and, even after the drizzle had passed, the heavy cloud cover made the night seem much darker than usual. The approach march took six hours and much of it covered boggy ground, which made the trek even more difficult for those who carried the assault ladders (made on 12 August) to help surmount the American parapet. After a brief rest, the column advanced as ordered at about 0200. The point force (referred to as "forlorn hope") consisted of part of the 8th Regiment's Light Company and its DeWatteville's counterpart. The light company of the 100th Regiment led the main body consisting first of the remainder of the 8th's Light Company, followed by the DeWatteville's Grenadiers, the light company of the 89th Regiment, and the bulk of the DeWattevilles and the 8th.[3]

Within minutes of moving, the column was fired upon by an American picket, skillfully led by Lieutenant William G. Belknap of the 23d Infantry. His force withdrew slowly, firing an additional two volleys before successfully gaining the American lines, literally just a few paces ahead of the attackers. As the U.S. garrison came alive, the forlorn hope and part of the DeWatteville Light Company moved along the lake shore, waded chest high out into the water, and circumvented the American abatis. But, as they organized to attack the rear of the Snake Hill position, they were, in turn, hit by the Ropes and Marston Companies, which were deployed for just such a contingency. U.S. forces turned back the British after some hard fighting, capturing an estimated 150 redcoats while the current swept away many others.[4]

Meanwhile, Fischer's main column tried to reach the U.S. positions at a point further inland in an effort to support the forlorn hope. The British charged at least five times into the abatis. Some groups did reach the base of the American positions, but were frustrated when they discovered that their 16-foot scaling ladders were nine feet too short—another engineering gaffe. Moreover, without having flints in their weapons, the men were unable to return the defenders' fire. Finally, the ferocious volleys from the Towson Battery and the 21st Infantry companies to its left proved overwhelming, forcing the attackers to withdraw in some confusion. In doing so, the troops collided with the main body of the 8th and the DeWattevilles, holding amongst the boulders along the shore. Soon, panic engulfed both forces and Colonel Fischer's column could not make any further contributions to the attack. Troops from the 21st Infantry pursued the retreating British for "upwards of a mile," and a few were captured. According to General Gaines, the first British rush against Snake Hill was not checked until it had gotten to the abatis, ten feet from the American earthworks. Gaines started to send some of the Rifles to support the Snake Hill defenders but held them back when he determined that resistance had been successful. A few of the men from the 4th Rifles attached themselves in the column to Captain Chunn's 17th Infantry Company on Towson's right.[5]

General Drummond's concept of a three-column converging movement proved too complicated. In the darkness, the timing could not be as precisely executed as he had intended. It appears that the Snake Hill fighting had ended before there was any contact with the other British columns. Some of the more nervous U.S. pickets forward of the Douglass Battery had to be ordered back to their positions after they withdrew, prematurely, upon hearing the uproar at Snake Hill.[6] The British left column, consisting of the 103d Regiment under Colonel Scott, finally made its appearance at 0300. The crunch of the men's feet along the lake shore alerted the U.S. troops. The 103d made two gallant efforts to close with the Americans, advancing to within 50 yards of the abatis. But, the surge was blown back by withering fire from Douglass' guns, from another gun rushed to the fight by Colonel MacRee, and from the defending infantrymen. The fire killed Colonel Scott along with an estimated 30 percent of his men, and forced the survivors of the 103d to withdraw under some pursuit from Captain Harding's militia. A few of these men gravitated to the third British column.[7]

This column, led by Colonel Drummond, made three probes against the curtain of Fort Erie proper. On the third try, in desperate fighting, Drummond's men wrested the northeast bastion from the defenders. The American defense, commanded initially by Captain Williams and Lieutenant Patrick McDonough, crumbled as both officers were killed when Drummond's men piled in, allegedly shouting, "no quarter to the Yankees." An officer from the 41st Regiment had planted a ladder against the bastion, allowing soldiers and sailors to struggle in, with Drummond among the first. The colonel had directed his men to keep their flints in their weapons, enabling them to engage effectively the first American defenders. Drummond was killed early in the fight, and soon all leadership disintegrated, as one officer after another was killed or wounded. A few British troops advanced into the lower levels of the bastion, but these men were killed or forced back by fierce resistance.[8]

After the British secured the northeast bastion, Major Jacob Hindman, the overall artillery commander, and Major William Trimble with the 19th Infantry troops led unsuccessful counterattacks. The American success at Snake Hill allowed General Ripley to send three companies from the 23d Infantry and the 17th Infantry company to the fort's aid. Earlier, a detachment from the 4th Rifles joined the fort's defenders, later, a larger force of 11th and 22d infantrymen from the reserve were led into the fray by Captain William Foster, 11th Infantry, and one of the assistant inspectors, Major Nathan Hall. These efforts proved unsuccessful, because of the limited approaches into the fort. Captain Alexander C. W. Fanning's battery helped isolate the attackers from any reinforcements, dominating all approaches to the bastion. Then, at 0500, just as it seemed as if British victory was possible, a tremendous explosion rocked the bastion.[9]

The British had turned a captured American gun on their opponents. Apparently, a spark from its discharge ignited the ready powder magazine on the floor below. An American survivor recalls a sudden hush, as if everything was being pulled into a vacuum, then "an unnatural tremor beneath our feet, like the first heave of an earthquake, and almost at the same instant, the center of the bastion burst up with a terrific explosion and a jet of flame, mingled with fragments of timber, earth, stone, and bodies of men, rose to the height of one or two hundred feet, in the air, fell in a shower of ruins, to a great distance all around."[10]

The explosion of the northeast bastion magazine completely shattered British resolve, killing or wounding nearly 400 men and leaving hundreds of others dazed and in shock. The debris hurled throughout the area caused further casualties on both sides and spread confusion. Lieutenant Fontaine was blown off the parapet into a ditch, where he was captured by Major Norton's warriors "who after taking his money, treated him kindly." The British survivors not captured broke contact and staggered back to their own lines as best they could, assisted somewhat by Major Norton's native troops. Norton's group had not been given any specific role in General Drummond's concept. So, when he learned of the situation, Norton assembled his men and advanced with the intention of assisting Colonel Drummond's column. Impeded by the brush and trees and the darkness, Norton reached the fort only in time to witness the explosion and to assist in the withdrawal. After holding briefly outside the American abatis, all British forces pulled back to their origional trenches, pursued by American artillery fire.[11]

The British feared an immediate counterattack, especially during the period before the survivors of the different attack columns could be regrouped. But none came. The Americans launched only a few desultory probes, as General Gaines seemed happy to settle for a defensive victory, and still faced the tasks of repairing the damage and caring for the casualties sustained in the encounter. The British had suffered an estimated 1,000 casualties; the Americans fewer than 90. Although Drummond was quick to blame the DeWattevilles for the plan's failure, the General had no one to blame but, perhaps, himself. He had conceived a high risk, complicated scenario, overmanaged and demoralized one of his columns, and made no apparent effort to influence the battle once it had been joined. He tended to blame others for his own shortcomings throughout the campaign.[12]

Fortunately for both sides, the American field medical system was established sufficiently to cope with the medical disaster represented by the British defeat. One field hospital under Doctor Troubridge, 21st Infantry, was set up in tents in the middle of the encampment, just in front of a permanent building, which served as General Gaines' quarters and sometimes as a surgery. This hospital cared for the British wounded and coordinated their evacuation to the

American shore. Most of these patients were sent to the hospital at Sandytown within a few days. It took another four days for the last of them to be moved from there to Williamsville. Civilians who saw the wounded passing in wagons remembered that many appeared to be badly burned. Healthy prisoners of war were evacuated directly to Williamsville.[13]

Casualties were cleared as quickly as possible from the northeast bastion so it could be repaired immediately. Lieutenant Douglass reported "more than 100 bodies were removed," as well as partial remains. The British dead were passed over the embankment in front of the Douglass Battery and were buried with honors in mass graves of 40 to 50 each. It took several hours to get the "wounded and burnt" out of the ruins and nearly two days to bury the dead. An estimated 200 British dead near Snake Hill were allowed to float down river, presumably without honors.[14]

A second field hospital established near Snake Hill under the auspices of the 23d Infantry, remained operational until the American withdrawal. A burial place located nearby, described by historian Benson Lossing as "just back of Towson's Battery," appears to have been used to bury soldiers who died of disease or injury before they could be sent to Sandytown.[15] Officers' remains, on the other hand, seem to have been returned to the United States for burial as a matter of routine. When Major Morgan was killed, for example, his body was sent on the same day from Fort Erie to Buffalo, where it was buried the following day at Park Meadow. In other cases, the quartermaster contracted with teamsters to carry officers' remains to locations outside the battle area, apparently at the request of their families.[16]

The Snake Hill area hospital came to be known unofficially as the "Fort Erie General Hospital." Documents requesting rations for the "sick and attendants" the month of August indicate as many as 200 men and five women were associated with the facility as staff or patients. These records, along with pay vouchers, suggest that the matrons—at the request of the surgeons— remained with their hospitals and served with their units throughout the siege at Fort Erie well into October. One duty of these matrons was to remove the personal effects of the deceased so they could be returned to the next of kin or to the government as appropriate. First Sergeants or adjutants performed this duty in the field, which explains the absence of such effects in most burials, especially in hospital settings. The wounded who could be evacuated first went to Sandytown. Many of the sick, however, went directly to Williamsville with little or no pause in the Buffalo area.[17]

In addition to the matrons, other civilians occasionally could be found in Fort Erie during the siege. Entries on the vouchers, submitted by rations contractors, indicate the periodic presence of groups or persons classed as "indigent families" and "refugees." In one case two "Canadian women" were issued flour. These civilians were encountered most commonly in July and again in October, during periods when it was probably most convenient for American loyalists living in Canada to process through the fort to the U.S. shore. Occasionally the families of deceased soldiers came to Fort Erie to settle the men's accounts. In one case, the wife of a 23d Infantry soldier, killed at Lundy's Lane, visited the fort from West Point, New York, on 17 October. She drew her late husband's back pay and retained bounty from the regimental paymaster and collected her husband's property from his old company. Her presence and that of local produce sellers and other civilians in such a dangerous place was not usual and raises the question of whether civilian casualties were incurred during the siege, although none have been reported.[18]

In the latter part of the siege, when General Porter's Brigade was reinforced with 1,500 New York militiamen on 9 and 10 September, a separate hospital was established under the direction of Hospital Surgeon Eli Hill, a veteran of several earlier militia call-ups. This facility appears to have been located west of Snake Hill, but worked closely with the hospital there, almost certainly sharing the same graveyard. Militia medical operations often were distinct from their federal counterparts, although they were similar in structure. Problems in matters of accountability for material and equipment and in requisitioning procedures existed because of the definition of what the federal government's responsibilities were for reimbursing the state when this property was expended in federal service. A standardized central issue system was developing in federal medical forces, but not amongst the militia, whose surgeons ordered and used items in quantities based only on their own judgement and training. Consequently, it often was simpler to keep militia medical facilities separate from their federal counterparts even when working in close association. Surgeon Hill's operation remained at Fort Erie until the second week of October.[19]

General Drummond decided to keep the pressure on the fort even after his disastrous attack. The arrival of the 82d Regiment from Kingston offset somewhat the recent British losses and provided fresh manpower to support Drummond's engineers. The shattered 103d Regiment was sent to garrison Fort Niagara while the 89th Regiment also was brought forward. Thus, manpower was not as much the immediate problem as was the constricting effect of the U.S. Navy's operation on Lake Ontario. Drummond's logistical resources were shrinking gradually without adequate resupply. Another problem was the weather, which was turning increasingly rainy and cool. Lacking tents, his men lived under appalling conditions in dugouts and shanties made from branches, which compounded the prospect of growing sick lists.[20]

Despite these problems, Drummond developed and reinforced the siege lines. Lieutenant Phillpotts began the day after the attack to improve the rear defenses and the access routes to the new line and to clear brush along the proposed line, itself. The pace of the work was hindered by the scarcity of the tools and the difficulty of grubbing tree roots, and soon the noise of the activity attracted U.S. picket patrols and harassing artillery fire from the fort. Work on the second battery itself began on the night of 25 August about 450 yards from Battery One and about 750 yards from Fort Erie. The men completed entrenching the next day and built gun embrasures that night. Meanwhile, work began on entrenchments extending to a third battery position.[21]

An American attack on 26 August briefly delayed completion of the battery and left six dead and 30 wounded of the 120 British pickets on the line. The aggregate of casualties from these brawls in the swamps and the brush of no-man's-land amounted to serious losses for both sides. Few prisoners were taken and the wounded, if they were fortunate, were dragged by their comrades to safety for treatment. American artillery fire further impeded British progress. Although U.S. gunners sent many rounds of solid shot over intended targets their use of explosive rounds proved devastating. Yet by the night of 29 August, Drummond's men had in place two long 18-pounders, one 24-pounder carronade, and an eight-inch howitzer. The next day, the British unmasked the battery and commenced firing. The American battery responded with counterfire so intense that the British engineers soon were forced to build overhead cover for their guns. Again the engineers had erred, setting the battery in a roll of ground which hid it from the fort, but also masked the gunners' view of their target. Therefore the emplacement was largely harmless to the U.S. defenders.[22]

The British engineers immediately shifted their efforts toward developing an access and defense for a third battery site, located about 500 yards southwest of Battery Number Two and about 400 yards from Fort Erie. Assisted by men from the newly arrived 6th Regiment, work on Battery Number Three was completed by dawn of 3 September. Its armament consisted of one long 24-pounder and an eight-inch mortar, both taken from Battery One. It also had two long 18-pounders, originally emplaced in the nearly worthless Battery Two. These guns were replaced by two brass eighteen-pounders shifted from Battery One. This transfer left one 24-pounder in the first battery to interdict U.S. shipping movements and to protect the line's shore flank.[23]

The Americans continued to work on their defenses, as well, and to patrol beyond their lines—both extremely hazardous undertakings. Lieutenant Douglass reported that daily losses during this phase of the siege averaged one in 16 men; hardest hit were the fatigue parties laboring on the fortifications. The British fired about 300 rounds a day into the American positions, using mostly solid shot but also shells and rockets. Battery Three pounded the works to try to effect a breach, while Battery Two harassed personnel. The Americans remembered the 30 days following the 15 August attack as the hardest of the siege. The continual attrition, hard work, and poor conditions proved too much for 70 men, who deserted.[24]

Chapter 6

SIEGE III, THE SORTIE

No one was immune from the rain of British shells. General Gaines was severely injured while sitting at a table in his quarters and evacuated on 28 August. Brevet Brigadier General James Miller, newly promoted, assumed command briefly until the convalescent General Brown could take charge on 2 September. Brown had not been idle while he was recovering. As early as 1 August he had written New York Governor Daniel Tompkins requesting an additional militia call-up. In the interim, he asked the regional militia commander, Major General Amos Hall, for men. By 19 August, Hall had produced fewer than 300, because of financial support limitations similar to those constraints discussed in connection with hospitals. Brigadier General Porter worked with state officials to expedite pay, supply, and contracting issues. As a result, a second call for militia on 21 August drew a much more favorable response from the men of Cayuga, Seneca, Ontario, Steuben, and Genessee counties. Soon, 4,000 men converged on the rendezvous point at Batavia, largely because of Porter's efforts and those of the Governor's representative, Colonel John B. Yates.

In the following days, it proved easier to get the men organized into regiments and companies and properly mustered than it did to get them supplied and equipped.[1] Supply deficiencies plagued every category. The federal and state arsenals already had been strained by earlier requirements imposed by the unprecedented attrition of the campaign. The state arsenal at Onondaga expended the remainder of its small arms stock on 31 August, issuing "70 English and three French muskets with bayonets" and 20 bayonets with scabbards. The previous day it had shipped to Batavia 122 British and four French muskets with bayonets and a miscellaneous collection of accoutrements to include 38 "unserviceable" cartridge boxes and belts. Such a variety of weapons were being deployed that standard ammunition and bayonets could not be issued. The countryside was scoured for weapons not turned in previously by militia already mustered out from earlier calls. The demand emptied the armories at Whitesborough and Canandaigua, as well as that at Onondaga. Captured British weapons and equipment also were issued. A limited supply of flints was available; however, knapsacks and blankets were hard to procure, which in part, explains General Brown's insistence that the men be given tents when they arrived at Fort Erie.[2]

The militias were not alone in experiencing supply problems as the siege progressed. The engineers' demand for tools and building materials was voracious. For example, in the first week of September, Colonel MacRee demanded 610 broadaxes "without delay." It was apparent from his requisitions that work on the fortifications was continuing at a furious pace. The supply system began to feel the added strain. The 9th Military District usually drew its ordnance and quartermaster supplies up the Hudson River directly from Philadelphia. However, operations in the Lake Champlain Valley were consuming equally vast resources. Further, the transportation net west of Utica was so underdeveloped that it placed a severe burden on the pipeline. The flow of goods to Buffalo, therefore, was shifted in part to cross Pennsylvania instead. Thus, by the end of July, cartridges and gunpowder were coming from Pittsburgh overland to Erie and then to Buffalo by boat.[3]

Perishables and regionally produced items were received from the contractors by the public store keeper, Ezra St. John, at Buffalo. They were held there, then sent to Buffalo Creek where they were loaded in open boats for the trip across to Fort Erie. Only one small storehouse operated at the fort; consequently, most goods had to be held in open storage, which accounted for a high degree of damage and waste. Bad weather also could impede the steady flow of fresh rations and contributed to an increasingly monotonous diet as the siege endured. Salt meat and hard bread became the staples. It is interesting to note the volume of quartermaster business conducted in the Buffalo area in support of actions beyond the scope of General Brown's campaign. Contracts for lake vessels indicate a steady movement of troops from eastern locations to Detroit. Throughout August, for example, elements of the 3d and 5th Infantry regiments - bag, baggage, and families in tow—embarked for western posts through Buffalo.[4]

Inspectors' comments reflected the increasingly uneven status of supplies.

U.S. Infantryman, 1813. (Parks Canada)

Lt. General Gordon Drummond (1772-1854), Commander of British Forces in Upper Canada. (McCord Museum of Canadian History, Montreal)

Winfield Scott wounded at the Battle of Lundy's Lane, 25 July 1814. The wound put him out of the war, but Scott survived to campaign in Mexico in 1848 and retire as General-in-Chief in 1861. The picture is from David H. Strother's Illustrated Life of Winfield Scott (1847). (Smithsonian Institution, Armed Forces History)

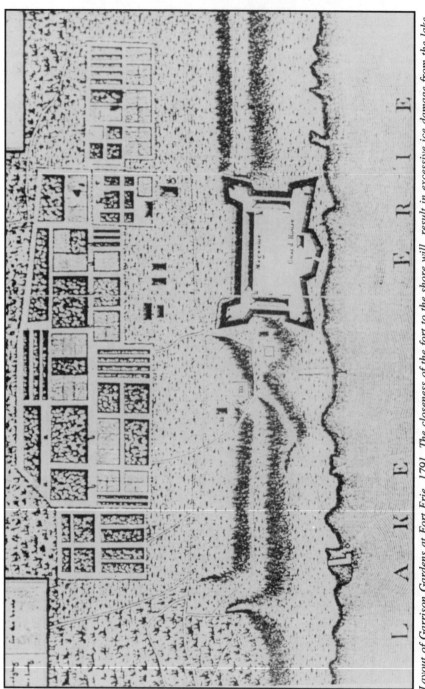

Layout of Garrison Gardens at Fort Erie, 1791. The closeness of the fort to the shore will result in excessive ice damage from the lake and cause its relocation more inland. (Public Archives of Canada)

Colonel Josiah Snelling cited the deteriorating condition of livestock resulting from the lack of balanced forage issues. Regarding the declining condition of individual equipment and clothing, he reported on 30 August, that more than 100 men in the rifle regiment were without shoes. Their condition, he said, was similar to that of the entire command. The clothing shortage worsened throughout September and October. By the end of the campaign, General Brown said the situation approached desperation. The remaining stocks in local depots as far east as Auburn had been absorbed by the reinforcements coming to Buffalo. He predicted a serious health crisis unless adequate clothing and footwear were made available immediately.[5]

The American logistical situation, although poor, was more promising than that of the British. General Drummond's soldiers were living under deplorable conditions. Since they still had no tents, the men lived in whatever temporary shelters they could contrive. As mentioned, their situation was worsened by two weeks of persistent rain, starting on 28 August and continuing on most days thereafter. Drummond was equally concerned about the limited flow of supplies to his force caused by the U.S. fleet's control of the mouth of the Niagara. He was stockpiling, slowly, a quantity of ammunition sufficient to support another possible attack. However, his letter to Sir George Prevost on 8 September suggests that he was beginning to lose confidence that his force could achieve anything further against the besieged Americans, and indicated that a British withdrawal was possible. Drummond's views did not shift even after he learned of the launching of the 110-gun HMS *Lawrence* on 10 September and the consequent predicted reversion of Lake Ontario's control to the Royal Navy.[6]

Part of General Drummond's discouragement may have stemmed from the attrition his units suffered during constant skirmishing and artillery exchanges with the Americans. The first serious U.S. probe occurred on 20 August, when a substantial force of riflemen advanced in the direction of Battery Two construction. The Glengarries and the British pickets and reserve engaged in an extended firefight lasting most of the day. Assisted with artillery fire, they forced the Americans to withdraw, taking their casualties into Fort Erie with them. The British moved their pickets closer to the fort to check a similar danger to the guns. However, this move posed too tempting a challenge to the Americans, who attacked in force again on 25 August. Major George M. Brooke of the 23d Infantry led a 100-man sally against the British. After a sharp fight, the Americans withdrew, collecting 30 British muskets. Brooke however, lost three men, including Captain Simeon D. Wattles, and counted four wounded.[7]

One of the most celebrated fights occurred on 4 September in conjunction with the unmasking of Battery Three. The American attack, spearheaded by a 40 man 21st Infantry picket guard led by Ensign Jeremiah Thomas, soon was joined by another 100 men from the New York Militia, led by Lieutenant Colonel Joseph Willcocks of the Canadian Volunteers. The fight lasted, intermittently, for about six hours before a rainstorm intervened, and the Americans withdrew at the command of Major Abraham Matteson. During the struggle, Colonel Willcocks and Lieutenant Thomas W. Roosevelt of the New York Militia were killed, among others. News of the turncoat Willcocks' death was a tonic to the besiegers, as they contended with another day of nearly continuous rain.[8]

U.S. rifle and artillery fire continued harrassing British labor parties working at Battery Three, and clashes persisted through the night of 5 September. Despite this, the battery finally was ready on the morning of the 6th in time to support the attack contemplated for the next day. But, General Drummond decided to delay the attack until additional reinforcements arrived and carried out a successful raid on U.S. picket post number four in front of Snake Hill, instead. The raid claimed 15 killed and seven wounded U.S. soldiers at the cost of two British casualties. Such successes in the brush fighting enabled the British engineers to complete construction of blockhouses at Batteries Two and Three, which afforded them added protection. Even before this last battery went into service, the Americans were experiencing daily losses from the besiegers' fire. The worst day for artillery deaths was 27 August, when Lieutenant Sylvanus Felton of the New York Militia was killed and 20 others were injured or later died. Both sides were beginning to show the strain of the standoff, especially at the high-command level. In many ways, the situation had become a question of the stubbornness or moral courage of the respective commanders.[9]

The steady grind and the bad weather seemed to have made General Drummond and his staff increasingly pessimistic. General Riall's replacement, General DeWatteville, arrived at the peak of the woodland skirmishing, assessed the situation, and advised a withdrawal. Drummond, himself, was convinced his artillery was inflicting little harm to the Americans and ordered ammunition husbanded to defend against a possible sortie in strength, which was being rumored by U.S. deserters and prisoners. Ammunition was so low at this point that it was no longer possible for the British guns to respond to the "brisk" U.S. fire, which the Americans began around the clock on 15 September. On 16 September, Drummond ordered the engineers to start evacuating Batteries Two and Three. By that evening, three of the guns were on their way back to Chippawa. The Americans would not let the remainder go unmolested.[10]

The tide of the war in late August compelled the convalescent General Brown to assume active command of his besieged forces on 2 September. The War Department's attention was now fragmented, with an increasing number of military flashpoints requiring additional support and guidance. To the south, where Major General Andrew Jackson was settling affairs with the Creek

Indians, rumors of increased British activity in Jackson's theater were supported by Royal Navy landings in August at Pensacola in Spanish Florida. In late August, several thousand British troops attacked Washington, burning the Capitol, the White House, and other government buildings. Meanwhile to the east, the Royal Navy continued to spread havoc throughout the Chesapeake Bay region. Clearly, the central government had larger worries beyond the situation at Fort Erie, which may explain Brown's sense of urgency and his early rise from his sick bed—any action that had to be taken would be accomplished with the resources within his command.[11]

When General Brown resumed command, the situation appeared critical. Brown was aware of the progress on Battery Three and concluded that the guns'continued slow pounding, characteristic of British tactics, could doom the fort. To counter the British threat, he began bringing over as many troops as possible to increase the offensive power of the garrison. Meanwhile, he initiated efforts to house the men as comfortably as possible in the increasingly rainy weather. A few veteran units returned after resting in Buffalo. Other newly arriving regular units were moved from the U.S. shore as soon as they trickled in from places as distant as Detroit, Sandusky, and Rutland, Vermont.[12]

Brown also directed General Porter to select the most reliable regiments from his New York Militia and bring them to Ft. Erie. Five regiments in addition to Lieutenant Colonel Hugh W. Dobbin's men, already deployed, were selected. A few men hesitated to cross the border, because they believed that the law specified they could be used only in defensive roles. General Brown ridiculed them, offering to provide a guard of their braver comrades to escort them home if they had so little courage. Finally, after a harangue from General Porter, the malcontents fell in with their more enthusiastic colleagues and marched to the docks. None of the New York Militiamen were in uniform, so Porter ordered them to wear red cloths around their necks or heads to show they were members of his brigade. General Brown directed that the movement of this large force proceed during the night of 9-10 September in order to conceal the possibility of an American attack from the British. The deployment of Porter's Brigade was helped greatly by the fortuitous arrival of four ships from Erie, Pennsylvania, bringing in reinforcements. The brig *Lawrence* and schooners *Lady Prevost*, *Caledonia* and *Porcupine* provided security, while their small boats helped carry the load. These ships later took up firing positions off the British water flank.[13]

Most of the militiamen crossed Lake Erie on the night planned without incident and set up a camp protected by rude sod and brush breastworks west of Snake Hill in cleared forest land along the Lake Erie shore. The rest of the New Yorkers crossed during the next two nights, along with the 150 men remaining in Major Thomas Jesup's 25th Infantry. Another 1500 New York militia held positions on the American shore, performing various security and support duties. All this movement did not go completely undetected. On 10 September, General DeWatteville suspected some kind of sortie could be afoot, one that he thought might include an amphibious assault.[14]

General Brown may have sensed a subtle shift in the tactical situation. British fire was slackening because of General Drummond's concern over the growing ammunition supply problem. In addition, Brown was aware that the British, without tents, were living in whatever temporary shelters they could contrive. With the advent of rain, he presumed the British sick list would grow rapidly, while the bad weather would not have the same adverse effects on his troops, who bivouacked, under shelter, either in floored tents or dug-outs. The image of continued British aggressiveness, as demonstrated by the completion of Battery Three and the fights around it, coupled with his assessment of their growing vulnerability, convinced Brown to risk a sortie to regain the initiative.[15]

Battery Three was situated so that it could enfilade a large part of the U.S. works, increasing the Americans'resolve to do something about it. Several of the U.S. officers talked vaguely about launching a sortie, and the concept was half-jokingly-endorsed by engineers MacRee and Wood. General Porter may first have raised the idea with General Brown, but whatever the source, Brown formally proposed a sortie at a council of war on 9 September. Although he received little encouragement from his subordinates, especially General Ripley, Brown persisted and worked with General Porter to secure the militia reinforcements that would be needed while he developed the final plan. In the meantime, American artillery fire increased considerably, hitting a tempo unmatched by the British gunners, frustrated by General Drummond's rationing of ammunition. An increase in picket skirmishing accompanied American probes into British lines, designed to acquire last-minute intelligence while masking the presence of Porter's force from the British scout's.[16]

General Brown knew, once the siege had settled into a semblance of routine, that General Drummond manned his forward lines with one brigade. The two other brigades rested, as they could, in the squalid camps two miles to the rear, beyond U.S. artillery range. Duty in the British line rotated daily. Brown's objective for the sortie was to maul the particular brigade on duty while destroying the batteries in the process. This would reduce the British artillery harassment and perhaps induce Drummond to lift the siege.[17]

The American commander worked on his plan in consultation with a few trusted officers but did not reveal his full scheme until late on the evening of 16 September, the day before the attack. In the meantime, however, the American artillery fire continued to increase, pounding the British positions. Pickets also expanded their activity on 16 September to protect pioneers hacking approaches through the forest to attack positions 150 yards from the British line.

These men were led by Lieutenants Donald Fraser and David Riddle of the 15th Infantry, members of Porter's staff. The two officers later became the guides for the attacking forces. The noise of the working party was masked by the sound of the artillery and periodic heavy rains.[18]

General Brown planned for a two-pronged thrust massed against Batteries Three and Two. The main thrust under General Porter was divided into two columns, headed by a large screening force. The recently arrived Colonel James Gibson of the 4th Rifles would precede the entire force with his men and the few remaining native troops. Porter's right column would be led by the popular engineer, Lieutenant Colonel Wood and comprised 400 1st and 23d Infantrymen, led by Major Brooke, as well as 500 New York Militiamen from the Dobbin, McBurney, and Fleming regiments. The New Yorkers in Colonel Wood's column were commanded by Major Hall, one of Brown's inspectors. Porter's other column consisted of the Hopkins, Churchill, and Crosby New York regiments, under the command of newly appointed Brigadier General Daniel Davis, an Ontario County farmer and experienced militia officer. Porter's objective was Battery Three. Once it had been destroyed, his force was to shift to Battery Two, where it would be assisted by a second column, led by Brigadier General Miller. This force consisted of Colonel Moody Bedel's 11th Infantry and elements of the 9th and 19th Infantries, led by Lieutenant Colonel Thomas Aspinwall. General Miller's force was to position itself in a ravine between the fort and the British lines, midway between the two targeted batteries. It could help Porter's men at Battery Three, if necessary, or join them in attacking Battery Two if Porter had been successful. Major Jesup and the 150 men remaining in his regiment, the artillery, and a number of convalescents comprised the rear area defenders in Fort Erie, itself.[19]

General Brown assigned command of the reserve to General Ripley almost as an afterthought. Brown had not kept his pessimistic subordinate informed during the last phases of the preparations for the sortie, but felt compelled to brief him early on the morning of the 17th. True to character, Ripley predicted a disaster. At first he said he wanted nothing to do with the enterprise. But then, he changed his mind and requested he be placed in charge of the reserve. Happy that Ripley did not demand a more active role, Brown agreed. The reserve, consisting of the 21st Infantry and two companies of the 17th Infantry, was ordered to deploy into the woods between the fort and Batteries One and Two to cover the main force's withdrawal back into the fort.[20]

On the morning of 17 September, under the cover of heavy artillery fire—described as "incessant" by one British soldier—the Americans moved to their attack positions. General Porter began his advance at about 1200. Guided by Lieutenants Fraser and Riddle, the large force advanced in fog and a light rain, which became heavier as they progressed. The inclement weather lulled the DeWattevilles and the 8th Regiment, on duty in the lines, into abstraction and helped mask the faint sounds of the U.S. approach. British work parties were busy removing the guns from Battery Three when, at about 1430, General Brown ordered Porter to unleash his brigade. The surprise was complete, and the defenders either ran or surrendered. In a matter of minutes, Porter's men captured and spiked the guns and Lieutenant Riddle, with the help of Quartermaster Lieutenant Archer Green, destroyed the adjacent blockhouse with explosives.[21]

The attackers then turned toward Battery Two, where they joined with General Miller's command, which had moved forward on General Brown's order to a point between the two target batteries. The commands linked at about 1500 and dashed into the second battery, taking the position amidst great confusion. Colonel Gibson was killed in this assault, and the indefatigable Lieutenant Riddle was wounded in the leg while straddling the remaining 24-pounder to spike it. Riddle would receive his second gallantry brevet of the campaign for his day's work. The American force then shifted toward the last battery.[22]

U.S. command and control was dissolving rapidly in the smoke and undergrowth and in the face of stiffening British resistance. As soon as the uproar at the lines was heard at the main British camp, every available man rushed forward, without regard to unit integrity. The 1st, 89th, and Glengarries attacked the Americans near Battery Three and in the connecting trenchlines. The 6th and 82d Regiments arrived in time to evict the first Americans from Battery One at bayonet point. General Davis was killed and Colonel Wood was mortally wounded and captured in the course of the fight.

During this melee, General Porter became separated from his command. Accompanied only by his orderly and another soldier, he blundered into a British company standing with arms at rest, apparently trying to decide what to do next. With the sounds of combat all around it, Porter tried to bluff his way out of the situation by shouting to imaginary forces behind him, grabbing weapons from the surprised troops, and declaring: "That's right my good fellows, surrender and we will take care of you!" One of the redcoats presented his bayonet and rushed Porter, knocking him to the ground with a slight wound to the hand. Only the fortuitous arrival of Captain John Richardson's Cayuga Rifle Company saved Porter and, in turn, captured the British Company.[23]

The 6th and 82d Regiments recaptured Battery Two in a fierce assault. A group of the 82d showed no quarter with the bayonet after their officer, Captain Robert Pattison, had been shot by American soldiers first appearing to surrender. General Porter later recalled that the maze of trenches, brush, abatis, and felled timber combined with the smoke and rain to make control irretrievable. The sun itself was so obscured that one U.S. prisoner escort detail lost its bearings and marched its charges into the British lines instead of to Fort Erie, its members thus becoming prisoners themselves. The battle rapidly devolved into a wild forest fight dominated by Major Norton's warriors and the now better-organized defenders.[24]

Sensing the shift in momentum, General Brown ordered Ripley's reserve forward to evaluate the situation and to direct a withdrawal, if appropriate. Ripley became separated from his force in the confusion and was seriously wounded soon after he joined Major Brooke's force. In the meantime, the fight had hit a crescendo near Battery One. Brown sent a courier to the 21st Infantry to assist General Miller's men on that flank. Somehow, Miller was able to communicate with his men sufficiently to begin a withdrawal. Seeing this, Brown got word to Porter to do the same, and soon the U.S. troops were streaming back with the British, native troops, and Glengarries in close pursuit. The British had regained their trenchline by about 1700. Brown estimated the whole affair to have lasted about an hour.[25]

The hour had been a costly one. U.S. forces sustained more than 500 casualties, losing many officers, with 12 killed, 22 wounded, and ten missing. The British lost more than 600 men, with more than half of them falling in the brigade on line when the Americans attacked. U.S. forces brought an estimated 400 British prisoners into the fort, but poor weather prevented shipping them to Buffalo until the afternoon of 19 September. Even then, the waters were rough. The approximately 200 Americans in British hands were marched around Lake Ontario to Kingston and Montreal. They later reported "kind" treatment from civilians throughout their ordeal, but very hard dealings with their captors. Those Americans who died in the British lines were buried by their foes in the trenches, which were soon to be abandoned. Ironically, had General Brown waited another two days, the British siege would have been lifted, anyway.[26]

Assault on the British Lines, 1814. Artist Unknown, Port Folio Magazine, 1815. *(Smithsonian Institution, Armed Forces History)*

Chapter 7

FINALE

The British continued withdrawing their hospital patients, heavy equipment, and stores on 18 September over virtually impassible, rain soaked roads. Some equipment, especially the heavy munitions, was moved by bateaux from a point near Battery One on the river shore. General Drummond justified his retrograde to Governor General Sir George Prevost by citing the increase in sickness caused by the continuing foul weather and the lack of adequate shelter, plus the obvious increase in U.S. strength as evidenced by the New York Militiamen, recently captured.[1]

Once the impedimenta was cleared, Drummond withdrew his main force at 2000 on 21 September. The British infantry abandoned what Drummond called the "lake in the midst of a thick wood" that had been their camp and trudged 1.5 miles north toward Frenchman's Creek. The troops left their campfires burning, and British pickets remained in contact with the Americans. Drummond advised Prevost that this movement restored his forces' mobility, however, the conditions of both the ground and his men hardly supported his explanation.[2]

At about 1400 on 22 September, Drummond's command withdrew further to a camp on Black Creek. General Drummond also dispatched the battered remnants of the DeWatteville and 8th regiments to Forts George and Niagara, where they helped repair heavy storm and water damage. In the meantime, General DeWatteville supervised a strong picket force, consisting of Major

Norton's native troops, the Glengarries, and a few dragoons. The U.S. forces had detected the withdrawal and on the morning of the 22d "sailed out" and destroyed the British camp which one of their officers described as "mostly fencing stuf [sic] and bushes." Then they pressed northward to regain contact. While DeWatteville skirmished with these Americans south of Frenchman's Creek, the British stores held at Black Creek were being shipped to Chippawa in bateaux. The latter operation was not accident free. At least one boat smashed onto Drake's Island and one of its crew was swept over the falls.[3]

The British main body pulled back once more to its final positions along the old Chippawa line, with pickets deployed forward along Black Creek and covering an area as far inland as Horn's Mill. General Drummond established his headquarters at Forsyth's by the Falls, while other units occupied Queenston Heights to guard against any surprise U.S. crossings. Major Norton's warriors were sent to Fort Niagara about 27 September in response to increased American activity. Meanwhile, General Brown's forces on the east bank were content to observe the British in their new positions. The siege of Fort Erie had lifted, but the drama continued as another American force closed into the area.[4]

Major General George Izard's Division was moving slowly into the region in response to an earlier call for help from General Brown. A British courier riding between Kingston and York had been captured around 7 September by a U.S. naval landing party from Sacketts Harbor. The contents of the papers he was carrying revealed that two more regiments were en route to reinforce General Drummond. This information inspired General Brown on 10 September to solicit Izard's aid. Brown asked for as much help as possible, fearing that the arrival of reinforcements would give the British the edge in manpower unless Izard could get a large part of his force to the Niagara front. The captured papers also may have influenced the timing of Brown's decision to launch the sortie against the British batteries.[5]

General Izard was one of the best trained flag officers in the American army. Born near London in 1776 of American parents, he was educated at various European military schools and commissioned into the U.S. Army from *L'Ecole du Genie* in 1797. He later resigned, but returned to service as a brigadier general in 1812. After working on the defenses of New York City, he commanded a brigade in the Champlain Valley until promoted to major general and assigned to command the U.S. Right Division. On 19 July, he had offerred to deploy his 5,000-man force along the St. Lawrence to threaten Kingston and thus pin down British forces that might otherwise go to assist in the Niagara area. His offer was ignored until 7 August, when Secretary Armstrong ordered him to move his men to Sacketts Harbor and to cooperate with the Navy in an attack on Kingston. If that proved unfeasible, he was to sail from Sacketts Harbor to Burlington Bay, where he would isolate General-Drummond's forces further east.[6]

General Izard protested these orders, because by the time he received them the tactical situation in the Lake Champlain area had changed, radically. It was obvious that substantial British forces were gathering at Montreal for a southward thrust. Izard proposed that he and his men remain at Plattsburgh to face this serious threat. Secretary Armstrong, unconvinced by Izard's argument, refused to change the orders for a westward deployment. Consequently, Izard, unwilling to take an unauthorized action, departed with nearly 4,000 troops on 27 August, en route to Sacketts Harbor by way of Utica. A week later, Secretary Armstrong was relieved of his position following the British attack on Washington, leaving no one fully in charge at the War Department for several critical weeks.[7]

On 3 September, the British under Governor General Prevost crossed into the United States, nearly a week after Izard had headed west. The large British force engaged in skirmishes as it moved southward. It then held north of a line along the Saranac River, defended by the remainder of the Plattsburgh garrison, led by Brigadier General Alexander Macomb. Both sides awaited the outcome of a naval battle for the control of Lake Champlain. U.S. Navy Lieutenant Thomas Macdonough defeated a hurriedly assembled British fleet on 11 September, causing Prevost to withdraw and ending the serious British threat in eastern New York. The critical U.S. victory was achieved with luck and good tactical leadership and without any guidance from Washington, which had focused too much on the Niagara at a very inopportune moment.[8]

The U.S. Right Division reached Sacketts Harbor on 17 September with 280 hard miles behind it. Lacking orders from Washington, and getting no encouragement for an attack on Kingston from Commodore Chauncey, General Izard decided to respond to Brown's request for help. He sent his dragoons and artillery over land and prepared to move the infantrymen in the fleet. Bad weather delayed their embarkation until 21 September, when the force sailed for the mouth of the Genessee River from which Izard's men set out for the west. The choice of landing there instead of at Burlington possibly reflected Chauncey's concern for the safety of his fleet and the possibility that the Right Division could be isolated that far west if lake control shifted. Izard's force of 4,300 men consisted of nine infantry regiments plus dragoons and artillery. The command left the Genessee on 24 March. A shortage of horses necessitated the use of 100 oxen to pull the heavy equipment and guns, which slowed the rate of march; the division did not reach Batavia until 27 September.[9]

At Batavia, Generals Brown and Izard met to discuss strategy and Izard as ranking officer assumed overall command. The two men decided that, first, Izard's force should attack Fort Niagara, while Brown's men held Drummond and his redcoats at Chippawa. Fort Erie, they agreed, was threatened no longer. Accordingly, Izard's men headed for Niagara, reaching Lewiston on 5 October. There, Izard and Brown conferred with General Porter and concluded that the absence of heavy guns for a siege underscored the need for all U.S. forces to consolidate north of Fort Erie and to operate together.[10]

The appearance of such a large force on the opposite bank fascinated, understandably, the British defenders on Queenston Heights. The full army could be seen south of Lewiston on the morning of the 6th. That afternoon, a U.S. command group was observed scouting various crossing points, all of which were well defended. During the night, twinkling campfires stretched for miles along the opposite side of the river. The next day, the U.S. force began to move south; its rear guard finally faded from the sight of the Queenston Heights observers at 0900. Extensive patrols were noted the remainder of the day.[11]

General Izard had moved to the Fort Schlosser area on 8 October with the intention of crossing the river at that spot; however, not enough boats were available. Consequently, on 9 October he moved his army to Black Rock and crossed into Canada on the 10th and 11th, camping two miles north of Fort Erie. The main body of the 17th Infantry had arrived at Fort Erie on board the *Niagara* on 6 October and was camped outside the fort. Izard attached the regiment to the 1st Brigade of his own division. On 13 October, he left a garrison under Major Jacob Hindman at the fort and took the rest of his force northward. He camped that night at Black Creek, then moved to Street's Creek the next day, prompting the deployment of British reserves to the Chippawa and to supporting positions along Lundy's Lane. Izard deployed from Street's Creek in battle order on the 15th and confronted General Drummond's force, now firmly established on the opposite bank of the Chippawa. He hoped, rather naively, that Drummond would rise to the bait, cross the Chippawa and repeat General Riall's mistake. When nothing happened, Izard deployed Towson's Battery of three six-pounders and a 5.5-inch howitzer and Captain Samuel B. Archer's two 18-pounders. An artillery duel ensued, in which four Americans were killed and two wounded.[12]

The armies lay on their arms in the intensely cold night, with the ground "too wet to sleep on," and continued to confront each other through the 16th. That day, Izard learned of the Navy's return to Sacketts Harbor and the subsequent reversion of the control of Lake Ontario to Sir James Yeo's Kingston fleet. As a result, he broke contact with the British on 17 October and moved his entire force southward to consider another tactic. The loss of naval support may also have started him wondering about any possible useful outcome from his activities.[13]

The following day, General Izard began probing the flank of the well-defined British position, sending Brigadier General Daniel Bissell's reinforced brigade about six miles west to Cook's Mills on Lyon's Creek. The brigade's primary mission was to seize or destroy British provisions rumored to be at the mill. The command consisted of Bissell's four infantry regiments, Captain Armstrong Irvine's company from the 4th Rifles, a small squadron of light dragoons under Lieutenant Philip Anspach, and a detachment of Captain Archer's artillery. The men marched on the morning of 18 October, following Black Creek part of the way on deplorable roads. The dragoons encountered and captured a British vedette, but, without further incident, the force reached the mills in the afternoon and set up camp. A pontoon bridge was built and Irvine's Rifles, Captain James Dorman's company, 5th Infantry, and Captain Thomas Horrell's company, 16th Infantry, were sent across to form a bridge-head defense. Lieutenant John Gassaway was sent further east of the bridge-head to set up a picket post on the road to Chippawa.[14]

British scouts quickly had detected General Bissell's movement. General Drummond immediately dispatched the Glengarries and seven companies of the 82d Regiment, all under the command of Lieutenant Colonel Christopher Myers, to shadow the move. As soon as Drummond learned that some of Bissell's force had crossed the creek, he ordered Colonel Hay, Marquis of Tweeddale, recently returned to duty and still suffering from his Chippawa wound, to reinforce Meyers. The Marquis took the remaining three companies of the 82d, the 100th Regiment, and the 104th Regiment Flank Companies and one six-pounder on a miserable night march through the cold mud. His force reached Colonel Meyer's position early on the morning of 19 October. Drummond ordered Tweeddale to determine the American intentions and to attack them if possible, but to take no unnecessary risks.[15]

The Glengarries already had tested Lieutenant Gassaway's picket in a series of skirmishes during the night. The next morning, Tweeddale forced back the American picket and advanced in line on the beachhead force to within about 500 yards of its position in a woodline. The men of the 100th behaved throughout with a studied coolness, almost bravado, which Tweeddale later learned was to show him that any recollections he may have had of their unsteadiness at Chippawa were unfounded. The Dorman and Irvine companies came under heavy fire for about 15 minutes, until General Bissell could get his main force deployed. Major Isaac Barnard led his 14th Infantry and advanced directly to support of the beachhead, with orders to hold the British force in place so it could be flanked. The 5th Infantry Regiment—led by one of its former officers, the Right Division Inspector General, Colonel Ninian Pinkney—maneuvered to get behind the British rear and capture the six-pounder. Tweeddale and Colonel Meyers detected this movement and, mindful of their orders not to over commit, smoothly broke contact and withdrew. Irvine's Rifles pursued them briefly, but to little effect.[16]

Initial reports of the contact and the distant sounds of battle were so alarming that General Izard immediately directed reinforcements be readied. The previous afternoon, Izard had ordered the 21st Infantry to rendezvous with Bissell. The regiment had slogged its way over what Captain Ropes called "the worst road I ever traveled without anything to eat or drink." The unit camped in the rain without shelter and dined on a few sheep purchased from a local farmer. The next morning, it continued toward Lyon's Creek as the rain persisted, only to encounter Bissell's force on its return march. "Much fatigued," the 21st joined the retreat. Bissell's men had pulled out at 1400 after they had buried friendly and enemy dead and destroyed 200 bushels of grain, but left the mills alone. Thus ended the affair at Lyons Creek. The Americans lost 13 killed and 53 wounded, the British one killed, 35 wounded.[17]

As morning broke on 21 October, U.S. units again appeared in force opposite Drummond's Chippawa positions. The British General was so unconcerned with the American presence that he went to a conference with Sir James Yeo on board one of the British ships standing off the mouth of the Niagara. By the time he returned, no American unit was in sight. Drummond immediately ordered his forces southward, including the newly arrived 90th Regiment, to determine his enemy's intentions. By daylight of the 23d, British scouts found the Americans positioned on the high ground opposite Black Rock, obviously on the defensive. The scouts, including some of Major Norton's warriors, again resumed positions along Black Creek, patrolling routinely well south of Frenchman's Creek. The continuing foul weather prevented General Drummond from deploying his main body, protected in their shelters along the strong Chippawa line. He was satisfied merely to keep an eye on the docile U.S. forces.[18]

General Izard, meanwhile, surmising that the Royal Navy's control of Lake Ontario obviated the opportunity for him to achieve any useful strategic objective, wished to end the pointless sparring with Drummond. The continuing inclement weather, coupled with the serious clothing shortages experienced throughout the command, further convinced him that the time had come to complete winter deployments. Both Izard and Brown shared rising concerns over the security of Sacketts Harbor, with so much of the 9th Military District's manpower concentrated so far from it.[19] General Izard must have made up his mind even as Bissell's men were dragging themselves back from Lyons Creek, because on 19 October he approved, immediately, General Brown's request to get to Sacketts Harbor as quickly as possible. Brown, the hero of the summer campaign, was on his way the next day, reaching the Harbor on the 30th. Six days later, General Drummond departed, having seen most of the force's tattered veterans shipped to York and Kingston and replaced by fresher units. Drummond left Major General Richard Stovin to watch the American remnants and to move the British forces into winter quarters.[20]

General Porter's Brigade received orders on 22 October to proceed to Batavia, where the men would be processed for discharge. The troops crossed the river by the 25th and were mustered out between 2 and 8 November, despite the fact that there was no pay for them. General Brown's Left Wing began a forced march toward Sacketts Harbor on 24 October under the leadership of Brigadier General William Winder, the victim of Stoney Point and Bladensburg. Winder pressed his men boldly eastward. Brown's tattered host of about 2000 men left Buffalo on the 28th and marched through the mud, sleet, and rain from dawn to dusk. Forbidden to use any buildings along the way, with little food and rarely seeing straw for bedding during the frozen nights, they pressed through Batavia on 1 November, Auburn the next day, finally reaching Sacketts Harbor on 13 November. By that time, only 1,500 troops were present for duty. Virtually every man had worn out a new pair of shoes issued just before the march; their blood-stained trail at the end of their trek reminded one officer of Valley Forge stories.[21]

The militia hospital at Fort Erie had closed on 19 October, and the sick and wounded were sent to Buffalo. The hospital was the last medical facility at Fort Erie. As late as 24 October, the Americans were still undecided about whether to retain the fort. General Izard had made tentative plans to establish a winter camp at Black Rock to support the fort. Thinking that he was outnumbered by the British, Izard engaged Captain Archer and nearly 100 men to improve the fort's defenses. Then, on 25 October increasingly rough weather convinced Izard that the oncoming winter would make it impossible to support the fort with any security.[22]

On that day, General Izard directed his chief quartermaster, Major John G. Camp, to gather the necessary men and boats to evacuate the troops and equipment from Fort Erie. The major enlisted 111 experienced boatmen from the units at Buffalo and hired another 130 discharged militiamen. An additional 30 officers and men were assigned to stand by at the docks at Buffalo and Black Rock. Izard also ordered Captain Archer to destroy the foundation of the block house he was building on Snake Hill and to demolish the whole site. His men set to work with such zeal that they broke nearly 20 picks and spades in the course of that day's work.[23]

Plans for the destruction of Fort Erie, hindered by continuing foul weather, were completed on 1 November, at which time General Bissel's brigade, the last remaining major tactical unit, left the fort. Major Hindman supervised the removal of the heavy equipment and guns; 15 guns remained on 1 November and were moved during the next three days. Then, on 5 November, the last troops, artillerymen, and engineers, placed the last explosive charges, boarded their boats, and rowed away as the fort erupted in total destruction.[24]

During November, nearly 1,000 hospital patients, as many as possible, were shipped across the state to Greenbush. Each day, hundreds passed eastward on the muddy roads through the villages of western New York. The nearly 2,000 patients who could not travel were gathered at the Williamsville Hospital and guarded by light artillery under Lieutenant Colonel Abraham Eustis. Construction continued throughout the month to accommodate the influx. General Miller led the 17th and 19th Infantries to winter quarters at Erie, Pennsylvania. The dragoons were dispersed to Batavia and the Genessee Valley for easier access to forage. The remainder of the U.S. Right Division built quarters for the winter between Buffalo and Black Rock. Soon, they began patrolling in force along the east bank again, raising periodic alarms. The British, for their part, were content to watch and spend their time building two new ships at Chippawa in anticipation of 1815 operations. The Niagara Campaign of 1814 had ended. News of the Peace of Ghent, signed on Christmas Eve, percolated into the area in early March, precluding any need for the new ships. Once more the Niagara Valley was at peace.[25]

The operations in which Fort Erie played such a prominent part have long been a source of great pride to Americans. Yet, on the surface, they seem pointlessly tragic. After all the death, destruction, and misery, the forces were back where they started from, both having lost many good men in the process. The concepts and direction of the whole campaign have earned well-merited criticism. For example, Secretary Armstrong's 28 February preliminary instructions to General Brown were confusing. They failed to indicate clearly that after Montreal, Kingston, unequivocally, was the next most important target in the 9th Military District. Once Brown had committed his forces, the Secretary believed that since control of the Lake Ontario probably was beyond U.S. grasp, the seizure of the Niagara Peninsula would be the next best prize. Considering that the occupation of terrain for negotiating purposes was a British aim, having an offset could have served some U.S. strategic purpose. Nonetheless, the generally accepted fatuity of Armstrong's view is not what really merits criticism; rather, it is his failure to coordinate the highly respectable forces of the Right and Left divisions in any kind of a combined operation. In short, the dynamic Brown and aggressive Scott were expected to achieve an objective without adequate resources. Ironically, the two soldiers with the professional acuity to perceive the outcome, Generals Ripley and Izard, did not have the moral courage or conviction to fight for a new strategy. Instead, they compromised, played along reluctantly, and in so doing ruined their military reputations.

Once his force was committed, General Brown's greatest weaknesses were in manpower and material support. Already operating below his requirement, he was forced to cope with inadequate reinforcement and insufficient resupply—problems that also plagued General Drummond, who experienced enormous difficulties with the flow of men and goods past Kingston. The relatively vast areas of frontier New York and Pennsylvania made any kind of large-scale, sustained operation extremely problematic. For the Americans, the difficulties in moving materiel were then compounded by Secretary Armstrong's proclivity to control the situation from Washington. This penchant restricted flexibility in the face of changing local situations, while it also stultified initiative on the part of local commanders. The slow movement of orders, approvals and requests made the whole system sluggish and unresponsive while virtually eliminating essential interservice cooperation.

The distances across New York necessitated the establishment of the intermediate depots mentioned in connection with the militia mobilizations. The depots eased the problem only partially. The costs of drayage were astronomical and rose in ratio to the distances covered. In the days of animal transport, forage demands often met or exceeded the value of the cargo. There never was sufficient forage, food and clothing along the lines of communication from Buffalo eastward to accommodate both the teams and men moving along them and the needs of the fighting forces across the Niagara. The slow movement of news meant that the logistical officers along this pipeline rarely were ready to react to the latest requirements imposed by the tactical situation. As a result, adequate materiel rarely was available when it was needed most, as witnessed by the August Militia call-up.

Things would have been much easier had the U.S. Navy controlled Lake Ontario, but no one with the responsibility in Washington or at Sacketts Harbor recognized this. The extent of the substantial achievements of Generals Brown and Izard must be judged against the light of difficulties posed by these supply and transportation problems and the absence of a higher coordinating system. It is remarkable they achieved so much.

As mentioned, Secretary Armstrong thought that local victories around Fort Erie would at least enhance general morale—and would be better than nothing. Although he has been criticized for this view, the fact is that General Brown's victories improved the morale of his countrymen. The images of Scott's grey line at Chippawa, the vicious nighttime fight at Lundy's Lane, and the courageous defense of Fort Erie ending with the dramatic sortie, all gave a positive legacy to the country's pride and self-confidence. The professionalism and courageous personal performances of so many of the participants bestowed a legacy of strength and self-respect to the U.S. Army which has endured. This respect crossed the battle line as well. Within a decade, the United States and Great Britain were tentatively cooperating on boundary issues and on matters of mutual concern in the Western Hemisphere. This new relationship is exemplified by the fact that Fort Erie was abandoned as a military post in 1823, the year of the Monroe Doctrine. All that remained was the small village of Waterloo and the Alexander Brother's storehouses, rebuilt for the third and final time.[26]

Perhaps Major Jesup best summarized the campaign in retrospect: ''We were all young soldiers, and the wonder should be, not that we blundered, but that we did not blunder more, and that our talented and veteran enemies should have out-blundered us.''[27]

1814 scene showing a U.S. general officer, left rear, U.S. Rifles in summer frocks and a sergeant musician, right rear, and a general staff officer talking with a field grade Rifles officer. (USA Center of Military History)

L'ENVOI

My first look at this hard fought campaign on the Niagara began as an attempt to explain how 28 American soldiers had found lonely graves on the Lake Erie shore. That explanation has led me to a more detailed appreciation of the campaign and the army that fought it. All who knew or know of General Scott have acknowledged that he was one of the U.S. Army's great trainers. However, exactly what he did, and what the results of his efforts were at the time of his rise to prominence, rarely have been demonstrated so graphically as they were in 1814.

Attempts to understand the graveyard's location have inspired a more detailed look at the medical and administrative operations of the 9th Military District. The operations proved to be reasonably efficient and sophisticated, debunking the stereotype of an inept army barely surviving any operational stress. Unquestionably, the American officers in charge of Brown's division had learned from bitter earlier experience. They presided over a reasonably responsive support system and a well-organized medical structure, capable of sustaining a large force in the field despite severe logistical limitations. The medical service developed into a form surprisingly similar to its modern counterpart.

Historical research and the archaeological analysis prompted by the discovery of the Fort Erie remains unequivocally confirmed that the graves were those of American soldiers. As a result, the Canadian government transfered their custody to the United States in a moving military ceremony held on the grounds of Historic Fort Erie on 30 June 1988. The Canadian military pall-bearers were members of some of the same historic units which had fought at the site so many years before. The 28 flag-draped coffins were transported to the National Cemetery at Bath, New York, in the Finger Lakes District from which so many of the U.S. forces had come. Nearly 175 years after their tragic passing, these forgotten soldiers played a role in reminding their coun-trymen of the U.S. Army's early sacrifices and achievements.

Fort Erie fell into ruins after the British Army abandoned it. It remained a tourist attraction for sometime thereafter, was used by Fenian raiders briefly in 1866, and then forgotten. The fort got a new lease on life in the 1930s when its restoration was seen as a solution to offsetting some of the effects of the Great Depression in the area. Reconstruction revealed the graves of the victims of 15 August just outside the fort, now marked by a monument. Once again, the mostly stone structure draws many visitors and more importantly, serves as a permanent memorial to the many men who performed their duty so long ago.

Annexes

NIAGARA CAMPAIGN OF 1814

In the past, one of the most frustrating aspects in studying the Fort Erie operations has been the absence of specific detail in published accounts. In most contemporary writings, authors have omitted full names, unit designations, or explanations of unit organization, even though much of that information was available, albeit in many disparate locations. The following annexes provide a solid reconstruction of U.S. unit organization and personnel based on the surviving data. Also included is a detailed chronology, which expands on the preceding narrative and also serves as a guide regarding specific incidents or dates. Finally, profiles of both typical and unusual U.S. units are provided, adding insight on unit careers and social composition. The bulk of this data pertains to the U.S. units.

- A. Chronology
- B. Order of Battle
- C. Unit Lineage
- D. Unit Strengths
- E. Officer Roster
- F. New York Militia
- G. Pennsylvania Militia
- H. Canadian Volunteer Regiment
- I. Indian Volunteer Corps
- J. Casualty Figures

K. Officer Casualties

L. Officer Mortalities

M. Soldier Mortalities—Descriptive

N. Soldier Mortalities—Rosters

O. Sample Company Analysis

P. Medical Facts

Q. Livestock

R. Enemy Prisoners

S. Weapons of the War of 1812

Annex A

CHRONOLOGY—
FORT ERIE OPERATIONS, 1812-1814

(Based on AG Letters, M 565, M 566;
SecWar Letters M221, M 222; RG 94, E 71, Eaton's Compendium)

1812

| 28 Nov. | American attack from Black Rock on Ft. Erie batteries is repulsed. Large number of American POWs taken (14th, 15th Infs., USN Tm). |

1813

28 May	Ft. Erie voluntarily abandoned by British.
29 May	Ft. Erie occupied by US troops, 12th US, COL Preston.
9 June	Ft. Erie evacuated by US troops.
12 Dec.	Ft. Erie reoccupied by British.

1814

11 Mar.	MG Brown's Div. begins move from Sackett's Harbor to Buffalo.
24 Mar.	BG Winfield Scott joins Brown's command at Batavia.
27 Mar.	Second increment of NY Militia from MG Amos Hall's Div. assumes 90 days duty on Niagara Frontier, relieving troops called up in January.

8 Apr.	BG Peter B. Porter and Jasper Parrish successfully negotiate with Iroquois for a corps of 500 warriors to be raised in support of the coming campaign.
20 Apr.	Headquarters at Buffalo, Winfield Scott in command while Brown is absent coordinating support and supervising defenses of Sacketts Harbor. Units embark upon period of intensive training.
2 June	Main body of 5th PA Volunteers leaves Erie, PA, on march to Buffalo. Arrives 14 June.
7 June	MG Brown resumes command in Buffalo.
15 June	11th Inf. arrives from Erie, PA (250 men).
19 June	Douglass' Co. of Bombardiers, Sappers, and Miners departs West Point for Buffalo.
21 June	Rear party 5th PA Volunteers departs for Buffalo by boat.
23 June	70 men from 22d Inf. (LT. Culbertson) arrive at Buffalo, attached to 9th Inf. until the remainder of the regiment arrives.
26 June	800 men from 23d Inf. arrive at Buffalo.
30 June	3 Companies from 22d Inf. (CPT King) join others with 9th Inf.
3 July	US forces envelop Ft. Erie. MAJ Thomas Buck, 8th Foot, surrenders garrison of 137 men from 8th Foot and 100th Foot. US:4 WIA 25th Inf.; UK:1 KIA.
4 July	5th PA Volunteers crosses Niagara River at Black Rock, marches to Chippawa, followed by 150 NY Cav. and 500 Iroquois (Porter's Brigade).
5 July	US forces encounter British below Chippawa River. *Battle of Chippawa—US*:61 KIA, 255 WIA, 19 MIA; UK:236 KIA, 322 WIA, 46 MIA.
6 July	Dead buried on site, wounded and prisoners sent to Buffalo.
8 July	British pull back to Ft. George and Burlington.
9 July	Scott's and Ripley's brigades reach Queenston Heights. Porter's brigade guards line of communications from Ft. Erie and Chippawa.
12 July	BG John Swift, NY Militia, killed near Ft. George.
18 July	St. Davids, U.C., burned by NY Militia under LTC Isaac W. Stone.
20 July	Americans probe defenses of Ft. George.
22 July	Unable to secure naval support, MG Brown lifts siege, pulls back.

25 July	US encounter British at Lundy's Lane. Battle lasted 1800-2400. Scott and Brown WIA, BG Phineas Riall WIA and captured. Scott's brigade decimated—US:171 KIA, 572 WIA, 110 MIA; UK:84 KIA, 559 WIA, 235 MIA. Dead buried on site.
26 July	BG Eleazer W. Ripley pulls US forces into Ft. Erie. Construction on defenses begins.
30 July	British advance party chases American pickets away from ferry position opposite Black Rock.
1 Aug.	British main body reaches Palmer's Tavern, six miles below fort. MG Brown requests additional militia.
2 Aug.	British close on fort, MG Gordon Drummond directs operations. Daily skirmishing begins. British main camp at Frenchman's Creek, two miles below fort; forward camp at Sherk and Madden farms.
2-3 Aug.	1st BN, 1st Rifle Regt. under MAJ Lodowick Morgan (240 men) repulse 600 British led by LTC J.G.P. Tucker at Scajaquada Creek below Buffalo on US side of Niagara River (0300-0400). US:2 KIA, 8 WIA; UK:12 KIA, 17 WIA, 5 MIA. (Buffalo was the US Logistical base; communication via rowboat from Sandytown.)
3 Aug.	First British siege guns are emplaced.
4 Aug.	BG Edmund P. Gaines assumes command of US forces. US Ontario fleet blockades mouth of the Niagara.
5 Aug.	1st Rifles under MAJ Lodowick Morgan and 4th Rifles under CPT Benjamin Birdsall are brought over from Buffalo; Swift's companies return from Lewiston.
6 Aug.	Rifles make "vigorous sortie." US:5 KIA, 4 WIA; UK:11 KIA, 3 MIA.
7 Aug.	British bombardment begins at sunrise.
10 Aug.	MAJ Lodowick Morgan, 1st Rifles, killed in skirmish while interdicting British work parties in their trenches (three KIA). American battery at Black Rock (NY Militia) fires on British flank. P.M.—US Schooners *Ohio* and *Somers* are captured; the *Porcupine* escapes.
13 Aug.	British barrage intensifies, sunrise to 8 p.m. On 13-14 Aug., US:10 KIA, 35 WIA, (including four officers).
1600, 14 Aug.	Heavy barrage resumes at sunrise. Just before sunset, American magazine blows up. LTC Victor Fischer's column departs for American left, moves four miles southwest to Lake Erie shore at Baxter's Farm. Rain persists until midnight.

2300	LTC Fischer's colomn moves from Baxter's Farm toward US position on Snake Hill. Order of march: Light Co. 8th Regt. (LT Young & guide SGT Powell, 19th Light Dragoons); Light Companies from Dewatteville's & 100th Regts.; elements Light Co. 8th Regts.; Dewatteville's Grenadiers; Light Co. 89th Regts.; rest of DeWatteville's; rest of 8th Regts. including 12 Royal Artymen (1000 men).
15 Aug.	British attack Ft. Erie (Snake Hill); contact US picket line. Under command of LT William G. Belknap, delays back into Snake Hill position, 12 casualties.

British dispositions: To attack Fort Erie—LTC William Drummond; one officer, 13 men Royal Arty., flank Companies 41 and 104 Regts., 50 marines, 90 sailors (360 men). To attack Douglass' Battery: COL Hercules Scott; 103 Regt. (700 men). Reserve: LTC J.G.P. Tucker; 1/Royal Scots, Glengarry L.I.; sqdn. 19th Light Dragoons.

US counterattack on northeast bastion first led by MAJ Jacob Hindman with a det. from 19th US, joined by 4th Rifles and elements of 11th, 19th and 22d US which formed in rear of Fanning's Battery.

British casualties: 147 captured at Snake Hill, 200 killed. 3 CPTs, 11 LTs, 350 men "lost" in Scott's column. 221 KIA including 14 officers, 174 WIA captured, 186 unwounded captured at bastion. Approx. 1000 total including 40 officers.

US casualties: 2 officers, 15 men KIA; 6 officers, 46 men WIA; 1 officer, 6 men MIA. Wounded and prisoners were sent to Buffalo.

19 Aug.	2d British Battery is completed, about 750 yards from fort; heavy bombardment resumes.
20 Aug.	Large skirmish, 40-50 American casualties, including LT Robert N. Yates and seven men KIA. Siege attrition averaged one of every 16 men each day. The Americans lost about 10-15 men per day in the siege: 16 Aug-1 Sep, 59 KIA, 147 WIA.
21 Aug.	Skirmish. US losses: 4 officers, 15 men. NY militia levied, 3,000 expected by 1 Sept. from Cayuga, Seneca, Ontario, Steuben, and Genesee Counties.
25 Aug.	Severe skirmish at 1500; MAJ George M. Brooke and CPT Simeon D. Wattles, both 23d Inf., led a patrol against British pickets. Wattles and two men were killed and six men were wounded.
27 Aug.	LT Felton, NY Volunteers, KIA and 20 others killed or

	wounded in arty. fire.
28 Aug.	BG Gaines wounded by arty.; BG Miller assumes command.
31 Aug.	3d British battery established, about 500 yards from fort.
2 Sept.	MG Brown resumes command.
4 Sept.	Severe skirmish. An 11th Inf picket reinforced with a detachment from the 21st US and a battalion of NY Volunteers repulsed British foray. LTC Joseph Willcocks, Canadian Volunteers and LT Roosevelt, NY Volunteers killed.
6 Sept.	Nearly 4,000 militiamen on station.
7 Sept.	British raid on US picket no. 4 (US:1 officer, 14 men KIA, 7 MIA; UK:1 KIA, 1 WIA).
7-14 Sept.	Rain daily.
10 Sept.	BG Daniel Davis' Brigade of Amos Hall's NY Militia Div. was called out on authority of BG Davis. Porter brought over 1,500 on the night of 9-10 Sept.; they camped west of Snake Hill. About 90 men from 21st Inf. and 350 regular army replacements join them. An additional 1,500 NY Militia deployed on US bank of Niagara. MG Brown requests support from MG Izard.
13-16 Sept.	Increased US arty. fire on British lines.
14 Sept.	400 Americans probe British lines; 1 officer KIA, 1 man MIA.
16 Sept.	American pioneers clear approaches to British lines.
17 Sept.	Brown's sortie: cloudy, light rain, increases to windy thunderstorms. Columns begin to form at 1200.
1430	Porter's three-part flank column leads out; COL James Gibson, part one, LTC Eleazer D. Wood, part two, BG Daniel Davis, part three. Battery #3 captured. Battery #2 captured, but Davis and Gibson are killed and Wood is mortally wounded. Battery #1 is taken briefly. Support: BG Miller. Reserve: BG Ripley. Ft. Erie: MAJ Jesup. Buffalo: COL Brady.
1630	Fierce British counterattack; Americans withdraw. (US:79 KIA, 216 WIA, 216 MIA, including 12 officers KIA, 10 MIA;UK:650 all categories, 115 KIA, 148 WIA, 400 MIA.)
18-19 Sept.	British siege guns are pulled back.
21 Sept.	British withdraw in the evening to positions on Chippawa River, leave pickets opposite Black Rock. MG George Izard departs Sackett's Harbor with 4,000 men.

26 Sept.	Izard's force reaches Batavia.
5 Oct.	Izard's force at Lewiston.
10 Oct.	Izard arrives at Black Rock, assumes overall command.
11 Oct.	Ft. Erie reinforced with 17th Inf. & 300 dragoons.
12 Oct.	Izard's force crosses Niagara.
13 Oct.	Izard's force advances with his Div. (3,500 regs.) and Brown's Div. (2,000 regs., 800 volunteers). MAJ Hindman in charge of Ft. Erie garrison.
15 Oct.	Arty. duel across Chippawa River; US:4 KIA, 1 WIA
19 Oct.	Battle at Lyon's Creek (Cook's Mills):
1900	Bissell's Brigade (5th, 14th, 15th, 16th Inf. Regts., Irvine's Co. of 4th Rifles, dragoons) engage Glengarry Light Inf. (US:13 KIA, 54 WIA, including 4 officers, 1 MIA; UK:1 KIA, 35 WIA.) Americans buried enemy & friendly dead on the field.
20 Oct.	Brown's Div. withdrawn, returns to US. Bissell pulls back from Lyon's Creek.
21 Oct.	Izard's force returns to Ft. Erie.
25 Oct.	MG Izard directs retrograde from Ft. Erie to begin and the fort prepared for demolition.
5 Nov.	Ft. Erie abandoned and destroyed.
9 Nov.	Militia discharged at Batavia.
13 Nov.	Brown's Div. closes into Sackett's Harbor.

Annex B

United States
WAR DEPARTMENT—MILITARY DISTRICTS

Effective 2 May 1813

Number One	—Massachusetts and New Hampshire
Number Two	—Rhode Island and Connecticut
Number Three	—New York from the Sea to the Highlands, and New Jersey excluding that part of the state which furnishes the first division of militia
Number Four	—New Jersey as defined (previously), Pennsylvania, and Delaware
Number Five	—Virginia south of the Rappahannock
Number Six	—North and South Carolina and Georgia
Number Seven	—Louisiana, the Mississippi Territory, and Tennessee
Number Eight	—Kentucky, Ohio, and the Territories of Indiana, Michigan, Illinois, and Missouri
Number Nine	—New York north of the Highlands, and Vermont
Number Ten	—Maryland, the District of Columbia, and that part of Virginia lying between the Rappahannock and Potomac Rivers

(Source: Army Register 1815)

United States
Left Division, 9th Military District
Order of Battle, Niagara Campaign 1814

MG Jacob Brown, Commanding General, 3–25 July; 2 September–10 October
MG Eleazer W. Ripley, Commanding General, 25 July–4 August
MG Edmund P. Gaines, Commanding General, 4–28 August

5 July Battle of Chippawa
<table>
<tr><td>1st Brigade</td><td>BG Winfield Scott
9th Inf. (6 companies), 22d Inf. (3 companies)—MAJ Henry Leavenworth
11th Inf.—COL John B. Campbell (WIA);
25th inf.—MAJ Thomas Jesup</td></tr>
<tr><td>2d Brigade</td><td>BG Eleazer W. Ripley
21st Inf., 19th Inf. (2 companies)—COL James Miller
23d Inf.—MAJ Daniel McFarland</td></tr>
<tr><td>Militia Brigade</td><td>BG Peter B. Porter
5th PA Volunteers—COL James B. Fenton
NY Mtd Volunteers (150)—CPT Claudius V. Boughton
Indian Corps (500)—LTC Erastus Granger</td></tr>
<tr><td>Artillery</td><td>MAJ Jacob Hindman
CPT Nathan Towson's (5 guns)
CPT Thomas Biddle's (3 guns)
CPT John Ritchie's (2 Guns)
CPT Alexander J. Williams' (5 guns)</td></tr>
<tr><td>2d Lt.Dragoons</td><td>CPT Samuel D. Harris' Co.</td></tr>
</table>

7 July   COL Hugh W. Dobbin's NY Volunteer Regt. arrives (600 men), attached to Porter's Brigade. Odell's Co., 23d Inf., arrives from Plattsburg.

9 July   CPT Douglass' Co. of Bombardiers arrives (50 men), assigned to siege train. Swift's Dobbins Regt., NY Militia joins Porter's Brigade.

14 July   22d Inf., COL Hugh Brady, arrives, assigned to 1st Brigade.

20 July   All but 50 Indians leave. Those left are formed as CPT Fleming's NY Light Co.

25 July Battle of Lundy's Lane
<table>
<tr><td>1st Brigade</td><td>BG Winfield Scott (WIA); LTC Thomas Aspinwall
9th Inf.—MAJ Henry Leavenworth*
11th Inf.—MAJ John McNeil (WIA)*
22d Inf.—COL Hugh Brady (WIA)*
25th Inf.—MAJ Thomas S. Jesup (WIA)*
<small>*cons w/9th Inf.</small></td></tr>
</table>

2d Brigade BG Eleazer W. Ripley
21st Inf., 19th Inf. (2 Companies), 17th Inf. (1 co)—
COL James Miller
23d Inf.—MAJ Daniel McFarland (KIA); MAJ
George M. Brooke
1st Inf.(150 men)—LTC Robert C. Nicholas (arrived
PM 25 July)

Militia Brigade BG Peter B. Porter
5th PA Volunteers—COL James B. Fenton Swift's
Regt. NY Militia—LTC Hugh W. Dobbin
Can. Volunteer. Regt.—LTC Joseph Willcocks
NY Mounted Volunteers—CPT Claudius V.
Boughton

2dLt Dragoons CPT Samuel D. Harris' Co.

Artillery MAJ Jacob Hindman
CPT Nathan Towson's (5 guns)
CPT Thomas Biddle's (3 guns)
CPT John Ritchie's (KIA); CPT John J. Fontaine's
(2 guns)
CPT Alexander J. Williams' (5 guns)
CPT David B. Douglass' Bombardiers (2 guns)

Misc. Militia Swift's Regiment NY Det. Militia (4 Companies at
Lewiston)
1 Co PA Volunteers at Buffalo
2 Companies NY Militia at Chippawa
1 Co (-) PA Volunteers at Ft Erie

1 Aug. 1st Rifle Regt (200 men)—MAJ Lodowick Morgan, arrives at
Buffalo from Sacketts Harbor

4 Aug. 2 Companies 1st Rifle Regt and 2 Companies 4th Rifle
Regt.—CPT Benjamin Birdsall, arrive from Erie, PA.

11 Aug. 2 Companies, 19th Inf. arrive at Buffalo from Erie, PA. LTC
Micah Brook's Regt., NY Militia, at Williamsville

15 Aug. Attack on Fort Erie

Left BG Eleazer W. Ripley
21st Inf.—LTC Eleazer D. Wood, CE
23d Inf., 17th Inf. (Co)—MAJ George M. Brooke
CPT Nathan Towson's (6 guns)

Center BG Peter B. Porter
5th PA Volunteers—MAJ James Wood
Swift's Regt., NYM—LTC Hugh W. Dobbins
CPT Thomas Biddle's (3 guns)

		CPT John J. Fontaine's (POW), CPT Alex. C.W. Fanning's (2 guns)
		1st & 4th Rifles—CPT Benjamin Birdsall (WIA); CPT L.G.A. Armistead
	Fort	MAJ William A. Trimble
		19th Inf. (2 Companies)—MAJ Trimble
		CPT Alexander J. Williams' (KIA); CPT J.W. Gookin's (3 guns)
	Right	LTC William MacRee, CE
		CPT Micajah Hardings' Co PA and NY Volunteers (120 men)
		CPT Claudius V. Boughton's NY Cav. Co. (100 men) dismounted
		CPT David B. Douglass' Bombardiers (50 men; 2 guns)
		9th Inf.—CPT Edmund Foster
	Reserve	LTC Thomas Aspinwall
		Companies 11th, 22d Inf., CPT Harris' Dragoons
	Black Rock	1st Inf.—LTC Robert C. Nicholas
	Buffalo	25th Inf.—LTC George McFeely
23 Aug.		90 recruits for 21st Inf. (LT Pratt) arrive
26 Aug.		Fenton's PA Volunteers discharged
29 Aug.		LTC Moody Bedel, 11th Inf., brings det. of reinforcements from VT.
30 Aug.		CPT Thomas Ramsey's Co, 1st Rifles arrives at Ft. Erie from Sandusky, OH; CPT John Lytle's Co, 4th Rifles arrives from Erie, PA; 23d Inf. reinforcements under 1LT John B. Truax arrive from Utica.
31 Aug.		4th Rifle Regt., COL James Gibson, arrives from Utica.
1 Sept.		22d Inf. sent to Buffalo, completes move on 10 Sept., 200 NY Cav. reach Buffalo
9 Sept.		25th Inf.—MAJ Thomas Jesup crosses from Buffalo (150 men)

NY Militia cross to Ft. Erie (1,500 men):
    LTC George Fleming's Regt.
    LTC Worthy L. Churchill's Regt.
    LTC James McBurney's Regt.
    LTC Caleb Hopkin's Regt.
    LTC Jedediah Crosby's Regt.
Remaining in Buffalo-Lewiston area:
    LTC James McMahan's Regt.
    COL William Vales' Regt.

LTC Mathias Leman's Regt.
COL Peter Allen's Regt.
LTC John Harris' Regt.
LTC Micah Brooks' Regt.

17 Sept. Sortie from Ft. Erie
  Main: BG Peter B. Porter
  Advance: 1st & 4th Rifles (200 men), CPT Fleming's Lt. Co.—COL James Gibson (KIA)
  Right Column: 1st Inf. & 23d Inf. (400 men, MAJ Brooke), 2d Lt. Dragoons (CPT Harris), Dobbin's Regt. (CPT N. Hall), McBurney's Regt., Fleming's Regt.—LTC Eleazer D. Wood (KIA)
  Left Column: Hopkins', Churchill's, & Crosby's Regts.—BG Daniel Davis (KIA)
  Ravine: BG James Miller
    9th & 19th Inf.—LTC Thomas Aspinwall (WIA)
    11th Inf.—COL Moody Bedel
  Reserve: BG Eleazer D. Ripley
    21st Inf., 2 Companies 17th Inf.
  Ft. Erie: MAJ Thomas Jesup
    25th Inf.
  Buffalo: COL Hugh Brady
    22d Inf.
    Elements, NY Militia

6 Oct. 17th Inf. Regt. arrives from Detroit (497 men)
10-12 Oct. MG George Izard's Div. crosses Niagara
  BG Daniel Bissell's Brigade
    5th Inf.—COL John D. Bowyer
    14th Inf.—MAJ Isaac D. Barnard
    15th Inf.—COL David Brearley
    16th Inf.—COL Cromwell Pearce
  BG Thomas A. Smith's Brigade
    4th Inf.—COL Robert Purdy
    10th Inf.—LTC Duncan L. Clinch
    12th Inf.—COL Isaac A. Coles
    17th Inf.—COL John Miller
  Artillery
    CPT Samuel B. Archer's Btry.
  2d Lt. Dragoons
  LTC Abraham Eustis

(Source: RG 94, E 71, Eaton's Compendium; E 53, E 55, Muster Rolls; RG 98, Unit Records)

British
Order of Battle, Niagara Campaign 1814
MG Gordon Drummond Commanding

1 July   The Right Div. under MG Gordon Drummond was deployed as follows:
103d Regt.; Militia—Burlington
8th Regt.; Glengarry Light Inf.—York
Niagara frontier units commanded by BG Phineas Riall
41st Regt.—Ft Niagara; 1st and 100th Regt., 19th LT. Dragoons (Det.), Prov. Dragoons (2 troops), Lincoln Co. Militia Flank Companies, Indians; all deployed west bank of Niagara from Ft. Erie to Ft. George

3 July   100th Regt. concentrated at Chippawa

5 July   8th Regt. arrives from York

7 July   Upper Canada Incorporated Militia deployed from Kingston to Ft Niagara.
89th Regt. and 104th Regt. Flank Companies sent from Kingston to York.
6th, 82d and 90th Regts. ordered from Montreal to Kingston.

8 July   Glengarry Lt. Inf. and 300 York Militia arrive at Ft. George.

23 July   104th Flank Companies reach 12 Mile Creek and are attached to 103d Regt..

25 July   MG Drummond with 103d Regt. joins Riall's force at Lundy's Lane.
89th Regt. arrives at Ft. George and Ft. Niagara.

29 July   DeWatteville's Regt. arrives at Ft Niagara.

8 Aug.   DeWatteville's Regt. fully closed at Ft. Erie, accompanied by 260 sailors and Royal Marines.

18 Aug.   82d Regt. arrived at Ft. Erie.
89th Regt. deploys from Ft. Niagara to Ft. Erie.
103d Regt. withdrawn to Ft. George.

24 Aug.   82d Regt. completes move to Ft. Erie.

2 Sept.   6th Regt. arrived at Ft. Erie.

8 Sept.   104th Regt. Flank Companies are withdrawn to Chippawa.

18 Sept.   97th Regt. at Chippawa.

23 Sept.   90th Regt. at Queenston.

19 Oct.   5 Companies of the 90th Regt. land at Burlington.

2 Nov.   37th Regt. and Arty. reinforcements land at Ft. George.

(Source: Right Division Orders, PAC, MG 19; E.A. Cruikshank, Documentary History...)

Annex C

UNIT LINEAGES

U.S. Unit Lineage
Perpetuation of War of 1812 Units in Modern U.S. Army

1814		1992
1st Infantry	-	3d Infantry
9th Infantry	-	5th Infantry
11th Infantry	-	6th Infantry
17th Infantry	-	3d Infantry
19th Infantry	-	3d Infantry
21st Infantry	-	5th Infantry
22nd Infantry	-	2d Infantry
23d Infantry	-	2d Infantry
25th Infantry	-	6th Infantry
26th Infantry		—
1st Rifles		—
4th Rifles		—
Towson's Battery	-	2/2 ADA
Fanning's Battery	-	2/3 ADA
Biddle's Battery		—
Williams' Battery		—
2 LT Dragoons		—

(Source: Organizational History Branch, USA Center of Military History)

Regional Affiliation of U.S. Units at Ft Erie, 1814

1st Infantry	-	New Jersey
9th Infantry	-	Massachusetts
11th Infantry	-	Vermont, New Hampshire
17th Infantry	-	Kentucky
19th Infantry	-	Ohio
21st Infantry	-	Massachusetts
22d Infantry	-	Pennsylvania
23d Infantry	-	New York
25th Infantry	-	Connecticut
1st Rifles	-	Pennsylvania, Maryland, Virginia, Kentucky, Tennessee
4th Rifles	-	New England, New York
Arty and Dragoons	-	At large
PA Volunteers	-	Cumberland, Franklin, Adams Counties
NY Volunteers	-	Cayuga, Seneca, Ontario, Steuben, Genesee Counties

(Source:*Army Register*1813; Fenton,*Journal...*; Hastings,*Tompkins Papers...*)

British Unit Lineage
Perpetuation of War of 1812 Units in Modern Forces

1812	1992
1st Regiment of Foot	Royal Scots
6th Regiment of Foot	Royal Regiment of Fusiliers
8th Regiment of Foot	Kings Regiment
41st Regiment of Foot	Royal Regiment of Wales (24/41st)
82d Regiment of Foot	Queen's Lancashire Regiment
89th Regiment of Foot	Royal Irish Rangers
100th Regiment of Foot	—
103d Regiment of Foot	—
104th Regiment of Foot	Royal New Brunswick*
Glengarry Lt. Infantry Fencibles	Stormont, Dundas and Glengarry Highlanders*
DeWatteville's Regiment	—
Royal Marines	Royal Marines
19th Lt. Dragoons	15th/19th King's Royal Hussars
Artillery, St Clair's Company	74th Mdm Battery
Artillery, Maclachlane's Company	—
Artillery, Holcroft's Company	—

*Canadian militia with a geographic claim to lineage
(Source: D.E. Graves, Directory of History, Nat. Defence Hq., Ottowa)

Annex D

Niagara Frontier 1814

Initial U.S. Strength, 1 July

Regiments	*Present for duty* Offs	Men	*Total* Pres & Absent	
9th Infantry	16	332	642	
11th Infantry	17	416	577	
22d Infantry	12	217	287	
25th Infantry	16	354	619	
Headquarters	4	—	4	
Total:	65	1,319	2,129	1st Brigade (Scott's) 30 June 1814
21st Infantry	25	651	917	
23d Infantry	8	341	496	
Headquarters	2	—	2	
Headquarters	2	—	2	
Total:	35	992	1,415	2d Brigade (Ripley's) 2 July 1814
Towson's Btry		89	101	
Biddle's		80	104	
Ritchie's		96	133	
Williams'		62	73	
Total:		317	411	MAJ Jacob Hindman's Artillery Corps

Pa Vols	753	MG P.B. Porter's Brigade, 2 July 1814
Indians	600	

(Source: RG 94, E 71; "Eaton's Compendium")

U.S Unit Strength as Shown by Ration Abstracts for the Months July through October 1814

Unit	July	Aug	Sep	Oct
1st Infantry	186		176	23
9th Infantry	435	279*	323*	293*
11th Infantry	490	295	334	334**
19th Infantry	161	*	*	11
21st Infantry	726	540	540	498
22d Infantry	274	264	251	**
23d Infantry	464	374	387	410
25th Infantry	357	288	290	*
Rifles	183	338	454	414
Artillery	380	285	324	362
Dragoons	68	56	74	412
Bombardiers	51	67	36	27
Willcocks'	56	13	**	—
NY Volunteers	620	483	1,500**	1,466
PA Volunteers	540	338	—	—
Indians	386	50		12
4th Infantry				555
5th Infantry				394
10th Infantry				322
12th Infantry				532
15th and 16th Infantries				844
17th Infantry				616
Lt. Artillery				440
Archer Artillery				181

(Based on RG 94, Box 14, Contractors Accounts, c1812-1820, William D. Cheever.)

Annex E

U.S. OFFICER ROSTER

Niagara Campaign, July-October 1814

1st Infantry
>LTC Robert C. Nicholas
>
>CPT John C. Symmes
>1LT Stephen Shea
>2LT Hilary Brunot
>
>1LT Lewis Bisell, WIA 25 July
>1LT Barony Vasques, WIA 25 July
>2LT John A. Shaw

9th Infantry
>LTC James Aspinwall, WIA 17 Sept.
>MAJ Henry Leavenworth, WIA 25 July
>MAJ Chester Lyman
>1LT Adj Loring Palmer, WIA 5 July
>1LT QM William Browning
>1LT Paym John Fowle, Jr.
>Surgeon Joseph Lovell
>Surgeon's Mate Thomas G. Mower
>
>CPT Abraham Hull, KIA 25 July
>CPT William J. Foster
>2LT Henry Willington
>
>CPT Thomas J. Harrison, WIA 5 July
>1LT William Browning, WIA 25 July

2LT Otis Fisher, WIA 25 July
ENS Joseph K. Jacobs, WIA 25 July
ENS George W. Jacobs, WIA 25 July

CPT Turner Crooker
1LT Joseph Gleason
1LT Stephen Turner, KIA 25 July

1LT Aaron Lewis
2LT Adolphus Burghart, KIA 25 July

CPT Jared Ingersoll, WIA 17 Sept.
1LT Ebenezer Childs, WIA 20 Aug., 17 Sept.
3LT Caleb Cushman, WIA 25 July
ENS Chesley Blake, WIA 25 July

CPT Samuel L. Allen
1LT David Perry, POW 25 July
3LT Elisha Brimhall, WIA 5 July

CPT Edmund Foster
1LT Daniel Chandler
3LT Patrick O'Flyng

11th Infantry
COL James B. Campbell, WIA 5 July
LTC Moody Bedel
MAJ John McNeil, Jr., WIA 25 July
MAJ Orsamus C. Merrill
1LT Adj David Crawford, WIA 17 Sept.
1LT Adj Newman S. Clark
2LT QM Hazen Bedel, WIA Aug.
2LT Paym Thomas Staniford
Surgeon Gordon P. Spencer
Surgeon's Mate T. Woodward
Surgeon's Mate John Sackett

CPT William S. Foster, WIA 25 July
1LT Henry J. Blake
3LT Isaac B. Davis, DOW 28 Sept.

CPT Valentine Goodrich, KIA 25 July
CPT John Bliss, WIA 25 July
2LT Enoch Cooper, WIA 25 July, 17 Sept.

3LT Benjamin Stevenson, WIA 25 July, 17 Sept.
3LT Humphrey Webster, WIA 25 July
ENS Thomas Dickey, WIA Sept.

CPT Horace Hale, KIA 17 Sept.
1LT William F. Hale, WIA 25 July, 17 Sept.
1LT Frederick A. Sawyer

CPT Malachi Corning
1LT James Wells
2LT Ezekial Jewett
2LT John V. Barron, WIA 25 July
ENS Elias Bedford, WIA 25 July

1LT Isaac Clark, Jr., WIA 17 Sept.
ENS John C. Walker
ENS Timothy Aldrich

17th Infantry Company
CPT John T. Chunn
1LT Thomas Mountjoy
ENS Mason Seward

19th Infantry
MAJ William A. Trimble, WIA 17 Sept.

CPT Alexander Hill
1LT John Carroll

1LT Carey A. Trimble
3LT Alexander Patterson, WIA 14 Aug.
ENS Nathan L. Reeves

CPT George Kesling
2LT Robert Stockton
3LT John McElwain
ENS Charles Cissna, WIA 15 Aug.

1LT William McDonald
2LT Abraham Fink
3LT James Nixon

1LT Charles L. Cass
2LT Andrew Bushness, WIA 15 Aug.
ENS Nicholas Neely, WIA 17 Sept.

(The 19th Infantry was in the process of consolidating with elements from the 17th, 26th, and 27th regiment during the summer of 1814 in accordance with the Act of 30 March 1814.)

21st Infantry
COL James Miller (prom Bvt. BGEN 25 July)
LTC Timothy Upham

MAJ Richard Pollard, resg 25 June
MAJ Joseph Grafton, resg 1 Sept.
MAJ Josiah H. Vose, assg 4 Aug.
MAJ William Bradford, assg 20 Aug.
1LT Adj John W. Holding
1LT QM James Craig
Surgeon Amasa Troubridge
Surgeon's Mate Josiah Everett
Surgeon's Mate Elisha L. Allen

1LT William Bowman
ENS Jeremiah Thomas, WIA 25 July
ENS Leven Jones, WIA 25 July
ENS John Bentley, KIA 17 Sept.

CPT James Proctor, resg 28 Jun
CPT Benjamin Ropes
1LT David Riddle (15th Inf. attached)
ENS William G. Camp, WIA 25 July

CPT Sullivan Burbank, WIA 25 July
CPT Lemuel Bradford, KIA 17 Sept.
3LT Nathanial Hinkley

1LT Benjamin F. Larned
1LT Daniel Henderson
1LT Ira Drew, POW
ENS Ezekial Bradwell

CPT Peres Loring
1LT Joseph Cilley, WIA 25 July
1LT James J. Fish, WIA 25 July

CPT Joseph Treat, Rel 25 July
1LT Aaron Bigelow, KIA 25 July
1LT Nicholas Hasdell, resg 28 July
2LT Edward Hall
ENS Calvin Cummings, WIA 17 Sept.

CPT Morrill Marston
2LT Paine Bracket
3LT Godfrey Belding
ENS Plate R. Greene
ENS Leonard Hoar

22d Infantry
COL Hugh Brady, WIA 25 July

MAJ H. Ralph Martin
MAJ John T. Arrosmith
1LT Adj John Greene
1LT QM John D. Kehr, KIA 25 July
3LT QM Charles J. Flemmings, appt 1 Aug.
1LT Paym Thomas Wright
Surgeon Edward Scull
Surgeon's Mate M.I. Cunningham, dism 17 Aug.

CPT Willis Foulk, WIA 25 July
2LT John Armstrong, DOW 28 Aug.
3LT David Kizer

CPT Thomas Lawrence
1LT George Ferguson, WIA 25 July
3LT Charles Hennings

CPT Jacob Cormack
2LT John R. Guy
2LT John Arrison
2LT James McKinney

CPT John Larkins, resg 1 Sept.
CPT Joseph Henderson, appt 2 Sept.
1LT John Culbertson, WIA 25 July
3LT John Brady
3LT Israel G. Ashbridge, resg 1 Oct.

CPT John Pentland, WIA 25 July
1LT William Sturgis, KIA 25 July
2LT Robert Hall

CPT Sampson L. King, WIA 5 July
2LT Robert M. Davidson, KIA 25 July
3LT George L. Wilkins
3LT John Semple

CPT William Morrow
1LT Samuel Brady
2LT Robert Bean, WIA 25 July

23d Infantry
MAJ Daniel McFarland, KIA 25 July
MAJ George M. Brooke, WIA 17 Sept.
1LT Adj John P. Livingston
1LT Paym Peter L. Hogeboom
1LT QM Zadock P. Morse, appt 19 July

Surgeon Silas Fuller
Surgeon's Mate John Gale

1LT Richard Goodell
ENS Isaac Webb

2LT Samuel Tappan, WIA 21 Aug.
3LT Frederick Philips

CPT Azariah W. Odell, WIA 25 July
1LT William G. Belknap, WIA 15 Aug.
2LT Samuel Spafford

CPT Simeon D. Wattles, KIA 25 Aug.
1LT Frederick Brown, WIA 17 Sept.
3LT Dudley Lamb, WIA 25 July

3LT John B. Truax (Det.

CPT Ephraim Gilbert, WIA 25 July
1LT Henry Whiting, WIA 25 July
3LT James S. Abeel, WIA 25 July
ENS Elijah T. O'Flying, KIA 17 Sept.

2LT Justus Ingersoll, WIA 25 July
3LT John P. Dieterich, WIA 25 July
ENS Joshua Brant

25th Infantry
MAJ Thomas Jesup, WIA 25 July
1LT Adj Ephraim Shaylor, WIA 25 July
1LT QM George McCrain, WIA 25 July
Surgeon's Mate Phineas Woodbury

CPT George Howard
1LT Thomas Seymour
2LT John Gifford, WIA 25 July

CPT Daniel Ketchum
1LT Joseph Hutchinson
ENS Andrew Phinchan

CPT Joseph Kinney, KIA 25 July
ENS Charles Burbridge
ENS Samuel Woodcomb

CPT John B. Murdock
1LT Edward White

CPT Thomas M. Read, WIA 5 July
2LT Henry DeWitt, WIA 5 July

3LT Talcot Patchin, WIA 5 July
ENS William C. Hunter, KIA 25 July

CPT Benjamin Watson
2LT DeLaFayette Wilcox, WIA Sept.
ENS Caleb Campbell

1st and 4th Rifles Combined
COL James Gibson, DOW 18 Sept.
LTC James McDonald
MAJ Thomas Chambers
MAJ Lodowick Morgan, KIA 12 Aug.
MAJ Joseph Selden
1LT Adj James S. McIntosh, WIA 3 Aug.
1LT Adj John Shortridge
1LT QM James H. Ballard
Surgeon William Henning
Surgeon's Mate Henry Field

1st Rifles
CPT Thomas Ramsey, WIA 17 Sept.
1LT James G. Gray
2LT Lambert Norton
3LT George L.B. Duplessis

CPT Joshua S.V. Hamilton, WIA 3 Aug.
2LT William Armstrong
2LT Peter Albright
3LT Samuel Cobb, WIA 17 Sept.

1LT Edward Wadsworth, WIA 3 Aug.
1LT William Arnold
2LT John Hanson

CPT Lewis G.A. Armistead, KIA 17 Sept.
2LT Josiah Hill
3LT Thomas L. Smith
3LT Henry B. Austin

1LT James H. Ryan
1LT Joseph C. Calhoun, Jr.
2LT Jacob Tipton
3LT George Davidson

4th Rifles
CPT Armstrong Irvine
1LT Abraham Schuyler

1LT Stephen Gaunt, WIA 17 Sept.
3LT Abraham Maury

CPT Benjamin Birdsall, WIA 15 Aug.
1LT Johathan Kearsly, WIA 20 Aug.
2LT Robert N. Yates, KIA 20 Aug.
3LT Richard H. Lee

CPT Matthew Magee
1LT George Getz
2LT R.R. Conrad
3LT William Gallup
ENS E.P. Conrad

CPT John Lytle
1LT John Polley
ENS John Page, Jr.

CPT Joseph Kean
3LT Elias Smur, DOW 22 Oct.

Light Dragoons
 CPT Samuel D. Harris
 2LT George Watts

Bombardiers, Sappers & Miners
 1LT David B. Douglass
 2LT Horace C. Story

Headquarters and Staff, Left Division, 9th Military District
 MGEN Jacob Brown, Commanding
 COL Charles K. Gardner, Adjutant General
 MAJ Roger Jones, Ass't Adjutant General
 COL Josiah Snelling, Inspector General
 MAJ Nathan Hall, Ass't Inspector General
 MAJ Azor Orne, Ass't Inspector General
 MAJ John G. Camp, Quartermaster
 CPT John B. Hogan, Ass't Quartermaster
 LTC William MacKee, Engineer
 MAJ Eleazer D. Wood, Ass't Engineer, KIA 17 Sept.
 CPT Loring Austin, ADC, DOW 5 Aug.
 CPT Ambrose Spencer, Jr., ADC

Annex F

NEW YORK MILITIA AND VOLUNTEERS

Headquarters, Porter's Brigade (effective 11 Sept. 1814)
    BGEN Peter B. Porter, Commanding General
    LT Donald Fraser (15th U.S. Infantry) Brigade Major
    LT David Riddle (15th U.S. Infantry) ADC
    QM LT Ephraim Webster
    ADJ Caleb Hopkins, Jr.
    CPT Robert Fleming (Indian Affairs)

Regimental Commanders
    LTC James McBurney
    LTC George Fleming
    LTC Caleb Hopkins
    LTC Isaac Crosby
    COL William Vale
    LTC Mathias Leman
    COL Peter Allen
    LTC William L. Churchill
    LTC Hugh W. Dobbin
(officers' rosters attached)

Swift's/Dobbin's Regiment of Detached New York Militia
(Seneca County)

Mustered 1 May, consolidated 1 Sept., mustered out at Batavia, 8 Nov.

COL Philetus Swift, commanding, 1 May-26 Aug.
LTC Hugh W. Dobbin, commanding, 26 Aug-8 Nov.; prom COL 1 Sept.
MAJ Shearman Lee, field officer
MAJ Abraham Matteson, field officer
LT Lodowick Dobbin, Adj
LT Archer Green, QM
LT Parmenio Adams, Paymaster
Dr. Guardner Wells, Surgeon
Dr. Samuel Howe, Surgeon's mate
Dr. Ira Wright, Surgeon's mate

CPT Joel B. Clark   65 men, 8 Nov.; 2 WIA
1LT Joseph Bancroft
2LT Benjamin F. Norris
3LT Moses Rice
ENS Rufus Hathaway

CPT Thomas Dewar   25 men, 8 Nov.
1LT Calvin Freeman
ENS Ephraim Stewart

CPT Moody R. Freeman   50 men, 8 Nov.; 1 died
1LT Stephen Smith
ENS Picket Broadaway

CPT Micajah Harding   57 men, 8 Nov.;
1LT Cyrenius Blackburn   2 KIA; 2 died
2LT William A. McClean
ENS Ichabod Baldwin

CPT William Hooper (KIA 25 July)   33 men, 8 Nov.; 1 KIA
1LT Thomas W. Roosevelt (KIA 4 Sept.)   4 WIA, 1 died

CPT William Hull   132 men, 8 Nov.; 2 KIA,
1LT Charles C. Tupper (WIA Aug.)   7 WIA, 1 died
2LT Sylvanus Felton (KIA 28 Aug.)
2LT Simeon Bacon

CPT Walter Warden, died   64 men, 8 Nov.; 2 KIA, 2 WIA
CPT William Ireland (discharged 13 Sept.)
1LT Jedediah Hunt (POW 25 July)
1LT Philo Cleaveland (res'd 1 July)

2LT Ebenezer Campbell
ENS Moses Goodfellow

CPT Nathaniel F. Knapp (WIA 17 Sept.)   160 men, 8 Nov.; 6 KIA,
CPT Julyius Tozer (attached)   1 WIA, 2 POW, 6 died
1LT Canvass White (attached)
1LT John C. Gilbert (discharged GCM Aug.)
2LT Joseph Hathaway
ENS Charles I. Jarvis (absent sick 20 Aug.)
ENS John Jones
ENS Isaac Wickwine
(Compiled from RG 94, Entry 55 Muster Rolls; Entry 510 Service Records)

New York Detached Militia, mustered 25 August, attached to Dobbins' Regiment, 6 September

CPT Phipps W. Hewitt—not mustered (20/31 deserted)
CPT James Colgrove   39 men, 8 Nov.; 1 KIA,
1LT William Bailey (WIA 17 Sept.)   3 WIA, 2 POW
2LT James Smith (disch 21 Sept.)
3LT Peter Samuel (disch 21 Sept.)
ENS Chauncey W. Smith

CPT John Fleming   39 men, 8 Nov.; 2 WIA
1LT John Reynolds   NYDM
ENS James Fleming

CPT Henry Parker   34 men, 8 Nov.; 2 KIA,
1LT Benjamin Nelson   2 WIA, 2 died, NYDM
ENS Silas Mills

CPT John Richardson   71 men, 8 Nov.; 1 WIA,
1LT John Alexander   Riflemen
2LT Silas Chatfield

CPT Tunis Swick (died)   48 men, 8 Nov.; 1 WIA,
CPT Comfort Butler (disch 13 Sept.)   1 POW, 2 died, Riflemen
1LT Tunis Covert, Jr., (disch 13 Sept.)
1LT William Pew
1LT Joseph Covert (disch 22 Sept.)
(Taken from National Archives muster rolls, RG 94, Entry 55;E510 Compiled Service Records; Peter B. Porter Papers, BECHS)

Stone's Battalion, New York Detached Militia

LTC Isaac W. Stone
CPT Adj William Pratt
Surgeon's Mate Simeon Hunt

CPT Claudius V. Boughton Mounted Company 101 men, 8 Nov.;
1LT Abel Parkhurst   3 KIA, 3 died, 12 POW
2LT Chauncey Deane
3LT Richardson Havin
Cornet James Gillis (POW 25 Aug.)

CPT Hope Davis (Lt. Inf.)   65 men, 12 July
1LT Ira Castle
2LT Solomon Close
ENS Thomas Jennison

(Based on National Archives muster rolls, RG 94, Entry 55; Compiled Service Records; Peter B. Porter Papers, BECHS, morning reports)

Casualties—Swift's/Dobbin's Regiment
New York Detached Militia

CPT Boughton's Co.
   PVT Ezra Barnes, POW 15 July
   Cornet James Gillis, POW 25 Aug.
   PVT Elijah Holford, POW 10 July
   PVT Cabel Hopkinson, POW 1 Oct.
   PVT Hugh Jenkins, killed 27 Aug.
   PVT Julius Kanny, POW 5 Aug.
   PVT Caleb Kimball, POW 17 Sept.
   PVT Alpheus Madden, died 10 Sept.
   PVT Patrick McGowen, POW 1 Oct.
   PVT James McNutt, POW 16 July
   PVT William Powers, POW 17 Sept.
   PVT John Rathburn, POW 5 Aug.
   PVT Timothy Rairden, POW 5 Aug.
   PVT Edward Van Dyke, POW 1 Aug.
   PVT Edgar Wells, KIA 17 Sept.
   PVT Calvin S. Wickson, died 18 Aug.
   PVT Zachariah Woodbeck, died 1 Sept.
   PVT Leonard Widner, KIA 27 Aug.
   PVT Jeremiah Woodman, POW 5 Aug.

CPT Clark's Co.
   SGT Isbel Ransome, WIA
   PVT William Hedge, WIA

CPT Colgrove's Co.
   1LT William Bailey, WIA 17 Sept.
   PVT David Casper, WIA 17 Sept.

PVT James Gillespie, KIA 17 Sept.
PVT Frederick Vaughn, POW 17 Oct.
PVT Bradley Wakeman, POW 17 Oct.
PVT Nathan Wickham, WIA 17 Sept.

CPT Fleming's Co.
PVT David Alger, WIA 17 Sept.
PVT Nathaniel Crowell, WIA 17 Sept.

CPT Freeman's Co.
PVT Hezekiah Hanford, WIA

CPT Harding's Co.
PVT David Clark, KIA
PVT Consider Hecomb, KIA 30 Aug., Ft. Erie
PVT John Morgan, died 15 Oct.
PVT Henry Sidley, died 18 Aug.
PVT Joshua Staples, died 25 Sept.

CPT Hooper's Co.
SGT James Bacon, died 13 Aug., in camp, Ft. Erie
PVT James Cronk, WIA 25 July
CPT William Hooper, KIA 25 July
SGT Joseph McClure, injured 8 Aug., at Buffalo Hosp
PVT Henry Murphy, WIA 25 July
PVT Mose M. Rogers, WIA 25 July, DOW 30 July
1LT Thomas W. Roosevelt, KIA 11 Sept.
PVT Daniel Ward, WIA 25 July

CPT Hull's Co.
PVT Asa Brooks, WIA 5 July
CPL Barnabus Donaghue, KIA 25 July
2LT Sylvanus Felton, KIA 28 Aug., by bombardment at Ft. Erie
PVT William Hedger, WIA 5 July, lost arms
PVT Elnathan Horton, died 16 Sept. at Ft. Erie
PVT Andrew Lawrence, WIA 12 July
PVT David Salisbury, WIA 17 Sept.
PVT Ebenezer Stone, WIA 17 Sept.
PVT Oran Stone, WIA 20 Aug., at Ft. Erie
PVT Walter Venight, WIA 17 Sept., severe
PVT William W. Wickham, KIA 28 Aug., at Ft. Erie

CPT Parker's Co.
PVT Charles Keyes, died 25 Oct.
PVT Nathaniel Mills, WIA 20 Sept.
PVT James Runyon, KIA 17 Sept.

PVT Hugh Stevenson, died 26 Oct.
PVT John Waddams, KIA 17 Sept.
MUS Jacob Winters, WIA 20 Sept.

CPT Richardson's Co.
PVT John Stoddard, WIA 17 Sept.

CPT Swick's Co.
PVT William Bloom, 18 Oct. died in the hospital at Ft. Erie
CPL Timothy Clarey, POW 17 Oct.
PVT David Dimmick, WIA 17 Sept.
PVT Peter Fisher, 18 Oct. died in the hospital at Ft. Erie

CPT Warden's Co.
PVT James M. French, WIA
PVT Jonathan Gray, WIA
PVT Ames Hewitt, KIA 25 Aug., Ft. Erie
1LT Jedediah Hunt, POW 25 July
PVT David Sparling, KIA 25 July

CPT Knapp's Co.
PVT Simon Adams, killed 3 Aug., at Black Rock by cannon shot
PVT Joshua Ames, died 26 Oct., at Williamsville Hospital
PVT Richard Blanchard, died 22 Sept., at Ft. Erie
PVT Henry Cashuss, WIA 5 Sept., by a bomb
PVT Josiah Charles, POW 25 July
PVT Mose Curricomb, died 22 Sept., at Ft. Erie
PVT Calvin Holmes, KIA 5 Sept., by a bomb
PVT Ezra Harvey, died 7 Oct., at Williamsville
PVT Daniel Liverman, died 1 Oct., at Williamsville
PVT Richard Page, KIA 5 Sept.
PVT John Paul, died 26 Sept., at Williamsville
PVT Phineas Pierce, KIA 4 Sept.
PVT Daniel Satterslee, died 2 Oct., at Williamsville
PVT James Simons, POW 25 July
PVT Elijah Wamsey, KIA 7 Sept.
PVT James Waver, KIA 4 Sept.
PVT John Wilhelm, DOW at Buffalo

New York Volunteer Units Vouchered for Travel from Home to Buffalo, RG
94, Boxes 89-90, OAG/QM Accts, MAJ John B. Hogan

Commander/Unit	Town	Vou Date	Remarks
Cayuga County:			
CPT Eliphalet Whittlesey, Co.	Aurelius	11 Aug.	

CPT John Marten, Co.	Ulysses	17 Aug.	
CPT Benjamin Horton, Co.		5 Sept.	
CPT Joseph Cone, Co.	Locke	5 Sept.	
CPT Joshua Harkin, Co.	Scipio	5 Sept.	
CPT John Bosworth, Co.	Scipio	5 Sept.	
CPT Alexander Price, Co.	Scipio	5 Sept.	
CPT William Bennett, Co.	Scipio	5 Sept.	
CPT William Watsen, Co.	Sempronius	6 Sept.	
CPT Martin Barber, Co.	Locke	6 Sept.	
ENS Ithaman Whipple, Det.		6 Sept.	18 men
CPT Samuel Love, Co.	Dryden	6 Sept.	Now Tompkins Co.
LT William Belknap, Co.		6 Sept.	
CPT Wadsworth, Co.		6 Sept.	NY LT Infantry
CPT James Dickson, Co.	Munton	6 Sept.	
CPT John Minser, Co.	Genoa	7 Sept.	
LTC George Fleming, Regt.	Aurelius	7 Sept.	2d Regt. NY det. mil.
ENS Benjamin Jayne, Co.	Sempronius	7 Sept.	
CPT John Richardson, Co.	Aurelius	7 Sept.	

Chatauqua County:

CPT James McMahan, Co.		31 Aug.	LTC McMahan's Regt.

Genesee County:

CPT W.D. Smith, Co.	Caledonia	30 Aug.	Now Livingstone County
CPT Elisha Kellog, Co.	Batavia	3 Sept.	W.L.Churchill's Regt.
LT Turner, Co.	Batavia	4 Sept.	
CPT Mitchell, Co.	Batavia	4 Sept.	Allen's Regt. CPT
CPT Benijah Holbrook, Co.	Riga	5 Sept.	
CPT Isaac Wilson, Co.	Middlebury	5 Sept.	
LT William Thayer, Co.	Pembroke	5 Sept.	
CPT Ira Wilson, Co.	Middlebury	5 Sept.	
CPT Elisha Mix, Co.	Lima	5 Sept.	
CPT Chester Warriner, Co.	Warsaw	5 Sept.	
COL William Vale, Regt.		5 Sept.	Det. Militia
CPT James Crittenden, Co.	Perry	6 Sept.	
CPT Chester Naramore, Co.	Caledonia	6 Sept.	Now Livingstone County
CPT Roger Kelsey, Co.	Bergen	7 Sept.	
CPT Daniel Buel, Det.	Leroy	7 Sept.	
CPT Josiah Hovey, Co.	Warsaw	7 Sept.	
CPT Elias Streeter, Co.	Riga	7 Sept.	
MAJ Roderick L. Stewart, Co.	Riga	8 Sept.	

CPT Ephriam Judd, Co.	Leroy	8 Sept.
CPT Chauncey Bill, Co.	Bergen	8 Sept.
ENS Robert Fulton, Co.	Parma	8 Sept. Now Monroe County
LT John Russ, Co.	Caledonia	8 Sept. Now Livingstone County
LT Martin Coe, Co.	Leroy	9 Sept.
LTC Mathias Leman, Regt.	Batavia	9 Sept.
ENS Isaac Leech, Co.	Murray	9 Sept.
Lt Peleg Burrows, Co.	Linden	9 Sept.
LT Jacob Tompkins, Co.	Alexander	9 Sept.

Seneca County:

CPT John Hull, Co.		4 Sept.
CPT William Ireland, Co.		4 Sept. NY Riflemen
CPT John Fleming, Co.		4 Sept.
CPT Comfort Butler, Co.	Ulysses	7 Sept. NY Riflemen
CPT James Colgrove, Co.		6 Sept. 145 Regt. NY Militia
CPT Tunis Swick, Co.		5 Sept.
CPT Henry Parker, Co.	Galin	5 Sept.

Steuben County:

CPT Crouch, Co.	Bath	29 Aug.
CPT John Silsbe, Co.	Bath	7 Sept.
CPT John Kennedy, Co.		7 Sept.
LT Abel Bullard, Co.		7 Sept.

Ontario County:

CPT Cost, Co.		13 Aug.
COL Peter Allen, Regt.	Honeoye & Bristol	3 Sept.
CPT Jenks Pullen, Co.	Phelps	3 Sept.
CPT John Markham, Co.	Lima	3 Sept.
CPT Nathan Bryan, Co.	Mendon	4 Sept.
CPT Roger Sutherland, Co.	Benton	4 Sept.
CPT Nathan Care, Co.	Penfold	4 Sept.
CPT John Henry, Co.	Benton	4 Sept.
CPT Timothy Mower, Co.	Canandaigua	5 Sept.
LT Joseph Luce, Co.	Palmyra	5 Sept.
LT Joseph Clarke, Co.	Naples	12 Sept.

Allegeny County:

CPT Nathaniel Ginger, Co.		13 Sept.

(Vouchers countersigned by John A. Graham, "Quartermaster of the 1,000 detached militia from the 7 Division of NYM.")

Annex G

PENNSYLVANIA VOLUNTEERS

5th Regiment of Penna. Vol. Militia in U.S. Service
(Adams, Cumberland, and Franklin Companies)

The 5th Pennsylvania Volunteer Regiment was formed from elements of the 1st and 2d Brigades of the 7th Militia Division (Cumberland and Franklin Counties) and the 2d Brigade of the 5th Militia Division (Adams County). Dunn's and Gordon's companies from the 6th Regiment, 2d Brigade volunteered in toto. The unit was called up 14-24 February 1814; mustered 4 March at Carlisle, PA; 18 March-30 May, part of Erie, PA, garrison; 31 May-13 June en route Buffalo; 4 July crossed into Canada; 26 August mustered out at Buffalo. Starting 10 July Alexander's, Dunn's and Moreland's Companies guarded prisoners en route to Albany.

COL James B. Fenton—Commanding
LTC Robert Bull, Second-in Command (KIA 5 July)
MAJ James Wood, Field Officer
MAJ Samuel Galloway, Field Officer (POW 5 July)
MAJ Ebenezer Wilson, Field Officer, transferred NYM
LT Thomas Poe, Adjutant (DOW 26 July)
LT Calvin Blythe, Adjutant, replaced LT Thomas Poe
CPT John Maclay, Quartermaster (WIA 25 July)
Dr. Samuel Mealy, Surgeon
Dr. William Simpson, Surgeon's Mate

CPT Samuel Gordon   Waynesboro, Franklin Co.
1LT William Dick (WIA 25 July)   Muster out 24 Aug. (71 men)
2LT William Patton
3LT James Burns
ENS William Miller

CPT William Alexander   Carlisle, Cumberland Co.
1LT Lindsey Spotswood   Muster out 24 Aug. (91 men)
ENS William Wright

CPT Samuel Dunn   Mercersburg, Franklin Co.
1LT James McConnell   Muster out 24 Aug. (71 men)
2LT Robert Foot
3LT John Favorite
ENS William Geddis

CPT George Hendel   Carlisle, Cumberland Co.
1LT David Everly   Muster out 24 Aug. (84 men)
2LT Peter Phillips
3LT Frederick Sharrets
ENS Michael Sanno

CPT John McMillan (WIA 25 July) Fairfield, Adams Co.
1LT Joseph Chamberlain   Muster out 24 Aug. (54 men)
2LT William Lynn
3LT Samuel Blythe

CPT Andrew Mitchell   Newville, Cumberland Co.
1LT Samuel McKeehan   Muster out 24 Aug. (62 men)
2LT James Mitchell

CPT David Moreland   Carlisle, Cumberland Co.
1LT Robert Thomson   Muster out 24 Aug. (111 men)
2LT John Neeper
ENS Amos Cadwallader

CPT James Piper   Newville, Cumberland Co.
1LT James Woodburn   Muster out 26 Aug. (51 men)
ENS Andrew Huston

CPT John Roberts (POW 5 July)   Carlisle, Cumberland Co.
1LT Thomas Reddick   Muster out 24 Aug. (74 men)
2LT John Gibson
3LT Jacob Cox

CPT Samuel White (POW 5 July)   Gettysburg, Adams Co.
1LT John Gardner   Muster out 24 Aug. (71 men)

2LT Samuel Gilliland
ENS John Graft
(Based on Pennsylvania Archives, series 6, vols VII, VIII, IX and series 7, index; RG 94 QM Accts-Hogan, Camp; Volunteer Orgs. & State Militia, War of 1812, Box 207, Fenton; Compiled Service Records, Boxes 4161, 4162)

Pennsylvania Militia Officers' Travel Vouchers, RG 94,
Boxes 89-90, OAG/QM Accts, Hogan—Voucher date 29 Aug.

Name	Destination, PA	County
COL James B. Fenton	Newville	Cumberland
MAJ James Wood	Greencastle	Franklin
LT Calvin Blythe, Adj.	Fairfield	Adams
LT William Lynn	Abbots' Farm	Adams
Dr. Samuel Malloy, Surgeon	Millerstown	Perry (Vou date 28 Aug.)
LT James Burns	Waynesboro	Franklin
LT Joseph Chamberlain	Gettysburg	Adams
CPT Samuel Gordon	Waynesboro	Franklin
LT Samuel Blythe	Fairfield	Adams
MAJ Ebenezer Wilson	Middlebury, NY	
LT John Gardner	Gettysburg	Adams
CPT Andrew Mitchell	Newville	Cumberland
CPT Samuel M. McKeehan	Newville	Cumberland
CPT John McMillan	Fairfield	Adams
ENS Andrew Huston	Newville	Cumberland
LT William Patton	Greencastle	Franklin
ENS John Graft	Gettysburg	Adams
LT James Woodburn	Mount Rock	Cumberland
LT John Gibson	Shippensburg	Cumberland
CPT George Hendel	Carlisle	Cumberland
LT William Dick	Mercersburg	Franklin
CPT James Piper	Newville	Cumberland
LT Samuel Gilliland	Gettysburg	Adams
Dr. William Simpson, Surgeon's Mate	Shippensburg	Cumberland
CPT John McClay, Regt QM		

Annex H

WILLCOCKS' CANADIAN VOLUNTEERS IN U.S. SERVICE

Joseph Willcocks was elected major of his detachment and other officers were selected when the unit was mustered locally by General Henry Dearborn at Ft. George, U.C., on 18 July 1813. A muster at the end of August shows eight officers and 66 men assigned and present for duty. The unit was given federal status in an Act of 24 February 1814. It ceased to exist as a distinct entity during July 1814, when its survivors were attached to LTC Hugh W. Dobbins' Regiment of New York Volunteers. The unit held its final muster on 15 June 1815 when the last 23 men on the rolls were discharged.

A total of 159 men, all residents of U.C., served in the ranks during the organization's existence. Forty-five of them were listed as AWOL or deserted. Six men died in service, one during the 1814 Campaign. Three men were captured, two of them on 25 July 1814, and two men were discharged to join the Regular Army. An Act of Congress passed on 5 March 1816 authorized a bonus of three months pay and a land grant to the honorably discharged men or their heirs. Total casualties: two officers and four men killed in action; two men died of disease; three men wounded and three men captured.

LTC Joseph Willcocks	Commanding (prom 13 Oct. 1813; KIA 4 Sept. 1814)
MAJ Benajah Mallory	1st field officer (Joined 12 Nov. 1813; promoted 19 Apr. 1814)

MAJ Abraham Markle   2d field officer (joined 8 Dec. 1813; promoted 19 Apr. 1814)

SURG Eliakim Crosby
ADJ Joseph Baker
QM Samuel Jackson, Sr.

CPT Gideon Frisbee
1LT Oliver Grace
2LT William Markle
3LT Eleazar Daggett

CPT William Biggar
1LT Joseph Huggins
2LT Abraham Cutler
ENS Samuel Jackson, Jr.

SURG John Dorman   (18 July - 8 Oct. 1813)
ADJ Joshua Totman   (KIA 1 Jan. 1814)

(Based on RG 94, Boxes 4161, 4162 War of 1812 Compiled Military Service Records; Records of Volunteer Units in U.S. Service)

Willcocks' Regiment of Canadian Volunteers
Roster of Enlisted Men, 1813-1815.

Allen, James PVT, AWOL as of 31 Mar. 1814
Allwood, David PVT, deserted 31 Mar. 1814
Archer, Johnathan PVT
Atwood, James B. PVT
Averill, David PVT
Beemer, Henry PVT, AWOL as of 31 Aug. 1814
Bennett, John PVT
Bennett, John H. PVT, AWOL 18 Aug. 1814
Bentley, Ira PVT
Bigelow, Abel PVT
Bradt, Emanius PVT, AWOL as of 31 Aug. 1813
Brown, Mathew PVT
Butner, William PVT enlisted in RA as of 31 Mar. 1814
Canfield, R.R. PVT, AWOL as of 31 Mar. 1814
Carley, Benj PVT
Cass, David PVT
Chamberlin, David PVT
Chapman, Adena, PVT, AWOL as of 31 Mar. 1814
Clark, James PVT, AWOL as of 31 Mar. 1814

Connaway, James SGT, AWOL as of 31 Mar. 1814 at 11 Mile Creek
Conway, Samuel PVT, AWOL as of 31 Mar. 1814
Curtis, Grove, PVT
Curtis, Leonard PVT, AWOL as of 31 Mar. 1814
Curtus, Daniel PVT
Dale, David PVT, died July 1814
Days, Jacob PVT
Dean, Silas PVT
Desscar, Oliver PVT, AWOL as of 31 Mar. 1814
Dibble, John PVT, AWOL as of 31 Mar. 1814
Dill, John PVT, died 16 Aug. 1813
Dotty, John PVT, AWOL as of 31 Mar. 1814
Eaton, John PVT, deserted as of 31 Mar. 1814
Farnum, Joseph PVT
Fassett, Jonathan PVT, AWOL as of 31 Mar. 1814
Felty, Ambrose PVT
Filly, Amna PVT
Follett, Abel PVT
Follett, Henry PVT
Force, John PVT
Fosgate, Silas PVT
Fow, John, PVT, AWOL as of 31 Aug. 1813
Fox, Amasa PVT
Franklin, Benjamin SGT, AWOL as of 31 Mar. 1814
Frasher, Samuel PVT, WIA 25 July 1814
Frink, H.B. PVT
Fuller, Daniel PVT, AWOL as of 31 Mar. 1814
Gardner, George T. PVT
Gilbert, Abner PVT
Gillis, Elias PVT
Gough, John PVT
Graves, Samuel PVT
Griffin, Joseph PVT
Harris, Joseph PVT
Harrison, Samuel PVT, deserted as of 31 Mar. 1814
Haskins, Adams PVT
Haskins, Elisha PVT
Havens, Robert PVT, POW Dec 1813, Near Niagara
Hendershot, Jacob S. SGM
Howell, Phineas PVT, AWOL as of 31 Aug. 1813
Huffman, William PVT
Ingram, William PVT, DOW Aug. 1813

Jackson, Josiah SGT, brevet 3LT by MAJ Mallory
Jackson, William D. PVT
James, William PVT
Johnson, John S. PVT
Jones, Nathan PVT
Jones, William PVT, deserted as of 31 Mar. 1814
Jonston, David PVT AWOL as of 31 Mar. 1814
Justine, Daniel PVT
Kackboard, Peter PVT, AWOL as of 31 Mar. 1814
Kain, John PVT
Kelley, George PVT
Lane, Jacob PVT
Lane, Peter PVT
Lappan, Anthony PVT
Larkins, Bradford PVT
Lepau, Anthony PVT
Lewis, Jonah PVT
Lewis, Russell PVT, deserted as of 31 Mar. 1814
Lloyd, Aaron PVT
Lloyd, Benjamin PVT
Lloyd, John PVT
Lockwood, John PVT died as of 31 Mar. 1814
Loop, Henry, PVT, deserted as of 31 Mar. 1814
Louge, R.M. PVT
Lovett, Joseph SGT, enlisted RA 20 Apr 1814 (pre-war deserter from 4th
    Inf)
Mallory, Abraham PVT
Mansfield, Isaac PVT
Marselius, Cary PVT
McCarter, William PVT
McCrany, Thomas PVT
McGarvin, James PVT "withdrew from the corps w/o permission" 31 Aug.
    1813
McGee, James PVT
McGee, William PVT
McLaughlin, Laughlin PVT
McGrigor, Robert PVT
Mead, Chauncey PVT
Millin, Enoch PVT, POW as of 31 Mar. 1814
Morse, Asa SGT
Moulton, Oliver PVT
Myers, Charles PVT

Myers, Joshua PVT
Newland, Cornelius PVT
Newton, Elijah PVT, AWOL as of 31 Mar. 1814
Olmstead, Enoch PVT, AWOL as of 31 Mar. 1814
Olmstead, Job PVT, AWOL as of 31 Mar. 1814
Olmstead, Moses PVT, AWOL as of 31 Mar. 1814
Onstone, Daniel, PVT, AWOL as of 31 Mar. 1814
Ousterhoudt, Lucas PVT
Palmer, David PVT, POW Dec 1813 at Black Rock, not exchanged
Piersons, David PVT, WIA 31 Aug. 1813, cannon shot broke thigh; medical discharge Apr. 1815
Pelton, Stephen CPL
Petinger, PVT
Philips, Daniel PVT
Pollock, James PVT
Prentice, Gilbert PVT
Proctor, Oliver CPL
Putnam, Franklin CPL, AWOL as of 31 Mar. 1814
Putnam, Peter CPL, AWOL as of 31 Mar. 1814
Reed, Joseph L. CPL
Reynolds, William CPL
Riley, Solomon CPL
Robinson, William CPL
Rogers, Thomas B. CPL, AWOL as of 31 Mar. 1814
Russell, Hezekiah PVT, AWOL as of 31 Mar. 1814
Safford, Philip PVT
Sales, Mordicai PVT, AWOL as of 31 Mar. 1814
Scott, John PVT
Seely, Silas H. PVT
Severcool, John PVT, AWOL as of 31 Mar. 1814
Shafer, Philipp PVT, AWOL as of 30 June 1814
Sherwood, Nathan PVT
Simons, John PVT
Smith, Charles PVT
Smith, John R. QM SGT
Smith, Luther SGT, WIA 25 July 1814
Smith, Nelson SGT
Smith, Oliver SGT, AWOL as of 31 Mar. 1814
Smith, Timothy S. SGT
Smith, William PVT, died in hospital 1 June 1814, sickness
Squires, Ephraim SGT
Stephens, Benjamin PVT

Stoddard, Nathan PVT
Strome, Samuel PVT, AWOL as of 31 Mar. 1814
Thomas, Seneca SGT
Throe, Benjamin PVT, AWOL as of Mar. 1814
Tille, Ambrose PVT
Tollett, Henry PVT
Tompkins, Samuel PVT
Tubs, Daniel PVT, deserted as of 31 Mar. 1814
Tufford, Philip PVT
Vanderburg, Jacob G. PVT
Wallace, William COMSY SGT
Wickham, Samuel QM SGT
Wilcot, Paul PVT, DOW Aug. 1813 at Lewistown, cannon shot in side
Wilder, Michael PVT
(Name spellings are as accepted as correct in Compiled Service Records.)
Based on RG 94, Boxes 4, 161-4, 162 Compiled Military Service Records

Annex I

NATIVE VOLUNTEERS

Indian Volunteer Corps, 1 June - 23 July 1814

Command and Staff
LTC Erastus Granger, Ind Dept
CPT Jasper Parrish, Ind Dept
CPT Robert Fleming, Ind Dept
Red Jacket
ADJ Caleb Hopkins, Jr.
QM Ephraim Webster
Insp. Edmund A. Trowbridge

Seneca Main Village
CPT Pollard
LT Jack Berry
LT Y.O.
ENS White Chief

Allegany & Cattaraugus
CPT War Chief
LT Big John
LT Black Snake
ENS Strong

Onondagas
CPT George
LT John Brown

Tuscaroras & Delawares
  CPT Long Beard
  LT T.C. Johnson
  ENS John Mountpleasant

Tonawandas
  CPT Cold
  LT Little Beard
  ENS John Sky

Stockbridge (until 6 Oct.)
  CPT Abner W. Hendrick
  LT Schuyler Hendrick
  ENS John Jacobs
(RG 94, Box 4272 War of 1812 Compiled Military Service Records, Corps of Indian Volunteers)

ANNEX J

U.S.CASUALTY DENSITY

(Campaign of 1814—Niagara Frontier)

	KIA	WIA
3 July—Capture of Ft. Erie:		
25th Infantry		4
5 July—Battle of Chippawa:		
9th Infantry	13	45
22d Infantry	18	44
25th Infantry	5	71
11th Infantry	15	60
21st Infantry	0	0
19th Infantry	3	2
23d Infantry	0	1
Artillery	4	16
PA Volunteers	3	2
Indians	9	8
25 July—Battle of Lundy's Lane:		
9th Infantry	16	90
11th Infantry	28	102
22d Infantry	39	90
25th Infantry	28	66
1st Infantry	11	20

21st Infantry	15	70
23d Infantry	10	52
Canadian Vols.	1	2
PA Volunteers	11	24
NY Volunteers	15	14
Artillery	10	35
2 Lt. Dragoons	1	2

3 August—Affair at Scajaquada Creek:

1st Rifles	2	8

1-30 August—Siege of Ft Erie (excluding 13-15 August):

Staff	0	1
Engineers	0	1
Artillery	1	1
9/19 Infantry	6	11
11th Infantry	5	17
21st Infantry	9	21
22d Infantry	4	15
23d Infantry	7	16
25th Infantry	3	10
1/4 Rifles	16	39
Volunteers	8	12

13-14 August—Cannonade at Ft. Erie:

Garrison	10	35

15 August—Battle of Ft. Erie:

Engineers	1	0
Artillery	4	4
9th Infantry	3	10
19th Infantry	5	16
22d Infantry	2	5
21st Infantry	2	6
22d Infantry	0	6
1/4 Rifles	0	3

September—Defense of Ft. Erie (excluding 17 September):

Artillery	6	8
1st Infantry	0	3
9/19th Infantry	2	6
11th Infantry	4	15
21st Infantry	8	6
22d Infantry	3	15

23d Infantry	4	7
25th Infantry	3	1
1/4 Rifles	0	6 (including det. 26th Inf.)
Volunteers	5	4

17 September—Sortie from Ft. Erie:

Engineers	1	0
Staff	0	1
9th Infantry	8	24
11th Infantry	4	25
19th Infantry	5	6
1st Rifles	11	19
4th Rifles	1	10
26th Infantry	0	0
1st Infantry	5	10
23d Infantry	19	26
2d Lt. Dragoons	1	0
Militia Staff	1	4
Dobbin's	4	29
McBurney's	2	9
Hopkin's	6	11
Fleming's	2	10
Churchill's	1	4
Crosby's	2	12
CPT Fleming's	1	1
Res Staff	0	1
21st Infantry	5	14

15 October—Cannonade at Chippewa:

Archer's Battery	2	1
5th Infantry	1	0
14th Infantry	1	0

19 October—Affair at Cook's Mill's (Lyon's Creek):

5th Infantry	5	14
14th Infantry	7	19
15th Infantry	0	1
16th Infantry	0	9
4th Rifles	0	11 (Irvine's Co.)

(Source: RG 94, Entry 71, Eaton's Compendium; Entry 53 Muster Rolls; RG 98 Unit Books)

Annex K

U.S. OFFICER CASUALTIES

(Campaign of 1814—Niagara Frontier)

5 July 1814 killed:
LTC Robert Bull, PA Vols

5 July 1814 wounded:
COL James B. Campbell, 11th Inf
CPT Sampson S. King, 22d Inf
CPT Thomas M. Read, 25th Inf
CPT Thomas Harrison, 42d Inf (attached 9th Inf)
1LT Loring Palmer, 9th Inf
2LT John V. Barron, 11th Inf
2LT Henry DeWitt, 25th Inf
3LT Talcot Patchin, 25th Inf
3LT Elisha Brimhall, 9th Inf

25 July 1814 killed:
MAJ Daniel McFarland, 23d Inf
CPT John Ritchie, Arty
CPT Abraham Hull, 9th Inf
CPT Joseph Kinney, 25th Inf
CPT Valentine R. Goodrich, 11th Inf
CPT William Hooper, NY Vols
1LT Aaron Bigelow, 21st Inf
1LT William Sturgis, 22d Inf

1LT Stephen Turner, 9th Inf
1LT John D. Kehr, 22d Inf
2LT Adolphus Burghardt, 9th Inf
2LT Robert M. Davidson, 22d Inf
Adj Thomas Poe, PA Vols (DOW 26 July)
ENS William C. Hunter, 25th Inf
CPT Ambrose Spencer, 29th Inf, ADC (DOW 5 Aug.)

25 July 1814 wounded:
MGEN Jacob Brown
BGEN Winfield Scott
1LT William J. Worth, 23d Inf, ADC
1LT Gerard D. Smith, 6th Inf, ADC
COL Hugh Brady, 22d Inf
LTC Hugh W. Dobbin, NY Vols
MAJ Henry Leavenworth, 9th Inf
MAJ John McNeil, 11th Inf
MAJ Thomas S. Jesup, 25th Inf
MAJ James Wood, PA Vols
CPT Thomas Biddle, Arty
CPT William S. Foster, 11th Inf
CPT John Bliss, 11th Inf
CPT John Pentland, 22d Inf
CPT Willis Foulk, 22d Inf
CPT Sullivan Burbank, 21st Inf
CPT Azariah W. Odell, 23d Inf
CPT John McMillan, PA Vols
1LT John Fowle, 9th Inf
1LT William Browning, 9th Inf
1LT George McClain, 25th Inf
1LT John Maclay, PA Vols
1LT William F. Hale, 11th Inf
1LT George W. Ferguson, 22d Inf
1LT John Culbertson, 22d Inf
1LT Barony Vasques, 1st Inf
1LT Lewis Bissell, 1st Inf
1LT Joseph Cilley, 21st Inf
1LT James Fish, 21st Inf
1LT Henry Whiting, 23d Inf
1LT Ephraim Shaylor, 25th Inf
1LT William Dick, PA Vols
2LT Henry M. Campbell, Arty
2LT Jacob Schmuck, Arty

2LT Otis Fisher, 9th Inf
2LT Enoch Cooper, 11th Inf
2LT James J. Fish, 19th Inf (attached 21st Inf)
2LT John Armstrong, 22d Inf
2LT Justus Ingersoll, 23d Inf
2LT Samuel Tappan, 23d Inf
3LT Caleb Cushman, 9th Inf
3LT Benjamin Stevenson, 11th Inf
3LT Humphrey Webster, 11th Inf
3LT Robert Bean, 22d Inf
3LT James S. Abeel, 23d Inf
3LT John P. Dieterich, 23d Inf
3LT Dudley Lamb, 23d Inf
3LT John Gifford, 25th Inf
LT O'Flynn, NY Vols
ENS Joseph K. Jacobs, 9th Inf
ENS George W. Jacobs, 9th Inf
ENS Chesley Blake, 9th Inf
ENS Elias Bedford, 11th Inf
ENS Nathan Thomson, 26th Inf (attached 11th Inf)
ENS Leven Jones, 21st Inf
ENS Jeremiah Thomas, 21st Inf
ENS William G. Camp, 2d Rifles (attached 21st Inf)

3 August 1814 wounded:
　CPT Joshua Hamilton, 1st Rifles
　1LT Edward Wadsworth, 1st Rifles
　1LT James S. McIntosh, 1st Rifles

12 August 1814 killed:
　MAJ Lodowick Morgan, 1st Rifles

14 August 1814 killed:
　1LT John Armstrong, 22d Inf (DOW 28 Aug.)

14 August 1814 wounded:
　CPT Thomas Biddle, Arty
　1LT Richard A. Zantzinger, Arty
　2LT John G. Watmough, Arty
　3LT John Patterson, 19th Inf

15 August 1814 killed:
　CPT Alexander J. Williams, Arty
　1LT Patrick McDonough, Arty

15 August 1814 wounded:

CPT Benjamin Birdsall, 4th Rifles
1LT John J. Fontaine (POW)
1LT William G. Belknap, 23d Inf
2LT Andrew Bushnell, 19th Inf
ENS Charles Cissna, 19th Inf

20 August 1814 killed:
2LT Robert N. Yates, 4th Rifles

20 August 1814 wounded:
1LT John Kearsly, 4th Rifles
1LT Ebenezer Childs, 9th Inf

21 August 1814 wounded:
1LT Samuel Tappan, 23d Inf

25 August 1814 killed:
CPT Simeon D. Wattles, 23d Inf

28 August 1814 killed:
2LT Sylvanus Felton, NY Vols

August 1814 wounded:
2LT Hazan Bedel, 11th Inf
LT Charles C. Tupper, NY Vols

September 1814 wounded:
2LT John W. Kincaid, Arty
2LT DeLaFayette Wilcox, 25th Inf
ENS Thomas Dickey, 11th Inf

4 September 1814 killed:
LTC Joseph Willcocks, CAN Vols
1LT Thomas W. Roosevelt, NY Vols

17 September 1814 killed:
BGEN Daniel Davis, NY Vols
COL James Gibson, 4th Rifles (DOW 18 Sept.)
LTC Eleazer D. Wood, CE
CPT Lemuel Bradford, 21st Inf
CPT Horace Hale, 11th Inf
CPT Lewis G.A. Armistead, 1st Rifles
CPT Daniel Buel, Crosby's Regt NY Vols
LT Thomas Besum, McBurney's Regt, NY Vols
LT W. Belknap, Fleming's Regt NY Vols
3LT Isaac B. Davis, 11th Inf (DOW 28 Sept.)
ENS John Bentley , 21st Inf

ENS Blakesley, McBurney's Regt NY Vols
ENS Elijah T. O'Flying, 23d Inf (DOW 18 Sept.)

17 September 1814 wounded:
MGEN Peter B. Porter, NY Vols
BGEN Eleazer W. Ripley
CPT William Biggar, CAN Vols, Actg ADC
1LT David Riddle, 15th Inf, Actg ADC
LTC Thomas Aspinwall, 9th Inf
MAJ William A. Trimble, 19th Inf
MAJ George M. Brooke, 23d Inf
CPT Jared Ingersoll, 9th Inf
CPT Thomas Ramsey, 1st Rifles
CPT Haie, McBurney's Regt NY Vols
1LT David Crawford, 11th Inf
1LT Ebenezer Childs, 9th Inf
1LT William F. Hale, 11th Inf
1LT Frederick Brown, 23d Inf
1LT Stephen Gaunt, 4th Rifles
1LT Joseph Gillett, Hopkins' Regt NY Vols
1LT Donald Fraser, 15th Inf (Bde Maj)
1LT William Bailey, Dobbin's Regt NY Vols
2LT Isaac Clark, 11th Inf
3LT Benjamin Stephenson, 11th Inf
3LT Samuel Cobb, 1st Rifles
ENS Nicholas Neely, 19th Inf
ENS Calvin Cummings, 21st Inf

15 October 1814 wounded:
Judge Adv Stephen Smith, Jr., ADC

19 October 1814 killed:
3LT Elias Smur, 4th Rifles

19 October 1814 wounded:
CPT Richard H. Bell, 5th Inf
1LT St. John Beckett, 14th Inf
3LT Martin Thomas, 16th Inf

Annex L

U.S. OFFICER MORTALITIES

No Known Disposition;
From Eaton's Compendium, RG94
and Adj. Gen. Roger Jones' Reports, RG94

1st Rifles
CPT Lewis G.A. Armistead, 17 Sept.

4th Rifles
2LT Robert N. Yates, 20 Aug.

1st Infantry
CPT Horace Hale, 17 Sept.

21st Infantry
CPT Lemuel Bradford, 17 Sept., shot in the neck, battleground Ft. Erie
ENS John Bentley, 17 Sept.

23d Infantry
CPT Simeon D. Wattles, 25 Aug.

Artillery
CPT Alexander J. Williams, 15 Aug.
1LT Patrick McDonough, 15 Aug.

Can Vols
LTC Joseph Willcocks, 11 Sept. (attached Swift's/Dobbins' NY Regt.)

NY Vols
  ENS Robert Felton, 28 Aug.
  LT Thomas W. Roosevelt, 11 Sept.
  BG Daniel Davis, 17 Sept.
  CPT Daniel Buel, Crosby's Regt., 17 Sept.
  LT Thomas Besum, McBurney's Regt., 17 Sept.
  LT William Belknap, Fleming's Regt., 17 Sept.
  ENS Blakesley, McBurney's Regt., 17 Sept.

Annex M

FT. ERIE, U.S. SOLDIER MORTALITIES

No Known Disposition; extracted from Company books, RG98

1st Infantry Regiment
    McConnoughy, Hugh, PVT, 13 Aug., killed
    McCalmon, James, PVT, 29 Aug., died
    Wimsie, Tyre, PVT, 29 July, died

9th Infantry—CPT Allen's Co.
    Calvin Wheaton, PVT, 31 July, wounded, died
    John St.Clair, CPL, 6 Aug., wounded, died
    David Palfrey, PVT, 17 Sept., killed in action
    Richard Jordan, CPL, 17 Sept., killed in action

9th Infantry—LT Chandler's Co.
    William Davis, CPL, 6 Aug., wounded
    Thomas Chandler, PVT, 17 Sept., killed in action
    Lemuel Pratt, PVT, 18 Sept., wounded
    Amos Pladbey, PVT, 18 Sept., wounded
    Samuel Haynes, PVT, 18 Sept., wounded
    Cornelius Wheeler, PVT, 18 Sept., wounded
    James Douse, PVT, 11 Aug., wounded

11th Infantry—CPT John Week's Co.
    Jeremiah Fuller, PVT, 15 Aug., Ft. Erie, cannon shot
    Edmund Day, SGT, 17 Sept., near Ft. Erie, shot in action

11th Infantry—CPT Corning's Co.
Jacob Burnham, SGT, 15 Aug., died of wounds
John Bassett, PVT, 15 Aug., died of wounds
Benjamin Lyndes, PVT, 15 Aug., died of wounds
John Carney, PVT, 21 Sept., died of wounds

11th Infantry—CPT John Bliss' Co.
William C. Waits, SGT, 27 Aug., killed by a single round shot while in his tent, Ft. Erie
Martin Cooley, PVT, 15 Aug., killed in the defense of Ft. Erie

11th Infantry—CPT John Bliss' Co. (vice Goodrich)
Daniel Blanden, PVT, 31 Aug., killed at Ft. Erie
Robert Miller, PVT, 4 Sept., killed at Ft.. Erie

21st Infantry—CPT Ira Drew's Co.
Jonathan Quimby, SGT, 17 Sept., shot in the body by grapeshot, battle-ground at Ft. Erie
Francis Hawke, PVT, 1 Sept., camp at Ft. Erie, shot in the head by cannon ball
Joseph Kelley, PVT, 17 Aug., on picket No 1, Ft. Erie, skirmishing

21st Infantry—CPT Morrill Marston's Co.
Angel Ham, PVT, 10 Aug.
Thomas Revere, PVT, 28 Aug., killed by a cannon ball
John A.M. Jackson, PVT, 26 Sept., killed in a skirmish
Charles Smith, PVT, 11 Oct.
John C. Beckwith, PVT
Nathan Case, PVT

21st Infantry—CPT Charles Proctor's Co.
George Trafford, PVT, 17 Sept., killed in action, Ft. Erie
Jonathan Rand, PVT, 4 Oct., sickness, Ft. Erie

21st Infantry—CPT Treat's Co.
Thomas Jackson, PVT, 13 Aug., killed at Ft. Erie
William Lancaster, PVT, 15 Aug., killed in action
Robert Ostrouds, PVT, 15 Aug., killed in action

21st Infantry—CPT Bradford's Co.
Elijah Butler, PVT, 4 Sept., killed on picket duty at Ft. Erie

21st Infantry—CPT Sullivan Burbank's Co.
Winthrop Baston, PVT, killed at Ft. Erie
Daniel Smothers, PVT, prisoner or killed at Ft. Erie
Moses Jewett, PVT, dead
Jeremiah Jordan, PVT, dead

Silas McLaughlin, PVT, dead
John W. Murphy, PVT, dead

21st Infantry—CPT Benjamin Ropes' Co.
Caleb Carr, PVT, 27 Aug., died of wounds at Ft. Erie
John Tobine, PVT, 17 Sept., killed in sortie, Ft. Erie

22d Infantry—CPT Thomas Lawrence's Co.
James Woods, PVT, dead 1814
Freeman Wheaton, PVT, dead 1814
Ezekial Gregg, PVT, dead 1814
Thomas Baley, PVT, dead 1814
Casper Bare, PVT, dead 1814
Frederick Cooke, PVT, dead 1814
James Fulton, PVT, dead 1814
William Phipps, PVT, 3 Sept., Ft. Erie, wounds
John Mason, PVT, 21 Aug. at Ft. Erie

22d Infantry—CPT Willis Foulk's Co.
Jeremiah Ballard, PVT, 17 Aug., Ft. Erie, 22d Regt Hospital of a lingering sickness
Andrew Taylor, PVT, 1 Sept., Ft. Erie, camp disease
William Bruce, SGT, 14 Aug., Ft. Erie Hospital, by a shot from the enemy during siege
Joshua Brown, PVT, 2 Sept., Ft. Erie Hospital, of wounds during siege
Jacob Bates, PVT, 30 Aug., Ft. Erie, killed by the enemy
Samuel Rossiter, PVT, 9 Sept., Ft. Erie, killed by the enemy
Jonathan Izard, PVT, Oct., of wound during siege at Ft. Erie
Adam Hallman, PVT, 7 Sept., Ft. Erie, sickness
Jacob Wilts, PVT, 26 Sept., Ft. Erie, of wounds received

22d Infantry—CPT Joseph Henderson's Co.
John Barnes, PVT, 21 Aug. at Ft. Erie
George Crouse, PVT, 24 Sept., killed
Israel Casper, PVT, 15 Aug., killed at Ft. Erie
Isaac Gilbreath, PVT, 30 Aug., died
John Hartman, PVT, 17 August, died
Adam Haughingberry, PVT, 2 Sept., died of wounds
William Harmon, PVT, 25 Aug., killed at Ft. Erie
Daniel Howell, PVT, 15 Aug., killed at Ft. Erie
John Woldruff, PVT, died at Ft. Erie

23d Infantry—LT Justus Ingersoll's Co.
John Sheffield, PVT, 31 Aug., Ft. Erie, killed in camp by shot
Daniel Cressey, PVT, 3 Sept., Ft. Erie, killed in camp by shot

Peter Cemercy, PVT 4 Sept., near camp at Ft. Erie, killed on picket guard
Archibald Reynolds, PVT, 18 Sept., Regt Hospital, Ft. Erie, died of wound received
Jonathan Johnson, PVT, 19 Sept., Regt Hospital, Ft. Erie, died of fever
Isaiah Adams, PVT, 20 Sept., Ft. Erie, died of diarrhea

23d Infantry—LT William Belknap's Co.
Jeremiah Daily, PVT, 14 Aug., Ft. Erie, cannonading, killed by a piece of a bomb shell
Job Bishop, CPL, 17 Sept., Canada, in action against the British
Jonathan Race, PVT, 17 Sept., Canada, in action against the British

23d Infantry—CPT Richard Goodell's Co.
A. Morgan, PVT, 1 Sept., Ft. Erie, killed
William Burgis, PVT, 6 Sept., Ft. Erie, sickness
Peter Tagert, PVT, 28 Sept., Ft. Erie, sickness
David Debois, PVT, 17 Sept., Ft. Erie, killed in action
Thadeus Hall, PVT, 17 Sept., Ft. Erie, killed in action
James Neville, PVT, 23 Aug., Ft. Erie, sickness
Francis Miller, PVT, 1 Aug., Ft. Erie, killed
Gardiner Kinione, PVT, 25 July, Ft. Erie, killed

25th Infantry—CPT Thomas Seymour's Co.
John French, PVT, at Ft. Erie
Francis Hernandez, PVT, wounded at Ft. Erie

25th Infantry—CPT Edward White's Co.
Ruel Jones, PVT, 1 Sept., died of wounds at Ft. Erie
John McKissick, PVT, 8 Oct., of sickness at Ft. Erie

25th Infantry—Daniel Ketchum's Co.
John McCannon, PVT, 18 Aug., Ft. Erie, cannon shot, killed instantly when a shot from the enemy passed through his body
Hiram Hard, PVT 28 Aug., Ft Erie, wounded by explosion of a shell and died same day
Samuel Powner, PVT, 2 Sept., Ft Erie, cause unknown
Alvin Smith, PVT, 6 Oct., Ft Erie, sickness

1st Rifles—CPT George Gray's Co. (Ala/Tenn Co.)
William England, PVT, 16 Aug., Ft. Erie, killed in action
George Fields, PVT, 6 Aug., Ft. Erie, killed in action
William Frost, PVT, 18 Aug., Ft. Erie, killed in action when on picket duty
Jesse Young, PVT, 6 Aug., Ft. Erie, killed while lying in his tent
Charles Harding, SGT, 17 Sept., Ft. Erie, killed in action
John Rowen, PVT, 6 Aug., near Ft. Erie, killed in action

Joseph Morrow, PVT, 17 Sept., Ft. Erie, killed in action
Aaron Sperling, PVT, 17 Sept., Ft. Erie, killed in action
Alisha Sharp, PVT, 17 Sept., Ft. Erie, killed in action
John McMahon, PVT, 17 Sept., Ft. Erie, when in action

1st Rifles—CPT William Smyth's Co.
Henry Cook, CPL, 20 July, died
Benjamin Owens, CPL, 20 July, unknown
John Brookart, PVT, 10 Aug., Ft. Erie, killed in action, shot
D. Frederick, PVT, 17 Sept., Ft. Erie, killed in action
John Batteace, PVT, near Ft. Erie, killed
Daniel Goble, PVT, 17 Sept., Ft. Erie, killed in action
James Lisles, PVT, 17 Sept., Ft. Erie, killed in action
George Rhea, PVT, 17 Sept., Ft. Erie, killed in action
Jonathan Stout, PVT, 17 Sept., Ft. Erie, killed in action

Artillery—CPT Alex C.W. Fanning's Co.
Joseph Schnyder, PVT, 3 Sept., Ft. Erie, killed in action
William Spalding, PVT, 31 Aug., died at Ft. Erie 1 Sept.;
both legs shot off
Samuel West, PVT, 1 Sept., Ft. Erie, killed
Jonas Sago, PVT, 3 Sept., Ft. Erie, killed in action

Artillery—CPT Alex. William's Co.
John Shute, PVT, 27 Oct., Ft. Erie, sick; died
Eben Edwards, PVT, 15 Aug., Ft. Erie, killed at Battle of
Philip Fagans, PVT, 15 Aug., Ft. Erie, killed
George Loughouse, PVT, 22 July, drowned in Lake Erie

Bombardiers—1LT David B. Douglass' Co.
Michael Carroll, PVT, 15 Aug., killed by falling debris

Annex N

U.S. FATALITIES

U.S. Deaths Throughout Period of Defense of Ft. Erie 1814
Extracted From RG 98

UNIT	NAME	RANK	DATE OF DEATH
19th Infantry	ABRAM, DESHAZE	SGT	08-16
23d Infantry	ADAMS, ISAIAH	PVT	09-20
23d Infantry	ADAMS, WILLIAM	PVT	09-17
23d Infantry	AGERMAN, DANIEL	PVT	09-17
23d Infantry	ALLEN, HORACE	PVT	09-10
23d Infantry	AMES, JOSIAH	PVT	07-29
First Rifles	ARMISTEAD, LEWIS G.A.	CPT	09-17
NY Volunteers	BACON, JAMES	SGT	08-13
25th Infantry	BALDWIN, EBENEZER	PVT	08-30
22d Infantry	BALEY, THOMAS	PVT	unknown
22d Infantry	BALLARD, JEREMIAH	PVT	08-17
22d Infantry	BARE, CASPER	PVT	unknown
22d Infantry	BARNES, JOHN	PVT	08-21
11th Infantry	BASSETT, JOHN	PVT	08-15
21st Infantry	BASTON, WINTHROP	PVT	unknown
25th Infantry	BATES, BOWELL	PVT	08-07
22d Infantry	BATES, JACOB	PVT	09- 02
First Rifles	BATES, JOSEPH	PVT	08-20
First Rifles	BATTEACE, JOHN	PVT	unknown
21st Infantry	BECKWITH, JOHN C.	PVT	unknown

NY Volunteers	BELKNAP, WILLIAM	LT	09-17
23d Infantry	BENJAMIN, JOHNSON	PVT	08-23
21st Infantry	BENTLEY, JOHN	ENS	09-17
NY Volunteers	BESUM, THOMAS	LT	09-17
11th Infantry	BILLINGS, DANIEL	PVT	08-15
23d Infantry	BISHOP, JOB	CPL	09-17
NY Volunteers	BLAKESLEY	ENS	09-17
NY Volunteers	BLANCHARD, RICHARD	PVT	09-22
11th Infantry	BLANDEN, DANIEL	PVT	08-31
NY Volunteers	BLOOM, WILLIAM	PVT	10-18
PA Volunteers	BORELAND, THOMAS	PVT	08-03
21st Infantry	BRADFORD, LEMUEL	CPT	09-17
First Rifles	BROOKHART, JOHN	PVT	08-10
22d Infantry	BROWN, JOSHUA	PVT	09-02
22d Infantry	BRUCE, WILLIAM	SGT	08-14
NY Volunteers	BUEL, DANIEL	CPT	09-17
23d Infantry	BURGIS, WILLIAM	PVT	09-06
11th Infantry	BURNHAM, JACOB	SGT	08-15
21st Infantry	BUTLER, ELIJAH	PVT	09-07*
17th Infantry	BUTLER, WILLIAM	PVT	08- 15
11th Infantry	CARNEY, JOHN	PVT	09-21
21st Infantry	CARR, CULET	PVT	08-27
First Rifles	CARTER, BURLOW	PVT	08-15
21st Infantry	CASE, NATHAN	PVT	unknown
NY Volunteers	CASHUSS, HENRY	PVT	09-05
22d Infantry	CASPER, ISRAEL	PVT	08-15
19th Infantry	CASTLE, GEORGE	PVT	09-17
23d Infantry	CEMERCY, PETER	PVT	09-04
9th Infantry	CHANDLER, THOMAS	PVT	09-17
NY Volunteers	CLARK, DANIEL	PVT	unknown
19th Infantry	COISIN, THOMAS	PVT	09-30
22d Infantry	CONELOUGE, MICHAEL	PVT	07-28
17th Infantry	CONNOR, JOHN	PVT	08-15
23d Infantry	COOK, PAUL	PVT	08-08
22d Infantry	COOKE, FREDERICK	PVT	unknown
11th Infantry	COOLEY, MARTIN	PVT	08-15
22d Infantry	COOPER, WILLIAM	PVT	08-10
25th Infantry	COUGH, GEORGE	PVT	08-15
First Rifles	COVEL, HENRY	CPL	07-20
22d Infantry	CRAINE, IRA	PVT	08- 03
First Rifles	CRASNER, PATRICK	PVT	08-15
23d Infantry	CRESSEY, DANIEL	PVT	09-03

22d Infantry	CROUSE, GEORGE	PVT	09-24
NY Volunteers	CURRICOMBE, MOSES	PVT	09-22
11th Infantry	CURTIS, JAMES	PVT	09-11
23d Infantry	CURTIS, NATHAN	CPL	08-31
23d Infantry	DAILEY, JEREMIAH	PVT	08-14
NY Volunteers	DAVIS, DANIEL	BGEN	09-17
9th Infantry	DAVIS, WILLIAM	CPL	08-24
11th Infantry	DAY, EDMUND	SGT	09-17
23d Infantry	DEBOIS, DAVID	PVT	09-17
21st Infantry	DOLINE, JOHN	PVT	09-17
9th Infantry	DOUSE, JAMES	PVT	08- 11
11th Infantry	DOYLE, PETER	PVT	09- 15
Artillery	DUNCAN, JAMES	PVT	08- 01
Artillery	EDWARDS, EBEN	PVT	08-15
First Rifles	ENGLAND, WILLIAM	PVT	08- 16
Artillery	FAGANS, PHILIP	PVT	08-15
23d Infantry	FARLEY, JOHN	PVT	09-17
21st Infantry	FARRER, HEZEKIAH	PVT	08-13
NY Volunteers	FELTON, ROBERT	ENS	08-28
First Rifles	FIELDS, GEORGE	PVT	08-06
19th Infantry	FISHER, JOSEPH	PVT	09-02
NY Volunteers	FISHER, PETER	PVT	10-18
23d Infantry	FITZGERALD, PETER	PVT	08-17
First Rifles	FLYNN, PETER	PVT	08-09
First Rifles	FREDERICK, D.	PVT	09-17
25th Infantry	FRENCH, JOHN	PVT	unknown
First Rifles	FROST, WILLIAM	PVT	08-18
11th Infantry	FULLER, JEREMIAH	PVT	08-15
22d Infantry	FULTON, JAMES	PVT	unknown
22d Infantry	GILBREATH, ISAAC	PVT	08-30
22d Infantry	GILCHRIST, JAMES	PVT	09-08
First Rifles	GOBLE, DANIEL	PVT	09-17
2d Infantry	GREGG, EZEKIAL	PVT	unknown
9th Infantry	GUBBEN, THOMAS	PVT	10-22
11th Infantry	GUILIAR, PHILIP	PVT	09-11
11th Infantry	HALE, HORACE	CPT	09-17
11th Infantry	HALL, BENJAMIN	PVT	08-15
22d Infantry	HALL, LAWRENCE	PVT	unknown
23d Infantry	HALL, THADEUS	PVT	09-17
22d Infantry	HALLMAN, ADAM	PVT	09-07

19th Infantry	HALMAN, STEPHEN	PVT	10-08
21st Infantry	HAM, ANGEL	PVT	08-10
NY Volunteers	HANFORD, HEZEKIAH	PVT	08-25
25th Infantry	HARD, HIRAM	PVT	08-28
First Rifles	HARDING, CHARLES	SGT	09-17
22d Infantry	HARMON, WILLIAM	PVT	08-25
22d Infantry	HARTMAN, JOHN	PVT	08-17
22d Infantry	HAUGHINGBERRY, ADAM	PVT	09-02
21st Infantry	HAWKE, FRANCIS	PVT	09-01
9th Infantry	HAYNES, SAMUEL	PVT	09-18
19th Infantry	HENDRICK, EDMUND	PVT	09-29
25th Infantry	HERNANDEZ, FRANCIS	PVT	unknown
NY Volunteers	HEWITT, AMES	PVT	08-25
25th Infantry	HIRAM, WARD	PVT	08- 28
NY Volunteers	HOCOMB, CONSIDER	PVT	08-30
NY Volunteers	HOLMES, CALBIN	PVT	09-05
NY Volunteers	HORTON, ELNATHAN	PVT	09-16
19th Infantry	HOUSMAN, ABRAHAM	CPL	09-17
22d Infantry	HOWELL, DANIEL	PVT	08-15
22d Infantry	IZARD, JOHATHAN	PVT	09-09
21st Infantry	JACKSON, JOHN A.M.	PVT	09-26
21st Infantry	JACKSON, THOMAS	PVT	08-13
NY Volunteers	JENKINS, HUGH	PVT	08-27
21st Infantry	JEWETT, MOSES	PVT	unknown
23d Infantry	JOHNSON, JONATHAN	PVT	09-19
19th Infantry	JOHNSON, WILLIAM	PVT	09-02
25th Infantry	JONES, RUEL	PVT	09-01
PA Volunteers	JONES, WILLIAM	PVT	08-05
21st Infantry	JORDAN, JEREMIAH	PVT	unknown
9th Infantry	JORDAN, RICHARD	CPL	09-17
21st Infantry	KELLEY, JOSEPH	PVT	08-17
NY Volunteers	KEYES, CHARLES	PVT	10-25
11th Infantry	KINDS, BENJAMIN	PVT	08-15
23d Infantry	KINIONE, GARDINER	PVT	07-25
PA Volunteers	LEASE, GEORGE	PVT	08-23
11th Infantry	LEE, DANIEL	PVT	09-17
PA Volunteers	LEOPARD, JACOB	PVT	08-19
First Rifles	LISLES, JAMES	PVT	09-17
2d Lt. Dragoons	LOOMIS, JUD	PVT	09-12
Artillery	LOUGHOUSE, GEORGE	PVT	07-22

11th Infantry	LYNDES, BENJAMIN	PVT	08-15
22d Infantry	MABIN, WILLIAM	PVT	08-15
NY Volunteers	MADDEN, ALPHEUS	PVT	09-10
22d Infantry	MASON, JOHN	PVT	09-01
11th Infantry	MAXFIELD, MOSES	CPL	08-29
1st Infantry	MCCALMON, JAMES	PVT	08-29
25th Infantry	MCCANNON, JOHN	PVT	08-18
23d Infantry	MCCLAY, JAMES	PVT	09
19th Infantry	MCCLINTOCK, JOHN	PVT	10-26
1st Infantry	MCCONNOUGHT, HUGH	PVT	08-13
23d Infantry	MCCORD, ANDREW	PVT	08-17
Artillery	MCDONOUGH, PATRICK	1LT	08-15
22d Infantry	MCFEE, GILBERT	PVT	09-20
25th Infantry	MCKISSICK, JOHN	PVT	10-08
21st Infantry	MCLAUGHLIN, SILAS	PVT	unknown
First Rifles	MCMAHON, JOHN	PVT	09-17
PA Volunteers	MELHORNE, HENRY	PVT	08-22
23d Infantry	MILLER, FRANCIS	PVT	07-30
11th Infantry	MILLER, ROBERT	PVT	09-04
PA Volunteers	MONSON, EDWARD	PVT	08
PA Volunteers	MOOR, JAMES	1SGT	08- 15
Artillery	MOORE, HENRY	CPL	08-05
22d Infantry	MOORE, WILLIAM C.	PVT	09-11
23d Infantry	MORGAN, A.	PVT	09-01
NY Volunteers	MORGAN, JOHN	PVT	10-15
22d Infantry	MORRISON, DANIEL	PVT	08-28
First Rifles	MORROW, JOSEPH	PVT	09-17
11th Infantry	MUNCELL, JOHN	PVT	08-17
21st Infantry	MURPHY, JOHN W.	PVT	unknown
23d Infantry	NEVILLE, JAMES	PVT	08-23
First Rifles	NORMAN, WILLIAM	PVT	09-01
19th Infantry	OSBORNE, GEORGE	PVT	09-17
21st Infantry	OSTROUDS, ROBERT	PVT	08-15
First Rifles	OWENS, BENJAMIN	CPL	07-20
9th Infantry	PALFREY, DAVID	PVT	09-17
17th Infantry	PAWLEY, JOHN	PVT	08-25
22d Infantry	PHIPPS, WILLIAM	PVT	09-03
NY Volunteers	PIERCE, PHINEAS	PVT	09-04
9th Infantry	PLADBEY, AMOS	PVT	09-18
25th Infantry	POWNER, SAMUEL	PVT	09-02
9th Infantry	PRATT, LEMUEL	PVT	09-18

21st Infantry	QUIMBY, JONATHAN	SGT	09- 17
23d Infantry	RACE, JONATHAN	PVT	09-17
21st Infantry	RAND, JONATHAN	PVT	10-04
23d Infantry	REUIFF, CHESTER	PVT	08-29
21st Infantry	REVERE, THOMAS	PVT	08-28
23d Infantry	REYNOLDS, ARCHIBALD	PVT	09-18
NY Volunteers	ROOSEVELT, THOMAS W.	LT	09-11
19th Infantry	ROOT, GABRIEL	PVT	08-15
23d Infantry	ROOT, THOMAS A.	PVT	09-17
22d Infantry	ROSSITER, SAMUEL	PVT	09-09
23d Infantry	ROW, JOSEPH L.	PVT	08-17
First Rifles	ROWEN, JOHN	PVT	09- 08
NY Volunteers	RUNYON, JAMES	PVT	09- 17
Artillery	SAGO, JONAS	PVT	09-03
11th Infantry	SANDERSON, ABEL	PVT	08- 25
Artillery	SCHNYDER, JOSEPH	PVT	09-03
23d Infantry	SCUDDER, SETH	PVT	09-12
Artillery	SEYMOUR, GERRARD	PVT	08-26
First Rifles	SHARP, ALISHA	PVT	09-17
3d Infantry	SHEFFIELD, JOHN	PVT	08-31
NY Volunteers	SHERMAN, WILLIAM	PVT	09-17
Artillery	SHUTE, JOHN	PVT	10- 27
NY Volunteers	SIDLEY, HENRY	PVT	08-18
21st Infantry	SIMONDS, JONATHAN	PVT	08-17
25th Infantry	SMITH, ALVIN	PVT	10-06
21st Infantry	SMITH, CHARLES	PVT	10-11
21st Infantry	SMITH, JESSE	PVT	08-16
First Rifles	SMITH, WILLIAM	PVT	08-16
21st Infantry	SMOTHERS, DANIEL	PVT	unknown
Artillery	SPALDING, WILLIAM	PVT	09-01
First Rifles	SPERLING, AARON		09-17
9th Infantry	ST. CLAIR, JOHN	CPL	08- 06
19th Infantry	STANSBERRY, JAMES	PVT	09-17
23d Infantry	STATTS, WILLIAM	PVT	08-17
NY Volunteers	STEVENSON, HUGH	PVT	10-26
23d Infantry	SWEET, JOHN	PVT	09-17
23d Infantry	TAGERT, PETER	PVT	09-28
22d Infantry	TAYLOR, ANDREW	PVT	09-01
21st Infantry	TOBINE, JOHN	PVT	09-17
21st Infantry	TRAFFORD, GEORGE	PVT	09-17
23d Infantry	TREE, NATHANIEL C.	PVT	09-17

19th Infantry	TRIMBLE, DANIEL	CPL	10-24
11th Infantry	UNKNOWN !1	PVT	10-12
First Rifles	UNKNOWN #10	PVT	09-08
First Rifles	UNKNOWN #11	PVT	08-21
23d Infantry	UNKNOWN #12	PVT	08- 24
11th Infantry	UNKNOWN #2	PVT	10-01
11th Infantry	UNKNOWN #3	PVT	09-17
19th Infantry	UNKNOWN #4	PVT	08-15
19th Infantry	UNKNOWN #5	PVT	08- 15
19th Infantry	UNKNOWN #6	PVT	08-31
19th Infantry	UNKNOWN #7	CPL	08-17
21st Infantry	UNKNOWN #8	PVT	08-27
First Rifles	UNKNOWN #9	PVT	09- 17
22d Infantry	VANGORDON, WILLIAM	PVT	08- 25
First Rifles	VAUCLEA, JONAS	PVT	08-20
11th Infantry	WAITS, WILLIAM c.	SGT	08-27
NY Volunteers	WAMSEY, ELIJAH	PVT	09-17
23d Infantry	WATTLES, SIMON D.	CPT	08-25
NY Volunteers	WAVER, JOHN	PVT	09-04
Artillery	WEST, SAMUEL	PVT	09-01
9th Infantry	WHEATON, CALVIN	PVT	07-31
22d Infantry	WHEATON, FREEMAN	PVT	unknown
9th Infantry	WHEELER, CORNELIUS	PVT	09-18
NY Volunteers	WICKHAM, WILLIAM	PVT	08-28
NY Volunteers	WICKSON, CALVIN S.	PVT	08-18
NY Volunteers	WIDNOR, LEONARD	PVT	08-27
Canadian Volunteers	WILLCOCKS, JOSEPH	LTC	09-11
Artillery	WILLIAMS, ALEXANDER	CPT	08-15
22d Infantry	WILLIAMS, JAMES	CPL	09-03
19th Infantry	WILLIS, AMOS	PVT	unknown
22d Infantry	WILTS, JACOB	PVT	09-26
1st Infantry	WIMSIE, TYRE	PVT	07- 29
22d Infantry	WOLDRUFF, JOHN	PVT	08-12
22d Infantry	WOODS, JAMES	PVT	unknown
NY Volunteers	WORDBECK, ZACHARIAH	PVT	09-01
4th Rifles	YATES, ROBERT N.	2LT	08-20
First Rifles	YOUNG, JESSE	PVT	08-06

Annex O

PROFILE OF TYPICAL U.S. UNITS

Sample Units
(RG 94, Entries 233-247, Unit Books)

Captain L. Bradford's Co., 21st Infantry
(Later CPT Lemuel Bradford's Co.)

The company was recruited first in June 1812; additional men were enlisted in February and March 1813 and again in March and April 1814. An additional large influx of men took place in the fall of 1814 in a merger with another company from the regiment. The original part of the company was recruited mostly from the northeast coastal areas of Massachusetts and the Androscoggin and Kennebec valleys of what is now southern Maine. A few men were enlisted in northern New York where the regiment was stationed. The men were a mix of five-year enlistees and those who had agreed to serve for the duration only. As of December 1814, three men had been discharged, one was missing in action, six had been killed in action, and eight had died (bowels, four; fever, two; inflammation of lungs, two).

Of the original 89 unit members, two were foreign born (Germany, Italy) while six were born in some state other than Massachusetts (NH, three; VT, one; NY, one; RI, one). The 58 men transferred in late 1814 had much more diverse backgrounds although most were recruited from the same regions, especially New York State. Seven of them were foreign born (Canada, three; Ireland, two; Portugal, one; Italy, one). Thirty-seven were born in some state other than Massachusetts (NH, 27; CT, three; NY, two; RI, two; VT, two; PA, one).

The original 89 men listed 16 occupations, foremost of which was farmer (44) followed by laborer (19). Other occupations are as follows: soldier five; carpenter two; housewright one; painter one; mason two; blacksmith one; wheelwright one; mariner one; coaster one; seaman one; cordwainer four; shoemaker two; tanner two; yeoman two.

Of the 58 additional men, again, most were farmers (26) or laborers (15). Other professions were: seaman, two; mariner, one; cordwainer, two; ropemaker, one; silversmith, one; merchant, one; hatter, two; cooper, one; cabinetmaker, two; shoemaker, one; soldier, one.

Thus, 106 of the 147 men in the company were farm workers or laborers.

The average age of the men was 27.5 years and the average height was 5 feet, 8.5 inches.

Roster
Captain L. Bradford's Co., 21st Regiment Infantry Vol 272

Name	Rank	Age	Height Feet/ Inches	Height Inches	Occupation	Birthplace
DWIGHT L. HARRINGTON	SGT	25	5 9.5	69.5	PAINTER	MA
JONATHAN L. QUIMBY	SGT	28	6 0	72	LABORER	MA
JOHN HUNTOON	SGT	24	5 7	67	LABORER	MA
WILLIAM EDDY	SGT	27	5 7.5	67.5	HOUSEWRIGHT	MA
SAMUEL MAGUIRE	SGT	22	5 10	70	FARMER	MA
MATHEW STEARNS	SGT	22	5 7.5	67.5	LABORER	MA
JOSEPH GARDNER	SGT	27	5 11	71	SOLDIER	MARBURG, GERMANY
FREDERICK FULLER	SGT	25	5 8	68	FARMER	CN

Average Age: 25 years
Average Height: 69.06 inches

Name	Rank	Age	Height Feet/ Inches	Height Inches	Occupation	Birthplace
JAMES FOWLER	CPL	19	5 5.5	65.5	HATTER	NH
ELIJAH BARTON	CPL	28	5 7	67	LABORER	MA
ASA HOLT	CPL	22	5 8.5	68.5	FARMER	MA
JOTHAN BUZZELL	CPL	20	5 8.5	68.5	LABORER	MA
WILLIAM WOODMAN	CPL	23	5 10	70	FARMER	MA
JOSEPH FURBUSH	CPL	29	5 11	71	TANNER	MA
SAMUEL PENNELL	CPL	24	5 6.5	66.5	CARPENTER	MA

Average Age: 23.57 years
Average Height: 68.14 inches

Name	Rank	Age	Height Feet/ Inches	Height Inches	Occupation	Birthplace
JOHN G. STAHL	MUS	27	5 3	63	SOLDIER	MA
ISAAC L. BENSON	MUS	22	5 8.5	68.5	HATTER	CN
JOHN RAYNES	MUS	18	5 9	69	LABORER	MA
JOHN ROGERS	MUS	21	5 6	66	CORDWAINER	MA

Average Age: 22 years
Average Height: 66.63 inches

Name	Rank	Age	Height Feet/ Inches	Height Inches	Occupation	Birthplace
HENRY ATKINSON	PVT	24	5 7	67	FARMER	MA
DANIEL BOYNTON	PVT	23	5 11	71	LABORER	VT

ARTHUR BOWING	PVT	18	5	5.5	65.5	LABORER	MA
THOMAS BLACKWELL	PVT	16	5	10.5	60.5	LABORER	MA
EZEKEAL BERZELL	PVT	25	5	5	65	SHOEMAKER	MA
AMOS BAKER	PVT	29	5	9	69	FARMER	MA
JOHN BRALEY	PVT	18	5	4.5	64.5	LABORER	MA
CHASE CLOUGH	PVT	31	5	7	67	SHOEMAKER	NH
THOS. N. CUSHING	PVT	22	5	8	68	CARPENTER	MA
STEPHNE CHASE	PVT	33	5	8	68	FARMER	MA
ABRAHAM CHADWICK	PVT	23	5	6.5	66.5	LABORER	MA
THOMAS CUNNINGHAM	PVT	15	4	11	59	LABORER	MA
SALTER COBB	PVT	19	5	9.5	69.5	FARMER	MA
JAMES COLBIRTH	PVT	39	5	9.5	69.5	FARMER	MA
LEVI DAVIS	PVT	15	5	5.25	65.25	LABORER	MA
JOSEPH DAVIS	PVT	21	5	11.5	71.5	MASON	MA
RICHARD DOOR	PVT	18	5	10.5	70.5	SOLDIER	MA
WILLIAM DALTON	PVT	18	5	5.5	65.5	FARMER	MA
CALEB EVENS	PVT	23	5	8.25	68.25	LABORER	MA
SETH FARROW	PVT	29	5	10.5	70.5	MARINER	MA
JOHN GLIDDEN	PVT	23	6	1	73	TANNER	MA
JOHN GORDON, JR	PVT	25	5	9.5	69.5	FARMER	MA
JOB HASKELL	PVT	18	5	8	68	FARMER	MA
JOHN HANSON	PVT	14	4	8.5	56.5	FARMER	MA
THOMAS HARRIS	PVT	35	5	8	68	FARMER	RI
JONATHAN HOLT, JR	PVT	19	5	10.5	70.5	FARMER	MA
WILLIAM HAMLIN	PVT	17	5	6.25	66.25	LABORER	MA
WILLIAM HAMILTON	PVT	17	5	6.25	66.25	LABORER	MA
DAVID HAMILTON	PVT	18	5	4.5	64.5	LABORER	MA
AVERY HART	PVT	18	5	8.5	68.5	FARMER	MA
EDWARD HARTWELL	PVT	32	5	10	70	SOLDIER	NH
JOHN HUGHS	PVT	30	5	8.5	68.5	CORDWAINER	MA
WILLIAM HUTCHINS	PVT	20	5	7	67	FARMER	MA
STEPHEN HUNT	PVT	39	5	11.5	71.5	FARMER	MA
JOEL HAMMOND	PVT	18	5	6	66	FARMER	MA
EDWARD HAMMOND	PVT	21	5	9	69	FARMER	MA
WILLIAM HART	PVT	18	5	7.5	67.5	FARMER	MA
CHARLES HYLER	PVT	19	5	5	65	COASTER	MA
ELISHA JAMES	PVT	22	5	7.25	67.25	FARMER	MA
JAMES JOHNSON	PVT	18	5	3	63	SOLDIER	MA
JOEL IRELAND	PVT	22	6	2	74	FARMER	MA
JEREMIAH JORDAN	PVT	46	6	0	72	FARMER	MA
DAVID KENDALL	PVT	41	5	9.5	69.5	FARMER	MA
ENOCH LEATHERS	PVT	45	5	7	67	CORDWAINER	MA
WILLIAM LIBBY	PVT	24	5	10	70	FARMER	MA
JAMES LOW, JR	PVT	19	5	10	70	FARMER	MA
DANIEL LAMBERT	PVT	26	5	6	66	FARMER	MA
AMMI MITCHELL	PVT	19	5	10.5	70.5	FARMER	MA
SILAS MESSENGER	PVT	21	5	7	67	FARMER	NY
ROBERT MARSHALL	PVT	21	5	7	67	FARMER	MA
BENJAMIN MARSHALL	PVT	18	5	2.5	62.5	FARMER	MA
JOHN NOBLE, JR	PVT	33	5	7	67	FARMER	MA
DAVID NILES	PVT	18	5	9.5	69.5	LABORER	MA

JOHN REVIS	PVT	14	4 7.75	55.75	FARMER	MA
DAVID ROLLINS	PVT	35	5 6	66	FARMER	MA
HUGH ROSS	PVT	30	5 10.25	70.25	FARMER	NH
SAMUEL ROBERTSON	PVT	23	5 10.75	70.75	MASON	MA
JUDAH SWIFT	PVT	23	5 4	64	SEAMAN	MA
WILLIAM SPEARIN	PVT	18	5 5.5	65.5	YEOMAN	MA
JAMES SPEARIN	PVT	18	5 7	67	FARMER	MA
URIAH SPEARIN	PVT	20	5 7.25	67.25	FARMER	MA
BENJAMIN SPEARIN	PVT	19	5 6.5	66.5	BLACKSMITH	MA
PEARSON SANBORN	PVT	37	5 7.5.	67.5	CORDWAINER	MA
EZEKIAL A. TURNER	PVT	23	5 7	67	WHEELWRIGHT	MA
JOHN TITCOMB	PVT	23	5 6	66	FARMER	MA
ASA TUTTLE	PVT	18	5 9.75	69.75	FARMER	MA
BENJAMIN WHIDDON	PVT	18	5 8	68	YEOMAN	MA
DANIEL WHITMAN	PVT	30	6 4.5	76.4	FARMER	MA
JOHN WARSON	PVT	19	5 5.5	65.5	FARMER	MA
TIMOTHY WHIDDEN	PVT	30	5 8	68	FARMER	MA
JOHN WHITTON	PVT	17	5 6.5	66.5	FARMER	MA
SAMUEL WHIDDEN	PVT	21	5 6	66	FARMER	MA
DANIEL H. WARREN	PVT	23	5 7	67	FARMER	MA
SOLOMON NICHOLSON	PVT	45	5 7	67	SEAMAN	MA
WILLIAM POLAND	PVT	36	6 2	74	MARINER	MA
EZRA PETERSON	PVT	29	5 7.5	67.5	CORDWAINER	NH
JOHN POTTER	PVT	34	5 9	69	FARMER	MA
JONAH BARKO	PVT	40	5 7	67	FARMER	NY
JOHN CUTLER	PVT	17	5 5.5	65.5	LABORER	MA
JOHN B. LAMO	PVT	32	5 4	64	LABORER	Montreal, Canada
WILLIAM CAREFOOT	PVT	20	5 9	69	LABORER	Ireland
DAVID MCLAUGHLIN	PVT	27	5 4.5	64.5	FARMER	NH
DANIEL SHERIDAN	PVT	48	6 0.5	72.5	FARMER	Ireland
WILLIAM WARNER	PVT	25	5 7.5	67.5	ROPEMAKER	MA
JAMES MERRILL	PVT	22	5 9	69	FARMER	NH
THOMAS D. MORRISON	PVT	16	5 4	64	FARMER	NH
SAMUEL NUTE	PVT	16	5 3	63	FARMER	VT
WARLAND WILLSON	PVT	21	5 7	67	FARMER	VT
THOMAS COOK	PVT	21	5 5.25	65.25	FARMER	NH
JAMES PECKHAM	PVT	31	5 6.25.	66.25	SILVERSMITH	RI
RUBEN FULKER	PVT	19	5 4.5	64.5	LABORER	NH
SAMUEL JACKSON	PVT	37	5 4.25	64.25	CORDWAINER	NH
FRANCIS THURSTON	PVT	15	5 3.5	63.5	FARMER	NH
JUAN CERA SIMELOZ	PVT	23	5 7	67	MERCHANT	Lisbon, PRT
FRANCIS MARTIN	PVT	27	5 4	64	FARMER	Quebec, Canada
WILLIAM MARSTON	PVT	17	5 8	68	FARMER	NH
SAMUEL CURTIS	PVT	22	5 9	69	FARMER	MA
EDWARD FOX	PVT	23	5 8	68	FARMER	CN
SAMUEL SMITH	PVT	25	5 8.5	68.5	FARMER	NH
BENJ. ROBINSON	PVT	25	5 5	65	COOPER	NH
JACOB PLACE	PVT	25	5 7.5	67.5	FARMER	NH

JOHN HOGANY	PVT	33	5 10.5	70.5	LABORER	MA
JOSHUA CHESLEY	PVT	27	5 9.5	69.5	SOLDIER	NH
JAMES ROBINSON	PVT	27	5 6	67	LABORER	NH
FRANCIS DULANO	PVT	42	5 6	66	LABORER	MA
ASA HASTINGS	PVT	21	5 10	70	FARMER	NH
SAMUEL ABBOT	PVT	22	5 7	67	LABORER	MA
JONATHAN REDMAN	PVT	36	5 6	66	LABORER	NH
JOHN HAYNES	PVT	33	5 10.5	70.5	LABORER	MA
JABEZ DAVIS	PVT	24	5 7	67	FARMER	MA
NATHAN DARLING	PVT	29	6 0	72	FARMER	VT
JONATHAN OTIS	PVT	42	5 10	70	LABORER	NH
JAMES COBURN	PVT	27	5 11	71	CABINETMAKER	NH
ROBY LYDSTON	PVT	21	5 8.5	68.5	SHOEMAKER	MA
JOHN VINCHAINE	PVT	19	5 8	68	LABORER	Livorno, Italy
HENRY GREEN	PVT	27	5 9.5	69.5	FARMER	PA
ROBERT FRIEND	PVT	21	6 1.25	73.25	FARMER	NH
WILLIAM FOSTER	PVT	14	4 10	58	LABORER	NH
PAUL WILLEY	PVT	40	5 8	68	FARMER	NH
WILLIAM FRENCH	PVT	23	5 6	66	FARMER	NH
RUFUS GRIDLEY	PVT	36	5 6.125	66.125	CABINETMAKER	MA
AMOS ALLEN	PVT	36	5 5.75	65.75	SEAMAN	NY

Average Age: 24.67 years
Average Height: 67.47 inches

Overall Averages—
Average Age: 24.56 years
Average Height: 67.57 inches

Personnel with Incomplete Data:
SETH BISKY   PVT
LEVI WITHAM   PVT   20
DANIEL BURWELL PVT

Captain Daniel McFarland's Company, 22d Infantry

The company was recruited between May and September 1812 from the southwestern part of Pennsylvania, especially Washington, Fayette and Allegeny Counties. All the 99 men had four year enlistments. Before May 1814, three men were discharged, 19 deserted, six were missing in action, three were killed in action and 23 had died of various diseases (inflammation of lungs, eight; fever, seven; dysentery, three; disorder of bowels, two; violent cold, one; dropsy, one, diarrhea, one).

Twelve men were foreign born (Scotland, one; Switzerland, one; England, one; Ireland, nine). Twenty-seven of the men were born in some other state than Pennsylvania (NJ, ten; MD, nine; VA, eight; DE, five; NY, two; NH, one; RI, one; MA, one). Thus, half the company was not native to Pennsylvania.

The men listed 25 different civilian trades or occupations. Farming (32) was the most common followed by laborer (11). Other occupations are as follows: joiner, two; carpenter, two; nailer, one; cabinetmaker, three; cooper, three; mason, three; bricklayer, one; stonecutter, one; blacksmith, six; forgeman, three; collier, one; cordwainer, one; sailor, one; shoemaker, seven; tailor, three; hatter one; watchmaker, one; potter, one; saddler, three; miller, two; baker, one; clerk, one; schoolmaster, one.

Average age of the men was 25.4 years and the average height was 5 feet 7.5 inches.

Roster
Captain D. McFarland's Co., 22d Infantry 1812-1813

Name	Rank	Age	Height Feet/Inches	Height Inches	Occupation	Birthplace
ANDREW FLANIGAN	SGT	25	6	72	JOINER	PA
GREENBURY HOOKE	SGT	25	5 7	67	WATCHMAKER	MD
JAMES CRAWFORD	SGT	23	6	72	LABORER	PA
ABEL INGRAM	SGT	32	6	72	CORDWAINER	DE

Average Age: 26.25 years
Average Height: 70.75 inches

Name	Rank	Age	Height Feet/Inches	Height Inches	Occupation	Birthplace
AMOS PRATT	CPL	27	5 9	69	FARMER	NJ
DUNCAN STEWART	CPL	37	5 6	66	SAILOR	Scotland
JOSEPH HEAFFER	CPL	19	5 9	69	COOPER	PA
JAMES CHAMBERS	CPL	22	6 2	74	FARMER	NJ
ALEXANDER MOORE	CPL	22	5 11	71	BLACKSMITH	DE
TOBIAS HENRY	CPL	33	5 7	67	FARMER	MD
HANS HAMILTON	CPL	24	6	72	BLACKSMITH	PA

Average Age: 26.29 years
Average Height: 69.71 inches

Name	Rank	Age	Height Feet/Inches	Height Inches	Occupation	Birthplace
WILLIAM JOHNSON	MUS	23	5 6.75	66.75	FARMER	PA
VALENTINE LOUDER	MUS	56	5 8.25	68.25	LABORER	MD

Average Age: 39.5 years
Average Height: 67.5 inches

Name	Rank	Age	Height Feet/Inches	Height Inches	Occupation	Birthplace
SAMUEL ALEXANDER	PVT	42	5 9	69	NAILER	Derry, Ireland
JOHN ANDERSON	PVT	19	5 9	69	FARMER	PA
WILLIAM BOWER	PVT	24	5 8	68	SHOEMAKER	NJ
BARNET BELFORD	PVT	25	5 6	66	FARMER	PA
WILLIAM BROWN	PVT	25	5 8	68	FORGEMAN	PA
JOHN BELL	PVT	25	5 9	69	LABORER	PA
DAVID CRAIG	PVT	26	6 0	72	COOPER	PA
JOHN CHRISTIE	PVT	26	5 9	69	COLLIER	Ireland
EDWARD COLE	PVT	32	5 6	66	PRINTER	PA
SOLOMON COOK	PVT	23	5 9	69	BLACKSMITH	NY
THOMAS CAMPBELL	PVT	21	5 9.5	69.5	BLACKSMITH	PA
JOHN CHANCE	PVT	30	5 9	69	FARMER	PA

Name	Rank	Age	Height		Occupation	Origin
STEPHEN CARMICHAEL	PVT	19	6 1.5	73.5	FARMER	PA
JAMES CANARY	PVT	19	5 6	66	FARMER	PA
BENJAMIN DAVIS	PVT	22	5 6	66	FARMER	VA
MANUEL DUNCAN	PVT	44	5 7.5	67.5	FARMER	Armagh, Ireland
SIMEON DANE	PVT	22	5 9.5	69.5	FARMER	NH
DAVID DAVIS	PVT	42	5 10.25	70.25	MASON	PA
PETER DEVON	PVT	29	5 7	67	BLACKSMITH	NJ
NATHAN ENOS	PVT	22	5 5.5	65.5	FARMER	NY
GEORGE ERVING	PVT		5 9.5	69.5	MILLER	PA
WILLIAM FLEMING	PVT	23	5 8	68	SHOEMAKER	VA
JAMES GADDIS	PVT	38	5 7	67	FARMER	PA
WILLIAM GIVON	PVT	29	5 11	71	SCHOOLMASTER	Ireland
WILLIAM GLASFORD	PVT	22	5 9	69	LABORER	PA
JOHN GERARD	PVT	28	5 6	66	SADDLER	VA
WILLIAM HOUSEL	PVT	23	5 6	66	FARMER	NJ
WILLIAM HOSICK	PVT	28	5 6	66	FARMER	PA
JOSHUA JOHNSON	PVT	38	5 11	71	MASON	PA
JOHN JONES	PVT	23	5 10.5	70.5	TAILOR	PA
JOSEPH JACKSON	PVT	24	5 6.5	66.5	FARMER	NJ
SAMUEL LANK	PVT	24	5 8	68	CABINETMAKER	DE
ROBERT LERVES	PVT	22	5 9	69	CORDWAINER	NJ
JAMES MOUNTS	PVT	23	6 0	72	FARMER	PA
HUGH MITCHELL	PVT	35	5 8.25	68.25	MASON	Down, Ireland
WILLIAM S. MOORE	PVT	23	6 0	72	FORGEMAN	PA
THOPHILUS MCDONALD	PVT	37	5 11	71	LABORER	Derry, Ireland
WILLIAM MCCREARY	PVT	25	5 7	67	CARPENTER	PA
ZADOCK MCINTIRE	PVT	21	5 8	68	FARMER	VA
JOHN MUSSER	PVT	23	5 10	70	BRICKLAYER	MD
SAMUEL MCCRILLACK	PVT	23	5 8	68	FARMER	PA
DAVID MORROW	PVT	31	5 7	67	SHOEMAKER	NJ
GEORGE MILER	PVT	38	5 6	66	LABORER	Zurich, Switzerland
MICHAEL MULVEY	PVT	19	5 4	64	STONECUTTER	MD
JOHN MCCOY	PVT	23	5 9	69	FARMER	PA
JAMES MARTIN	PVT	27	5 9.5	69.5	LABORER	PA
WILLIAM MERCER	PVT	40	5 9	69	COOPER	VA
WILLIAM MOORE, JR.	PVT	23	5 10	70	FARMER	PA
WILLIAM MORGANTHAL	PVT	27	5 7	67	SHOEMAKER	PA
ROBERT MCCANN	PVT	20	5 8	68	FARMER	PA
ARCHIBALD MCMILLAN	PVT	22	5 6	66	FARMER	PA
CHARLES ODENBAUGH	PVT	41	5 7.5	67.5	CABINETMAKER	MD
DAVID PERKINS	PVT	19	5 9	69	SHOEMAKER	PA
LEVI PENINGTON	PVT	35	5 9	69	MILLER	DE
JOHN PARKS	PVT	19	5 7	67	LABORER	England
JAMES POLLOCK	PVT	21	5 8	68	FARMER	Donegal, Ireland
JOHN RICHARDS	PVT	41	6 0.6	72.6	FORGEMAN	PA
JOHN RAY	PVT	42	5 9	69	LABORER	Ireland

Name	Rank	Age	Height	Inches	Occupation	State
SAMUEL ROBB	PVT	38	5 11	71	CARPENTER	PA
WILLIAM RUSH	PVT	24	5 8	68	CLERK	DE
WILLIAM RODGERS	PVT	35	5 7	67	FARMER	PA
BENJAMIN SPRAGUE	PVT	23	5 10	70	FARMER	RI
BILBE SHEPHERD	PVT	24	5 5	65	FARMER	NJ
JAMES STILL	PVT	31	5 7	67	SHOEMAKER	NJ
B. LEVI STEWART	PVT	41	6 1	73	BLACKSMITH	MA
WILLIAM SMITH, JR.	PVT	25	5 9.5	69.5	TAILOR, HATTER	MD
WILLIAM L. SMITH	PVT	23	5 10	70	LABORER	Derry, Ireland
JACOB SOUCLERS	PVT	18	5 8	68	FARMER	VA
JOHN SHIPE	PVT	38	5 8	68	SADDLER	VA
FREDERICK TAYLOR	PVT	24	5 10	70	SHOEMAKER	MD
JOSEPH TAYLOR	PVT	19	5 8	68	TAILOR	MD
MICHAEL TEATER	PVT	27	5 7.5	67.5	CABINETMAKER	PA
HYRONEMEUS TOWART	PVT		5 6	66	BAKER	PA
AMOS UPDEGRAF	PVT	43	5 9	69	SADDLER	PA
ABRAHAM VALELY	PVT	21	5 7	67	FARMER	PA
CHARLES WILLIAMS	PVT	21	6 0	72	FARMER	PA
GEORGE WALLACE	PVT	22	5 10.5	70.5	LABORER	PA
JOHN WHITION	PVT	24	5 8	68	FARMER	PA
JOSEPH WALLACE	PVT	21	5 5.5	65.5	POTTER	PA
FIELDING WILLIAMS	PVT	34	5 6	66	HATTER	VA
THOMAS WALLACE	PVT	35	6 0	72	CORDWAINER	PA

Average Age: 27.44 years (does not include unknown ages)
Average Height: 68.51 inches

Overall Averages—
Average Age: 27.57 years
Average Height: 68.67 inches

Personnel with Unknown Data:
BANJAMIN JOHNSON
JOHN LAWRENCE
JAMES REED
JAMES STEWART   JOINER
ARNOLD WARNER

Annex P

MEDICAL DATA

U.S. Medical Personnel, Niagara Frontier 1814
(RG 94, Entry 407, QM Accounts and Returns)

Allen, Elisha L.	Surgeon's Mate, 21st Inf.
Allen, E.S.	Surgeon's Mate, 5th Inf.
Aspinwall, E.	Hospital Surgeon's Mate
Bates, James	Hospital Surgeon's Mate.
Benjamin, Stephen	Wardmaster, Williamsville G.H.
Bronaugh, James C.	Surgeon, Buffalo G.H. (4th Rifles)
Brownell, Richmond	Acting Asst. Apothocary Gen.
Bull, E.W.	Chief Hospital Surgeon, Williamsville G.H.
Coote, C.N.	Hospital Surgeon's Mate, NY Militia
Cunningham, M.I.	Surgeon's Mate, 22d Inf. (dismissed 17 Aug.)
Dade, H.	Surgeon's Mate, 10th Inf. (Arty.)
Entwistle, Thomas	Steward, Williamsville G.H.
Everett, Josiah	Surgeon's Mate, 21st Inf.
Faulkner, James	Surgeon's Mate, Willcocks' Regt.
Field, Henry	Surgeon's Mate, 4th Rifles
Fuller, Silas	Surgeon, 23d Inf.
Gale, John	Surgeon's Mate, 23d Inf.
Green, Henry	Acting Surgeon's Mate, 25th Inf.
Hayes, Adam	Hospital Surgeon, 9th Mil. Dist. Staff
Henning, William	Surgeon, 4th Rifles
Hill, Eli	Hospital Surgeon, NY Militia
Horner, W.E.	Surgeon's Mate, Williamsville G.H.

Howe, Samuel	Surgeon's Mate, Swift's/Dobbin's Regt.
Hunt, Henry	Surgeon, 15th Inf.
Hunt, Simeon	Surgeon's Mate, NY Militia
Johnson, Jeremiah	Surgeon, NY Militia
Lovell, Joseph	Surgeon, 9th Inf.
Malloy, Samuel	Surgeon, PA Volunteers
Madison, W.S.	17th Inf.
Martin	17th Inf.
Marvin, Mather	Surgeon, McMahon's Regt., NY Militia
Mealy, Samuel	Surgeon, 5th PA Volunteers
Mower, Thomas G.	Surgeon's Mate, Arty.
Pratt, Clark	Hospital Steward, 23d Inf.
Sackett, John	Surgeon's Mate, 11th Inf.
Scull, Edward	Surgeon, 22d Inf.
Sheldon, Chauncey L.	Surgeon's Mate, Swift's/Dobbin's Regt.
Simpson, William	Surgeon's Mate, 5th PA Volunteers
Smythe, Robert	Surgeon, 23d Inf. (except 27th Inf. Sep)
Spencer, Gordon P.	Surgeon, 11th Inf.
Tavett	Surgeon, NY Militia
Thomas, William	Chief Hospital Surgeon, Buffalo
Trimble, James	Surgeon's Mate, Arty.
Troubridge, Amasa	Surgeon, 21st Inf.
Wear	4th Rifles
Wells, Guardner	Surgeon, Swift's/Dobbin's Regt.
Williams, William	Surgeon, 17th Inf.
Wolcott, A.	Surgeon, 94th Regt, NY Militia
Woodbury, Phineas	Surgeon's Mate, 25th Inf.
Woodward, T.	Surgeon's Mate, 11th Inf.
Wright, Ira	Surgeon's Mate, Swift's/Dobbin's Regt.

U.S. Hospitals, Niagara Frontier 1814
(RG 94, Entry 407, QM Accounts and Returns)

Ft. Schlosser	General Hospital, 1 July-1 Aug.
Williamsville	General Hospital, 1 Aug.- 15 Mar. 1815, Raphael Cook's property.
	Medical storage depot, June-Feb. 1815, Abel Aspenwall's house & barn.
Ft. Erie	Militia Brigade Hospital, Sept.-Oct.,
	23d Inf. Regt., 13 July-13 Oct.
	21st Inf. Regt., Aug.-16 Sept.
	22d Inf. Regt., Aug.-10 Sept.

Buffalo	General Hospital, 9 Sept.-9 Dec., Luke Draper's house.
	General Hospital, 9 July-9 Jan. 1815, W. David's house.
	1st Rifle Regt. Hospital, 26 Aug.-31 Oct., Jonathan Olmstead's house.
	4th Rifle Regt. Hospital, 26 Aug.-30 Sept., Nathan Dudley's house.
	22d Inf. Hospital, 10 Sept.-15 Oct., Ethan Ludlow's house.
	McMahan's & Allen's NY Militia Regts., 25 Aug.-31 Oct., Samuel Edsell's house.
Black Rock	Militia Hospital, 4 July-1 Oct., Cyrenius Chapin's house.

Annex Q

PRESENCE OF LIVESTOCK

U.S. Livestock in 1814 Niagara Campaign
RG94, OAG/QM Accts; RG98 QM File, Left Division

The quartermaster reported 450 horses in Upper Canada on 17 July; 79 with the line units, the remainder with the trains. About 220 horses were present in the fort during the siege and sortie phases.

Forage reports on or about 12 August indicate that the artillery retained 112 horses at Ft. Erie. Each battery still had nearly a full authorization of animals (24 to 29). This figure was reduced to about nine horses per battery by 20 September. A total of 32 horses was considered the battery's full strength.

Other units reporting horses at Ft. Erie were:

LT Douglass' Engineer Co.	20 horses, 8 Aug.
CPT Harris' Dragoon Co.	45 horses, 12 Aug.
	70 horses, 1 Oct.
LT Deane's NY Volunteer Cav.	15 horses, 13 Aug.
Ft. Erie Command & Staff	28 horses, 7-31 Aug.

Eight yoke of oxen (16) were at Ft. Erie beginning on about 9 Aug.

Annex R

BRITISH POW'S AND DESERTERS

British Prisoners taken 15 August
(RG 94, OAG/QM Accounts., IG Report.)

CPT Colclough, 103d
LT Murray, 103d
Sail Master Charles Hyde, Royal Navy

     10 SGT 103d
      1 SGT DeWatteville
      2 SGT G. Legion
      1 SGT Marine

      7 sailors
      2 Corp 8th
      2 Corp Royal Scots
      2 Corp 41st
      1 Corp 103d
      3 Corp DeWatteville
      1 Corp 100th
PVTS
      2 —8th
      8 —18th
      3 —89th
    21 —104th
      2 —100th
    91 —103d

```
  2 —1st
  6 —R. Marine
 79 —DeWatteville
  5 —Royal Scots
  6 —41st
  2 —G. Legion
227 —Total
```

British Prisoners taken 17 September
(RG 94, OAG/QM Accounts.; IG Report).

MAJ Winter, DeWatteville
MAJ Charles DeVillette, DeWatteville
CPT R. Zehndes, DeWatteville
CPT Hecker, DeWatteville
CPT R. Stiges, DeWatteville
LT/Adj Mermot, DeWatteville
LT/Adj DeBerry, DeWatteville
LT Heicken, DeWatteville
CPT Bradbridge, 8th
LT Maincie, 8th
ENS Mathison, 8th

SSGT	4	DeWatteville
SGT	7	DeWatteville
CPL	7	DeWatteville
MUS	1	DeWatteville
PVT	112	De Watteville
PVT	91	Grenadiers
PVT	1	Dragoon
PVT	9	R. Artillery
SGT	8	8th
CPL	9	8th
PVT	65	8th
SGT	3	Royal Scots
PVT	15	Royal Scots
SGT	1	6th
PVT	9	6th Regiment
PVT	8	82d
SGT	1	89th
CPL	1	89th
PVT	19	89th

LTC Malone Burwell in the militia taken at Ft. Talbot, 16 Aug., paroled 16 June 1815.

Register of Deserters from the Enemy
(RG 98, OAG/QM Accounts; RG 98 QM File, Left Division)

August 1814

15	Glengarry Regiment including one SGT
7	DeWatteville
4	82d
5	8th
31	Total

September 1814

55	Dewatteville
4	114th
11	Glengarry
9	8th
1	Royal Scots
2	87th
1	6th
19	LT Dragoon
82	Total

Annex S

WEAPONS OF THE WAR OF 1812

The infantrymen on both sides carried muskets, shoulder weapons with smooth bores. They were loaded from the muzzle by ramming a charge and projectile down the barrel with a ram-rod. The British Tower musket, or Brown Bess, was a durable .71-calibre flintlock that could be loaded and fired five to six times a minute by a trained man. The U.S. musket Model 1795 had a slightly tighter tolerance for its .65-calibre projectile and, consequently, could be loaded only three to four times a minute. Neither weapon was particularly accurate. However, this mattered little as any battlefield quickly became obscured by smoke from muskets and artillery. What did matter was how rapidly and, in general, accurately a battalion could hurl lead as a group at their enemy counterpart. Post-war estimates indicated that one shot out of 30 in infantry engagements "took effect." Many Americans attempted to increase these odds by adding buckshot to their ball projectile, an action considered barbarous by the British. The relatively slow-moving lead projectiles, which could penetrate five inches of oak at 30 yards, often inflicted horrendous wounds when they flattened out on impact.

Artillery provided greater lethality on the battlefield. Forces employed two types of artillery weapons: the gun, or cannon, featured a smooth bore capable of firing a variety of projectiles on a flat, line of sight, trajectory; the howitzer was designed to hurl projectiles on a more curved trajectory to hit such targets as men in fortifications who could not be reached by a flat shot. A mortar could fire a round with an even greater curve of trajectory. The calibers of the guns were measured by the weight of the shot they fired, while howitzers were identified by the diameter of their bore. Six-pounder guns were the type most commonly used by field artillery. Twelve and 18-pounders were used more often in stationary situations; however, during the Niagara Campaign, General Brown deployed these weapons as part of his artillery reserve. Higher calibre weapons were almost always used in fixed situations, such as during the siege of Fort Erie, when units employed 24-pounders and the eight-inch howitzer.

The artillery guns were reasonably accurate to about half a mile, and could fire a variety of ammunition. Solid shot, the traditional cannon ball, was especially effective against massed infantry or cavalry. It also was used in counterbattery fire to break up an opponent's guns. Solid shot from heavier guns could be used to break walls, as well (a 24 pound shot could penetrate six inches of oak at 100 yards, for example). Hot shot was solid heated so as to have an incendiary effect. The artillery also could fire bombs, or explosive shells, as well, which were hollow spheres filled with gunpowder and equipped with a slow burning fuse ignited when the main round was fired. These rounds were especially effective against men and horses in the open. A third type of round was case or canister, which consisted of lead balls and metal scraps in a metal container and was used against a nearby enemy. The round was most effective when fired from about 700 yards and was relied upon as final protective fires for the guns. A final type of round, used only by the British, was shrapnel. This was a shell loaded with powder and projectiles and was especially effective against troops in the open.

The War of 1812 is associated also with the use of rockets, as commemorated in the U.S. National Anthem. The Congreve rocket had an effective range of about 1,800 yards and a maximum range of three miles. It was fired from a copper tube mounted on a tripod. The rocket consisted of a case of sheet iron with a cylindrical conical head screwed into it. The lower part of the iron case carried the main charge and featured a bushing, which allowed insertion of a 12 to 16 foot stick that served as a stabilizer and part of the means of launch. The explosive head ranged in weight equivalents of artillery, from six- to thirty-two pounders. The rocket was more spectacular than dangerous because its accuracy was very poor. At best, it could be used to scare militiamen or to harass area targets. A Royal Marine artillery rocket detachment supported British operations on the Niagara frontier in 1814.

(Sources: James L. Babcock, "Campaign of 1814 on the Niagara Frontier" (1963); Gay DeVernon, *A Treatise on the Science of War...* (1817); R. Alan Douglas, "Weapons of the War of 1812" (1963); Donald E. Graves, *Sir William Congreve and the Rocket's Red Glare*, Bloomfield, Ontario,: Museum Restoration Service, 1989.)

Bibliography

COMMENT ON SOURCES

The basis for this paper has been the holdings of the U.S. National Archives at Washington, D. C. Other archives, published documentary collections and memoirs, and secondary sources have been used as appropriate. The primary sources used consisted of personnel records, supply and fiscal documentation, and correspondence among and between commanders, staff officers, and War Department officials. These consist, for the most part, of practical accountability documents for men, equipment, and money. Their perusal in quantity gives an excellent picture of the daily operations of General Brown's command. Since most of them deal directly or indirectly with aspects of pecuniary liability, it is reasonable to presume they are accurate. Commanders' reports are less detailed and critical but still give a reasonable picture of events. Memoirs are less reliable when dealing with matters outside the immediate experience of the writer, but still are useful for documenting personal experiences. Modern secondary sources in some cases report actual errors, while in others the brevity of the treatment leaves an incorrect impression. This study's principal reliance on the documentation produced by those responsible for the daily operations of General Brown's force has attempted to reveal the most reliable documentation possible, while providing some of the perspective of those who fought there.

Books & Dissertations

Adams, Henry, *The War of 1812*, H.A. DeWeerd, ed., Washington: Infantry Journal, 1944.

Ashburn, Percy M., *History of the Medical Department of the United States Army*, Boston: Houghton, Mifflin, 1929.

Auchinleck, G., *A History of the War Between Great Britain and the United States of America During the Years 1812, 1813, and 1814*, London: Arms & Armour Press, 1972 (repr. 1855 ed.)

Babcock, Louis L., *The Siege of Fort Erie, An Episode of the War of 1812*, Buffalo: Peter Paul Book Company, 1899.

Baylies, Nicholas, *Eleazer Wheelock Ripley and the War of 1812*, Des Moines: Brewster & Company, 1890.

Beauchamp, William M., *A History of the New York Iroquois*, New York State Museum Bulletin 78, Archaeology 9, Albany: New York State Education Department, 1905.

Beirne, Francis F., *The War of 1812*, New York: E.P. Dutton and Company, 1949.

Berton, Pierre, *Flames Across the Border: The Canadian–American Tragedy, 1813-1814*, Boston: Little, Brown and Company, 1981.

Bingham, R.H., *The Cradle of the Queen City*, Buffalo: Buffalo Historical Society, 1927.

Bingham, Robert, *Address at Opening of Restored Ft. Erie*, 6 July 1939. Ft. Erie Public Library.

Bowler, R. Arthur, ed. *War Along the Niagara: Essays on The War of 1812 and Its Legacy*, Youngstown, New York: Old Fort Niagara Association, Inc., 1991.

Bradford, Robert D., *Historic Forts of Ontario*, Belleville, Ontario: Mika Publishing Company, 1988.

Brannan, John, ed., *Official Letters of the Military and Naval Officers of the U.S. During the War with Great Britain*, Washington: 1823.

Brown, Fred R., *History of the 9th U.S. Infantry 1799-1909*, Chicago: R.R. Donnelly, 1919.

Brown, Harvey E., *The Medical Department of the United States Army from 1775 to 1783*, Washington: Surgeon General's Office, 1873.

Caffrey, Kate, *The Twilight's Last Gleaming: Britain vs. America , 1812-1815*, New York: Stein and Day, 1977.

Callan, John F., *The Military Laws of the United States Relating to the Army, Volunteers, Militia, and to Bounty Lands and Persons, From the Foundation of the Government to the Year 1863*, Philadelphia: George W. Childs, 1863.

Carnochen, Janet, *Inscriptions and Graves in the Niagara Peninsula*, Niagara Historical Society No. 10, Niagara Falls: *The Times*, 1902-03.

Clarke, William P., *Official History of the Militia and National Guard of the State of Pennsylvania*, 3 vols., Philadelphia: 1909.

Coles, Harry L., *The War of 1812*, Chicago and London: University of Chicago Press, 1965.

Court Martial, *Proceedings of a GCM, Held at Ft. Independence, (Boston Harbor) for the Trial of Major Charles K. Gardner...Preferred Against Him by MGen. Ripley*, Boston, 1816.

Crosswell, Daniel, "American Invasion of the Niagara Frontier," Unpublished thesis, University of Wisconsin/Milwaukee, 1957.

Cruikshank, E.A., ed., *Documentary History of the Campaign Upon the Niagara Frontier*, 9 Vols., Welland, Ontario: 1907.

Cruikshank, E.A., ed., *Documents Relating to the Invasion of the Niagara Peninsula by the United States Army Commanded by General Jacob Brown in July and August 1814*, Niagara-on-the-Lake: Niagara Historical Society, No.33, 1920.

Cruikshank, E.A., *The Old Fort at Ft. Erie*, Welland: Tribune- Telegraph Press, 1930.

Cruikshank, Ernest, *Drummond's Winter Campaign, 1813*, Lundy's Lane Historical Society.

Cullum, G.W., ed., *Campaign of the War of 1812*, New York: James Miller, Publisher, 1879.

DeVernon, Gay, *A Treatise on the Science of War and Fortification*, 2 vols., New York: J. Seymour, 1817.

Douglas, John, *Medical Topography of Upper Canada*, London: Burgess and Hill, 1819.

Douglass, David B., *The American Voyager; The Journal of David Bates Douglass*, Sidney W. Jackman & John F. Freeman, eds., Marquette, Michigan: Northern Michigan University Press, 1969.

Dunlop, William, *Recollections of the American War 1813-1814*, Toronto: Historical Publishing Company, 1905.

Dunlop, William, *Tiger Dunlop's Upper Canada...*, Toronto: McClelland & Stewart, 1967.

Elliot, Charles W., *Winfield Scott, The Soldier and the Man*, New York: MacMillan Company, 1937.

Elting, John R., *Amateurs, To Arms! A Military History of the War of 1812*, Chapel Hill: Algonquin Books, 1991.

Everest, Allan S., *The War of 1812 in the Champlain Valley*, Syracuse: Syracuse University Press, 1981.

Fenton, J., *Journal of the Military Tour by the Pennsylvania Troops and*

Militia under the Command of Col. James Fenton, to the Frontiers of Pennsylvania and New York, Carlisle, PA: George Kline, 1814.

Forest Lawn: Its History, Dedications, Progress,...Names of Lot Holders, etc., Buffalo: Thomas, Howard & Johnson, 1867.

Gillett, Mary C., *The Army Medical Department, 1775-1818*, Washington: Army Center of Military History, 1981.

Goodhue, Josiah F., *History of the Town of Shoreham, Vermont...*, Middlebury, Vermont: A.H. Copeland, 1861.

Graham, Lloyd, *Niagara Country*, New York: Duell, Sloan & Pierce, 1949.

Graves, Donald E., "Joseph Willcocks and the Canadian Volunteers: An Account of Political Disaffection in Upper Canada During the War of 1812," Unpublished M.A. thesis, Carlton University, 1982.

Graves, Donald E., ed., *Journal of Sir John Le Couteur*, Societe Jersiaise, St. Helier, unpubl.

Hall, Henry, *The History of Auburn*, Auburn, New York: Dennis Brothers & Company, 1869.

Hampton, Celwyn E., *The Twenty First's Trophy of Niagara*, Ft. Logan: 1909.

Hannay, James, *A History of The War of 1812*, Toronto: Morang and Company, Ltd., 1905.

Hastings, Hugh, ed., *Public Papers of Daniel D. Tompkins, Governor of New York, 1807-1817*, 3 vols., New York & Albany: Wynkoop, Hallenbeck, Crawford Company, 1898.

Hickey, Donald R., *The War of 1812: A Forgotten Conflict*, Urbana and Chicago: University of Illinois Press, 1989.

Hill, Henry W., *Municipality of Buffalo, New York; a History 1720-1923*, 4 vols., New York: Lewis Publishing Company, 1923, Vol. I, pp. 115-58.

Hitsman, J. Mackay, *The Incredible War of 1812: A Military History*, Toronto: University of Toronto Press, 1965.

Horsman, Reginald, *The War of 1812*, New York: Alfred A. Knopf, 1969.

Hough, Franklin B., *A History of Jefferson County in the State of New York...*, Albany: Joel Munsell, 1854.

Irving, L. Homfray, *Officers of the British Forces in Canada During the War of 1812-15*, Welland, Ontario:1908.

Izard, George, *Official Correspondence with the Department of War Relative to the Military Operations of the American Army Under the Command of Major General Izard on the Northern Frontier of the United States in the Years 1814, 1815*, Philadelphia: Thomas Dobson, 1816.

Jacobs, James R. and Tucker, Glen, *The War of 1812: A Compact History*, New York: Hawthorne Books, 1969.

Jenkins, John S., *The Generals of the Last War with Great Britain*, Auburn: Derby, Miller & Company, 1849.

Johnson, Allen, ed., *Dictionary of American Biography*, 11 vols. w/supplements, New York: Charles Scribner's Sons, 1927-64.

Johnson, Crisfield, *Centennial History of Erie County...*, Buffalo: Mathews & Warren, 1876.

Ketchum, William, *Authentic and Comprehensive History of Buffalo*, Buffalo: Rockwell, Baker & Hill, 1865.

Kieffer, Chester L., *Maligned General; The Biography of Thomas Sidney Jesup*, San Rafael, California: Presidio Press, 1979.

Kimball, Jeffrey, "Strategy on the Northern Frontier, 1814," Unpublished Phd. thesis, Louisiana State University, 1969.

Klink, Carl F. and Talman, James J., eds., *The Journal of Major John Norton, 1816*, Toronto: The Champlain Society, 1970.

Kropf, Richard C., *Notes on Surgeons of the Indian Wars and [the] War of 1812*, Mimeo, Columbus, Ohio: Anthony Wayne Parkway Brd, 1957.

Landon, Harry F., *Bugles on the Border: The Story of the War in Northern New York*, Watertown, New York: Watertown Daily Times, 1954.

Linn, J.B., and W.H. Egle, *Muster Rolls of Pennsylvania Volunteers in the War of 1812*, Baltimore: Genealogical Publishing Company, 1956 (repr.. 1890 ed.).

Lossing, Benson J., *Pictorial Field Book of the War of 1812*, New York: Harper, 1869.

Lundy's Lane Historical Society, *The Centenial Celebration of the Battle of Lundy's Lane July 25th 1914*, Niagara Falls, 1919.

Mahon, John K.,*The War of 1812*, Gainesville: University of Florida Press, 1972.

Mann, James, *Medical Sketches of the Campaigns of 1812, 13, 14...*, Dedham, Massachusetts: H. Mann & Company, 1816.

Marquis, Thomas G., *Battlefields of 1814*, Toronto: Ryerson, 1930.

Mason, Philip P., ed., *After Tippecanoe: Some Aspects of the War of 1812*, Westport, Connecticut: Greenwood Press, 1973 (repr. 1963 ed.).

McCauley, I.H., *Historical Sketch of Franklin County*, Chambersburg, 1876.

McRee, William, *Memoir of Colonel William McRee, USE*, Wilmington, North Carolina: 1834.

Michigan Daughters of the War of 1812, *What So Proudly We Hailed*, Ann Arbor, 1964.

Nead, Benjamin M., *Waynesboro, the History of a Settlement in Franklin Co.*, Harrisburg: Harrisburg Publishing Company, 1900.

Owen, David A., *Fort Erie (1764-1823): An Historical Guide*, Niagara Falls, Ontario.: Niagara Parks Commission, 1986.

Park, S.J. and Nafziger, G.F., *The British Military: Its System and Organization, 1803-1815*, Cambridge, Ontario: RAFM Company, Inc., 1983.

Peterson, Clarence S., *Known Dead During the War of 1812*, mimeo, Baltimore: 1955.

Pfeiffer, Susan and Williamson, Ronald F., eds., *Snake Hill: An Investigation of a Military Cemetery from the War of 1812*, Toronto and Oxford: Dundurn Press, 1991.

Porter, Peter A., *American Niagara Frontier in War of 1812...*, (1915, approx.).

Pratt, Julius, *The War of 1812, vol V in Alexander Flick, ed., History of the State of New York*, New York: 1935- 37.

Raddall, Thomas H., *The Path of Destiny*, New York: Popular Library, 1957.

Ripley, Eleazer W., *Facts Relative to the Campaign on the Niagara in 1814*, Boston: Patriot Office, 1815.

Roosevelt, Theodore, *The Naval War of 1812*, Annapolis, Maryland: Naval Institute Press, 1987 (repr. 1882 ed.).

Schneider, David H., "The Training and Organization of General Winfield Scott's Brigade and the Life of the Regular Soldiers In It," Unpublished M.A. thesis, University of Florida, 1976.

Schweitzer, George K., *War of 1812 Geneology*, Knoxville, 1983.

Scott, Winfield S., *Memoirs of Lt. Gen. Scott, LLD*, 2 vols., New York: Sheldon & Company, 1864.

Seibel, George A., *The Niagara Portage Road: 200 Years, 1790-1990*, Niagara Falls, Ontario: City of Niagara Falls, 1990.

Shrauger, Carol, et al., *Williamsville, New York: Where The Past Is Present*, Village of Williamsville Historical Society, 1985.

Silver, James W., *Edmund P. Gaines, 1777-1849; Frontier General*, Baton Rouge: LSU, 1949.

Skeen, C. Edward, *John Armstrong, Jr.: A Biography*, Syracuse, New York: Syracuse University Press, 1981.

Sketch of the Life of General Nathan Towson, US Army, Baltimore: N. Hickman, 1842.

Stagg, J.C.A., *Mr. Madison's War: Politics, Diplomacy, and Warfare in the Early American Republic, 1783-1830*, Princeton: Princeton University Press, 1983.

Stanley, George F.G., *The War of 1812, Land Operations*, MacMillan of Canada in Collaboration with the National Museum of Man, National Museums of Canada, 1983.

Starke, Elliot, *History of Cayuga County, New York*, Syracuse: D. Mason & Company, 1879.

Stephen, Leslie & Lee, Sidney, *Dictionary of National Biography* 21 vols. w/ supplements, London: Oxford University Press, 1921-22.

Stone, William L., *The Life and Times of Red Jacket*, New York: Wiley, Putnam, 1841.

Treat, Joseph, *The Vindication of Captain Joseph Treat, Late of the 21st Regiment, US Infantry*, Philadelphia, 1815.

Turner, Wesley, *The War of 1812: The War That Both Sides Won*, Toronto and Oxford: Dundurn Press, 1990.

U.S. Army, Adjutant General's Office, *Index of Awards of Claims of the Soldiers of the War of 1812*, Baltimore: Genealogical Publishing Company, 1969.

U.S. Congress, *American State Papers: Documents, Legislative and Executive of the Congress of the U.S., Class V Military Affairs, Class IX Claims*, Washington: Gales & Seaton, 1832-61.

U.S. Congress, *United States Pensioners, War of 1812, Mexican and Civil War*, Washington: Government Printing Office, 1883.

U.S. Senate, Document 100, 16 Congress, 2d Session, 1820-1821, "Statement of the Number of Militia from Each State...During the War of 1812."

U.S. War Department, *Subject Index, 1809- 1860, General Orders, AGD, Subject Index of the WDGO's 1 Jan. 1809 to 31 Dec. 1860*, Washington: Government Printing Office, 1886.

Watmough, John G., *A Brief Sketch of the Services of John G. Watmough...When an Officer in the United States Army*, Philadelphia, 1835.

Way, Ronald L., "Defenses of the Niagara Frontier," Unpublished M.A. thesis, Queen's University, 1938.

White, Leonard D., *The Jeffersonians: A Study in Administrative History, 1801-1829*, New York: MacMillan Company, 1959.

White, Patrick C.T., *A Nation on Trial: America and the War of 1812*, New York: 1965.

White, Samuel, *A History of American Troops...under General Gaines, Brown, Scott and Porter*, Baltimore, 1830 (repr. 1896, George P. Humphrey, Rochester, New York).

Wilkinson, James, *Memoirs of My Own Times*, 3 vols., Philadelphia: Abraham Small, 1816.

Wilner, Merton M., *Niagara Frontier: A Narrative and Documentary History*, 5 vols., Chicago: S.J. Clarke Publishing Company, 1931.

Zaslow, Morris, and Wesley B. Turner (eds.), *The Defended Border: Upper Canada and the War of 1812*, Toronto: Macmillan, 1964.

Articles

Anderson, Fanny J., "Medical Practices During the War of 1812," *Bulletin of the History of Medicine*, 16 (1944): 261-75.

Ashburn, Percy M., "American Army Hospitals of the Revolution and War of 1812," *Bulletin of Johns Hopkins Hospital*, 46 (1930): 47-60.

"Assault on Fort Erie, or, Two Ways of Telling a Story," *Littell's Museum of Foreign Literature*, 43 (1834): 427-35.

Ayars, Charles W., "Some Notes on the Medical Service of the Army, 1812-1839," *Military Surgeon*, 50 (1922): 505-524.

Babcock, James L., ed., "Campaign of 1814 on the Niagara Frontier," *Niagara Frontier*, 10, No. 4 (1963): 121-178.

Babcock, L.L., "The Siege of Ft. Erie," *Proceedings of the New York State Historical Association*, VII, 1909.

"Biographical Sketch of Major Thomas Biddle," *Hazard's Register of Pennsylvania*, X, No. 8 (Aug. 25, 1832): 121-128.

"Biography of Colonel Jacob Hindman," *Portico*, 3 (1816): 38-52.

Brady, William T., "The 22d Regiment in the War of 1812," *Western Pennsylvania Historical Magazine*, 32 (1949): 56-60.

Brooke, St. George T., "The Brooke Family in Virginia," *Virginia Magazine of History and Biography*, vols. 11 (1904), 12 (1905), 13 (1906), 14 (1907): 11 pp. 445-447, 12 pp. 102-103 (George Mercer Brooke).

Buffalo and Erie Counties Historical Society Publications:

Dorsheimer, William, "Buffalo During the War of 1812," vol I (1879): 185-198.

Hodge, William, "Buffalo Cemeteries", vol. I (1879): 49-75.

Hall, Amos, "Militia Service of 1812-1814 as shown by the Correspondence of MGen. Amos Hall," vol. V (1902): 26-62.

O'Reilly, Isabelle M., "A Hero of Ft. Erie," vol. V (1902): 63-93.

Bird, William A., "The Sortie From Fort Erie," vol. V (1902): 95-98.

Severance, Frank, "Papers Relating to the War of 1812 on the Niagara Frontier," vol. V (1902): 98-109.

Longslow, Richard, "A Niagara Falls Tourist of...1817," vol. V (1902): 110-124.

Severance, Frank, "The Story of Captains Jasper Parrish, captive...," vol. VI (1903): 527-538.

Severance, Frank, "Personal Recollections of Captains Jones & Parrish," vol. VI (1903): 539-546.

Salisbury, Hezekiah, "A Guardsman of Buffalo...a Participant in the War of 1812," vol. IX (1906): 311-370.

Howe, Eber D., "Recollections of a Pioneer Printer," vol. IX (1906): 375-406.

Howe, Eber D., "Life of General Ely S. Parker," vol. XIII (1919).

Harris, Samuel D., "Service of Capt. Samuel D. Harris; a Sketch of His Military Career...2d Light Dragoons...," vol. XXIV (1920): 327-342.

Severance, Frank H., "William Hodge Papers," vol. XXVI (1922): 169-314.

Severance, Frank, "War Losses on the Niagara Frontier," vol. XXIX (1925): 249-319.

Bingham, Robert W., ed., "Niagara Frontier Miscellany," vol. XXXIV (1947).

Colquhoun, A.H., "The Career of Joseph Willcocks," *Canadian Historical Review* VII (Dec. 1926): 287-293.

Crombie, John N., "The 22d U.S. Infantry: A Forgotten Regiment in a Forgotten War," *Western Pennsylvania Historical Magazine 60* (1967): 133-47, 221-31.

Crombie, John N., "The Papers of Daniel McFarland," *Western Pennsylvania Historical Magazine 61* (1968): 101-25.

Cruikshank, Ernest, "The Siege of Fort Erie, August 1st - September 23d 1814,"*Lundy's Lane Historical Society Publications*, Welland: *Tribune* Office, 1905.

Doan, Daniel, "The Enigmatic Moody Bedel," *Historical New Hampshire 25*, No. 3 (1970): 27-36.

Douglas, R. Alan, "Weapons of the War of 1812," *Michigan History 47* (1963): 321-326.

Douglass, David B., "An Original Narrative of the Niagara Campaign of 1814," John T. Horton, ed., *Niagara Frontier II*, No. 1 (1964): 1-36.

Duncan, Louis L., "Sketches of the Medical Service in the War of 1812," *Military Surgeon 81* (1932): 436-40, 539-42; 82 (1932): 48-56.

Edgar, James D., "The Army Medical Department in the War of 1812," *Military Surgeon* Vol. 60, No. 3 (March 1927): 301-313.

Einstein, Lewis, ed., "Recollections of the War of 1812 by George Hay, Eighth Marquis of Tweeddale," *American Historical Review* XXXII (1926-27): 69-78.

Emerson, George D., "General Scott at Lundy's Lane," *Proceeding of the New York State Historical Association* vol.. VIII, Albany: J.B. Lyon Company, 1909: 60-66.

Ferguson, Allan J. "Militia Medicine in New York, 1812," *Military Collector and Historian 35*, No. 4 (1983): 167-168.

Forman, Sidney, "The U.S. Military Philosophical Society, 1802- 1803," *William & Mary Quarterly* 3d series, 2 (July 1945): 273-285.

Frederiksen, John C., ed., "Chronicle of Valor: The Journal of a Pennsylvania Officer in the War of 1812," *Western Pennsylvania Historical Magazine* 67 (3) (1984): 243-284.

Graves, Donald E., "The Canadian Volunteers, 1813-1815," *Military Collector and Historian 31* (Fall 1979): 113-117.

Graves, Donald E., "'Give the Damned Yankees No Quarter', The Life and Death of Lt. Col. William Drummond, Tarnished Hero of the War of 1812," Unpublished essay, 1992.

Green, E., "Some Graves in Lundy's Lane," *Niagara Historical Society Publications* No. 22 (1912).

Green, Ernest, "New Light on the Battle Of Chippawa," *Welland County Historical Society Papers and Records* vols. III, Welland: Welland Publishing Company, 1927.

Guelzo, Carl, "Fort Erie: High Point of a Low War," *Military Review* 38, No. 10 (Jan 1959): 50-57.

Hager, Fred E., "Thomas Sidney Jesup," *Quartermaster Review* 11 (1931): 14-47.

Hall, James A., "Biographical Sketch of Major Thomas Biddle," *Illinois Monthly Magazine* 1 (1831): 549-561.

Hanks, Jarvis, "A Drummer Boy in the War of 1812: The Memoir of Jarvis Frary Hanks," Lester Smith, ed.,*Niagara Frontier 7* (1960).

Hitsman, J. Mackey, "The War of 1812 in Canada," *History Today* XII, No. 9 (September 1962): 632-639.

Holley, George W., "The Sortie from Fort Erie," *Magazine of American History* VI (1881): 401-413.

Homer, W.E., "Surgical Sketches: A Military Hospital at Buffalo, New York, in the Year 1814," *Medical Examiner and Record of Medical Science 9* (1853) 1-25, 69-85.

Jay, William, compiler, "Table of the Killed and Wounded in the War of 1812," *Collections of the New York Historical Society* 2d series, 2·(1849): 447-466.

Kerley, Robert L., "The Militia System and the State Militias in the War of 1812," *Indiana Magazine of History 73*, No. 2 (1977): 102-124.

Kimball, Jeffrey, "The Battle of Chippawa: Infantry Tactics in the War of 1812," *Military Affairs* XXXII (1968): 169-186.

Kimball, Jeffrey, "The Fog and Friction of Frontier War: The Role of Logistics in American Offensive Failure During the War of 1812," *The Old Northwest* vol. 6 (1980): 323-343.

Kochan, James L., "22d US Infantry Regiment, 1812-1813," *Military Collector and Historian 33* (1981): 164-165.

Livingstone, John, "General Nathan Towson," *Sketches of Eminent Americans*, New York: Craighead, 1854: 381-422.

McGinnis, George, "The Part That Buffalo, New York, Played in the War of 1812," *Military Surgeon* LXXXVI (1940): 393-395.

McKee, Marguerite, "Services of Supply in the War of 1812," *Quartermaster Review 6* (1917): 45-55.

Martin, John D., "The Regiment DeWatteville: Its Settlement and Services in Upper Canada," *Ontario Historical Society Papers and Records* LXII (1960): 17-30.

Norton, Jacob P., "Jacob Peter Norton, A Yankee on the Niagara Frontier in 1814," Daniel R. Porter, ed., *Niagara Frontier 12* (1965).

Parker, Arthur C., "The Senecas in the War of 1812," *New York State Historical Association Proceedings 15* (1916): 78-90.

Phalen, James M., "Surgeon James Mann's Observations on Battlefield Amputations," *Military Surgeon 87* (1940): 463-466.

Riddell, William R., "Benajah Mallory, Traitor," *Ontario Historical Society Papers and Records* XXVI (1930): 435-449.

Ripley, Eleazer W., "Biographical Memoirs of Major General Ripley," *Port Folio* XXV (1815): 108-136.

Ropes, Benjamin, "Benjamin Ropes' Autobiography," *Essex Institute Historical Collections 91* (January 1955): 105-127.

Sawyer, B.G., "The War of 1812 and Biographical Sketches," in Abby M. Hemenway, ed., *Vermont Historical Gazeteer* vol. I: 574-81.

Severance, Frank H., "General Brown at Chippawa, July 5, 1814," *Proceedings of the New York State Historical Association* vol. VIII, Albany: J.B. Lyon Company, 1909: 33-37.

"The Siege of Ft. Erie," *United States Military Magazine 2* (1840): 65-73.

Smith, C. Charles, "Memoirs of Colonel Thomas Aspinwall," *Massachusetts Historical Society Proceedings 3* (1891): 30-38.

"Sortie from Ft. Erie," *United States Military Magazine 1* , No. 12 (1840).

Stacy, C.P., ed., "Upper Canada at War, 1814: Captain Armstrong Reports," *Ontario History* XLVII (1956).

Steppler, Glen A., "Logistics on the Canadian Frontier, 1812-1814," *Military Collector and Historian 31* (1979): 8-10.

Tuttle, Mary M., "William Allen Trimble," *Ohio Archaeological and Historical Society Journal* 14 (1905): 225-246.

Wainwright, Nicholas B., "The Life and Death of Major Thomas Biddle," *Pennsylvania Magazine of History and Biography* 104 (1980): 326-344.

Walker, Joseph E. "A Soldier's Diary for 1814," *Pennsylvania History* 12 (1945): 292-303.

Wyman, Hal C., "Remarks on the Surgery of the War of 1812," *Physician and Surgeon* 29 (1907), 203-209.

Archival Sources

Adams County Historical Society, Gettysburg, PA 17325:
  Gettysburg Compiler 11 May, 1876.

American Antiquarian Society, 185 Salisbury Street, Worcester, MA 01609:
  Two letters by Sergeant Hector Shields, 25th Infantry in regard to the Battle of Chippawa.

Author's collection, Rt.2, Box 3005, Front Royal, VA 22630: Auburn, NY, *Cayuga Patriot*, 1814-1815.

Buffalo & Erie County Historical Society, 25 Nottingham Court, Buffalo, NY

17216: Peter Porter Papers: A.C. Goodyear Collection, including Chippawa, Ft. Erie: Jarvis Hanks, Memoir.

Cornell University Library, 101 Orin Street, Ithaca, NY 14853: John G. Camp Papers (QM during Niagara Campaign).

Dartmouth College, Baker Library, Hanover, NH 03755: John W. Weeks correspondence in regard to Chippawa and Lundy's Lane.

Geneva Historical Society, 543 S. Main Street, Geneva, NY 14456: Papers of General Hugh Dobbins, NY Militia.

Library of Congress, Washington, DC: Jacob Brown Correspondence: Thomas S. Jesup on Niagara Campaign; Amasa Trowbridge on Battles of York, Ft. George and Ft. Erie; Letters of Capt. John McNeil, 11th Infantry; Military reports, rosters and correspondence of Col. Jacob Kingsbury, 1st Infantry; E.P. Gaines Papers.

Massachusetts Historical Society, 1154 Boylston Street, Boston, MA 02215: 1812 Collection, including letters of Jacob Brown concerning various Niagara campaigns.

Minnesota Historical Society, 690 Cedar Street, St. Paul, MN 55101: Two orderly books by Lt. Lawrence Taliaferro, 1st Infantry.

Missouri Historical Society, Jefferson Memorial Building, St. Louis, MO 63112: Small collection 1st and 17th Infantries muster rolls; Memoirs of Capt. Louis Bissell, 1st Infantry, including his role in the Ft. Erie sortie; Correspondence of Col. Jacob Kingsbury, 1st Infantry.

National Archives, Washington, DC:
Documents—

RG 15–Veterans Administration: War of 1812 Pension Application Files. Post Revolutionary War Series of Bounty Land Applications.

RG 49–Bureau of Land Management: Entries 13-18 Bounty Land Warrants, 1812-1855.

RG 92–Office of the Quartermaster General: Entry 225, Consolidated Correspondence File "Medical," "Batavia," "Brady." Entry 562, QM Cemeteries. Entry 563, QM Cemeteries.

RG 94–Records of the Adjutant General's Office: Entry 53, Muster Rolls of Regular Army Organizations 1784–Oct. 31, 1912. Entry 55, Muster Rolls of Volunteer Organizations, War of 1812. Entry 71, Returns of Killed and Wounded in Battles or Engagements with Indians, British, and Mexicans, 1790-1848 (Eaton's Compendium). Entry 85, Register of Returns and General Information Relating to the Army. Entry 89, Register of Enlistments, 1798-1914. Entry 91, Regular Army Enlistment Papers. Entry 95, Certificates of Disability, 1812-1899. Entry 125, Miscellaneous Records, 1812-1815. Entry 126, Index to Miscellaneous Records, 1812-1815. Entry 407,

QM Accounts and Returns. Entries 309, 312, 320, 321, 323, Commissioned Officers. Entry 510, Compiled Service Records.

RG 98–Records of US Army Commands, 1784–1821: Entries 35-40, Headquarters and 1st Div (Right Wing) 1813-15, 9th Military District. Entries 41-51, 2d Div (Left Wing), 1812-15, 9th Military District Entries. 52-60, Miscellaneous Records, 9th Military District. Entry 78, Records of Bvt. MGen. E.P. Gaines, 1814-19. Entries 96, 97, 99, 1st Infantry Books. Entry 102, Capt. Fanning's Co, 2d Arty, Co Book. Entry 104, Capt. Williams' Co, 2d Arty, Co Book. Entry 105, Capt. Fanning's Co, 2d Arty, Clothing Book. Entry 114, Capt. Fanning's Co, 2d Arty, Clothing Book. Entries 199-207, 11th Infantry Co Books. Entries 233-240, 21st Infantry Co Books. Entries 241-247, 22d Infantry Co Books. Entries 252-259, 25th Infantry Co Books. Entries 367-371, 1st Rifles Co Books.

RG 99–Office of the Paymaster General, 1799-1912 Entry 1, Letters Sent 1814. Entry 7, Letters Received 1814.

RG 153–Office of the Judge Advocate General Court Martial Case Files 1814-1815.

RG 156–Records of the Chief of Ordnance Entry 3, Correspondence

RG 159–Records of the Inspector General of the Army Entry 1, Inspection Reports 1814-1836, 1842.

Microfilm—

Office of the Adjutant General: M602 Index to Compiled Service Records of Volunteer Soldiers who Served During the War of 1812; M233 Register of Enlistments in the U.S. Army, 1798-1914; M566 Letters Received, 1805-1821; M565 Letters Sent, 1800-1890; M711 Register of Letters Sent, 1812-1889.

Office of the Secretary of War: M220 Reports to Congress; M221 Records, Main Series, 1801-1870; M222 Letters Received, 1789-1861; M127 Letters Sent to the President, 1800-1863; M6 Letters Sent concerning Military Affairs; M370 Misc Letters Sent, 1800-1809; M22 Register of Letters Received, Main Series, 1800-1870; M7 Confidential Letters Sent.

Veterans Administration: M313 Index to War of 1812 Pension Application Files.

Bureau of Land Management: M848 War of 1812 Military Bounty Land Warrants, 1815-1858.

Miscellaneous: M41Peter B. Porter Papers.

New Hampshire Historical Society, 30 Park Street, Concord, NH 03311: Papers regarding 11th Infantry and 2d Dragoons, including muster rolls and supply requisitions; letters of Capt. John McNeil, 11th Infantry; Letters of Col. Moody Bedel, 11th Infantry.

New Jersey Historical Society, 230 Broadway, Newark, NJ 07104: Muster rolls of NY and PA militias.

New York Historical Society, 170 Central Park West, New York, NY 10024: 14 letters of Richard Goodell, 23d Infantry; 47 pieces by Capt. John Mc-Neil, 11th Infantry; Diary of Col. G. McFeely, 25th Infantry; Orderly book of 25th Infantry; John M. O'Connor Papers—muster rolls, reports Ft. Erie, 1814 (60 items).

New York State Library, Cultural Education Center, Empire State Plaza, Albany, NY 12203: Letters of Thomas S. Jesup, 25th Infantry; Paddick Papers on 1814 Niagara Campaign.

Oneida Historical Society, 318 Genessee Street, Utica, NY 13502: Col. Nathan Williams' correspondence with Jacob Brown.

Pennsylvania Historical Society, 1300 Locust Street, Philadelphia, PA 19107: No. 998 Pennsylvania Vols. in War of 1812 and Civil War.

Pennsylvania History and Museum Commission, Box 126, Harrisburg, PA 17120: John Witherow Journal on the 1814 Niagara Campaign; 5th Pennsylvania Infantry (Simon Snyder Papers).

Public Archives of Canada, Ottowa, Canada: DeWatteville Papers, Ms Gp. 24, F96. Joseph D. Mermet Letters in Jacques Viger Papers, Saberdache Bleu, Vols. 4 and 5, M8.

Public Records Office, London, United Kingdom: George Philpotts Diary, War Office 55, Vol. 860: 135-144.

St. Lawrence University Museum, Canton, NY: Orderly Book kept at Ft. Erie.

Tulane University, Tilton Library, New Orleans, LA 70118: Materials on New York Militia affairs by Asa B. Sizer.

United States Army Military History Institute, Carlisle Barracks, PA 17013: Diary of Amasa Ford, 23d Infantry, regarding 1814 Niagara Campaign (copy); Letter, Thomas Jesup to Maj. William McDonald; Stuart Goldman Collection.

United States Military Academy, West Point, NY 10996: 13 letters of Col. James Miller, 21st Infantry.

University of Michigan, Clements Library, Ann Arbor, Michigan 48104: Collection of Jacob Brown and Winfield Scott on the Niagara Campaign (60 items regarding Niagara 1814); Accounts of the Battles of Stoney Creek and Ft. Erie in John Kearnsey Memoirs, Lucus D. Lyon Papers; Papers of Surgeon William H. Wilson on the Northern Frontier.

University of Rochester Library, Rochester, NY 14627: 32 letters of Nathanial Rochester regarding militia affairs.

Vermont Historical Society, Monpelier, Vermont 05002: David Crawford and John McNeil, 11th Infantry, papers.

Wisconsin Historical Society, 816 State Street, Madison, WI 53706: Correspondence by Capt. John Symmes, 1st Infantry...Lundy's Lane and Ft. Erie; Letters of Capt. William Armstrong, 1st Rifles in re Ft. Erie; Diary of Jacob Norton regarding Izard's activities, 1814.

Notes

Chapter 1

1. A good recent overview of the background to the war may be found in Donald R. Hickey, *the War of 1812. A Forgotten Conflict*, (Urbana and Chicago: Univ. of Ill. Press, 1989).

2. Carl F. Klink and James J. Talman, eds., *The Journal of Major John Norton 1816* (Toronto: The Champlain Society), p. 6; Robert D. Bradford, *Historic Forts of Ontario* (Belleville, Ont.: Mika Publ. Co.), pp. 39, 41; Ronald L. Way, "Defences of the Niagara Frontier," (M.A. Thesis, Queen's Univ., 1938), pp. 28-36; David Owen, *Fort Erie (1764-1823) An Historical Guide* (Niagara Falls, Ont: Niagara Parks Commission, 1986), pp. 19-41; Louis L. Babcock, *The Siege of Fort Erie: An Episode of the War of 1812* (Buffalo: Peter Paul Book Co., 1899), pp. 8, 10.

3. Lloyd Graham, *Niagara Country* (New York: Duell, Sloan, and Pearce, 1949), pp. 69, 71. Scajaquada Creek was often referred to as "Conjocta."

4. Graham, *ibid.*, p. 73; Bradford, *ibid., p. 43;* Way, *ibid.*, pp. 34-6; Robert W. Bingham, ed., *Niagara Frontier Miscellany* (Buffalo: The Buffalo Historical Society, 1947), p. 143. The Indian reserve was bounded approximately by Seneca Street, Indian Church Road, and Buffalo Street in modern Buffalo.

5. Graham, *ibid.*, pp. 89-90; Bradford, *ibid.*, pp. 43-44. One battery was at the foot of Bertie Street, Fort Erie, one by the international R.R. bridge and one at Frenchman's Creek.

6. Klink and Talman, *ibid* pp.302-303; Hugh Hastings, *Public Papers of Daniel D. Tompkins, Governor of New York 1807-1817* 3 Vols. (New York and Albany: Wynkoop, Hallenbeck, Crawford Co., 1898), I: 79-80.

7. Chester L. Kieffer, *Maligned General: A Biography of Thomas S. Jesup* (San Rafael, CA: Presidio Press, 1979), p. 12. One of the POW's was Lt. Jesup, who would return in 1814 as a major commanding the 25th Infantry Regiment during the siege and sortie at Fort Erie; Theodore Roosevelt, *Naval War of 1812* (Annapolis, MD: Naval Institute Press, 1987, reprint of 1882 ed.), p. 158.

8. Roosevelt, *ibid.*, p. 160; Graham, *ibid.*, pp. 91-93. Winfield Scott would distinguish himself on the Niagara Frontier. He was born near Petersburg, Virginia, in 1786. He briefly attended William and Mary and studied for the bar before entering the army in 1809. He served at New Orleans under Generals James Wilkinson and Wade Hampton until assigned as a lieutenant colonel to Smyth's command in 1812. Following the war, the 6 foot, 5 inch general was a national hero. He distinguished himself as pacifier and negotiator several times along the Canadian border and during the Cherokee Indian Removal. He became general-in-chief in 1841, conducted a brilliant campaign in Mexico in 1847-48, and later ran on the 1852 Whig ticket for president. He retired in November 1861 and died at West Point in 1866. Winfield Scott, *Memoirs of Lt. Gen. Scott LLD,* 2 vols. (New York: Sheldon and Co., 1864): passim; Allen Johnson, ed., *Dictionary of American Biography* 11 vols. (New York: Charles Scribner's Sons, 1927-64), VIII: 505- 511.

9. Hastings, *ibid.*, I: 80; John R. Elting, *Amateurs To Arms!: A Military History of the war of 1812* (Chapel Hill: Algonquin Books, 1991), pp. 40-41.

10. Elting, *ibid.*, pp. 47-48; George F. G. Stanley, *The War of 1812 Land Operations* (Macmillan of Canada in Collaboration with the National Museum of Man, National Museums of Canada, 1983), pp. 124-131, 135.

11. Elting, *ibid.*, p. 51; Stanley, *ibid.*, p. 136; Roosevelt, *ibid.*, pp. 310-311.

12. Allen Johnson, ed., *Dictionary of American Biography II* vols. (New York: Charles Scribner's Sons, 1927-64), VIII: 99-100. After the War, Porter returned briefly to Congress, was Secretary of State in Albany, then served as an international boundary commissioner. He was John Q. Adams' Secretary of War, 1828-29, before retiring to private business ventures in western New York. Porter died at Niagara Falls in 1849.

13. Graham, *ibid.*, pp. 95, 97; Klink and Talman, *ibid.*, p. 310-311.

14. Elting, *ibid.*, p.51; Bradford, *ibid.*, p. 44; Klink and Talman, *ibid.*, p. 317.

15. Newark is now Niagara-on-the-Lake; Elting, *ibid.*, p. 120-121; Graham, *ibid.*, p. 97; Stanley, *ibid.*, p. 181-182.

16. Bradford, *ibid.*, pp. 44-45; Klink and Talman, *ibid.*, p. 326; George

A. Seibal, *The Niagara Portage Road: 200 Years, 1790-1990* (Niagara Falls, Ont.: City of Niagara Falls, 1990), p. 259.

17. Hannay, *ibid.*, pp. 152-158, 167-168; Stanley, *ibid.*, p. 193; Donald E. Graves, "The Canadian Volunteers," *Military Collector and Historian 31* (Fall 1979): 113.

18. Hannay, *ibid.*, pp. 171-172; Graham, *ibid.*, p. 98.

19. Graham, *ibid.*, p. 99; Stanley, *ibid.*, pp. 216, 273.

20. Leslie Stephens and Sidney Lee, *Dictionary of National Biography* 21 vols. (London: Oxford University Press, 1921-22): VI: 27-28; Drummond would be knighted in 1815 for his services along the Niagara. He returned to Britain that year, where he commanded a variety of units, gaining promotion to general in 1825. He died in London in 1854.

21. Hannay, *ibid.*, pp. 230-231; Graham, *ibid.*, p. 102.

22. Graham, *ibid.*, p. 105; Bingham, *ibid.*, p. 148; Hannay, *ibid.*, pp. 231-233; Hastings, *ibid.*, III pp. 408, 411, 449; Ernest Cruikshank, *Drummond's Winter Campaign 1813* (Lundy's Lane Historical Society, n.p., n.d.), pp. 26-28. Prior to burning Buffalo, the British deployed and paused in the vicinity of the junction of Niagara and Mohawk Streets.

23. Babcock, *ibid.*, p. 14; Owen, *ibid.*, p. 49.

Chapter 2

1. C. Edward Skeen, *John Armstrong, Jr, A Biography* (Syracuse New York: Syracuse University Press, 1981), p. 179; Henry Adams, *The War of 1812*, H. A. DeWeerd, ed. (Washington: Infantry Journal, 1944), p. 169.

2. U.S. National Archives (herewith referred to as N.A.), Microfilm M6, Secretary of War, Letters Sent (LS), Armstrong to Wilkinson 24 March 1814, Armstrong to Izard 24 March 1814.

3. John S. Jenkins, *The Generals of the Last War With Great Britain* (Auburn: Derby, Miller and Co., 1849), pp. 13-60. Brown became general-in-chief of the Army in 1821 until his death in 1828.

4. John D. Morris, "General Jacob Brown and the Problems of Command in 1814," R. Arthur Bowler, ed., *War Along the Niagara* (Youngstown, New York: Old Fort Niagara Assoc., Inc., 1991), p. 30; Skeen, *ibid.*, p. 177.

5. N.A., Microfilm M222, Secretary of War Letters Received (LR), Brown to Armstrong, 21 March 1814; N.A., (LS), Armstrong to Brown, 20 March 1814; Jeffrey Kimball, "The Battle of Chippawa: Infantry Tactics in the War of 1812," *Military Affairs*, XXXII, (1968): 170.

6. Winfield S. Scott, *Memoirs of Lt. Gen. Scott LLD, 2 Vols (New York: Sheldon and Co., 1864), I: 115-118*; Morris, *ibid.*, p. 30; Skeen, *ibid.*, p. 178.

7. N.A., Microfilm M127, Letters Sent to the President, Armstrong to Madison, 30 April 1814; Adams, *ibid.*, p. 171.

8. N.A., *ibid.*, Armstrong to Madison, 30 April 1814; J. Mackay Hitsman, *The Incredible War of 1812. A Military History* (Toronto: University of Toronto Press, 1965), p. 190.

9. Morris, *ibid.*, p. 37; Skeen, *ibid.*, p. 180; Kimball, *ibid.*, p. 177; Carl Guelzo, "Ft Erie: High Point of a Low War," *Military Review* 38, No. 10 (January 1959): 51; Jacob Brown, Letter to Secretary of War, 14 April 1814 in E.A. Cruikshank, *Documents Relating to the Invasion of the Niagara Peninsula by the United States Army Commanded by General Jacob Brown in July and August 1814* (Niagara-on-the-Lake: Niagara Historical Society, Publ. No. 33, 1920), pp. 15-16, 26 (Hereinafter, "Cruikshank, DR").

10. Adams, *ibid.*, pp. 170, 172; Hitsman, *ibid.*, p. 191.

11. Skeen, *ibid.*, p. 180; Cruikshank, *DR*, Jacob Brown Letters to Secretary of War, 30 April, 17 June, pp. 26-27.

12. Adams, *ibid.*, p.171; Hitsman, *ibid.*, pp. 188-189.

13. Hitsman, *ibid.*, p. 189; John K. Mahon, *The War of 1812* (Gainesville, Florida: University of Florida Press, 1972), p. 266; S. J. Park and G. F. Nafzinger, *The British Military: Its System and Organization, 1803-1815* (Cambridge, Ont.: RAFM Co., Inc., 1983), p. 109.

14. Hitsman, *ibid.*, p. 192; James Hannay, *A History of the War of 1812* (Toronto: Morang and Co., Ltd, 1905), pp. 306-307; Joseph E. Walker, "A Soldier's Diary for 1814," *Pennsylvania History,* 12, (1945): pp. 297-298.

15. Stephen and Lee, *ibid.*, p. 979.

16. Hitsman, *ibid.*, p. 192; Mahon, *ibid.*, p.266; George F. G. Stanley, *The War of 1812: Land Operations* (Macmillan of Canada in Collaboration with the National Museum of Man, National Museums of Canada, 1983), pp. 302-303.

17. Donald E. Graves, "I Have a Handsome Little Army..., A Re-examination of Winfield Scott's Camp at Buffalo in 1814" in R. Arthur Bowler, ed., *War Along the Niagara: Essays on the War of 1812 and Its Legacy* (Youngstown, New York: Old Fort Niagara Assoc. Inc., 1991), pp. 47-8; Jacob Brown, Letters to Secretary of War 20 April, 7 June 1814, Cruikshank, *DR ibid.*, pp. 8, 27; Kimball, *ibid.*, p. 172; N.A. Record Group (RG) 98, vol. 442, AG Orders, Northern Army 9th Military District, 14 May 1814.

18. Flint Hill is the area between Scajaquada Creek and Chapin Farm (S. W. corner Main Street and Jewett Parkway); Frank H. Severance, "William Hodge Papers," *Publications of the Buffalo Historical Society* XXVI (1922): 181.

19. N.A. RG 159, Report by Major Nathan Hall, AIG, Sacketts Harbor, 30 June 1814; Graves, *ibid.*, p. 49-50.

20. Library of Congress, (LC), Thomas Jesup Papers, Vol. I, pp. 183-192.

21. The pace was 26 inches at a rate of 75 or 100 per minute. N.A. RG 94, Entry 125, Box 134 (Miscellaneous Documents and Orders), General Orders, April to June 1814. The information in this and subsequent paragraphs unless noted otherwise is based on this source.

22. See Annex B for the order of battle.

23. Winfield S. Scott, *Memoirs of Lt. Gen. Scott, LLD,* 2 Vol. (New York: Sheldon and Co., 1864), I: 121.

24. N.A. RG 94, Entry 510, Compiled Service Records, Fenton's Regiment, 5th Pennsylvania Volunteers.

25. The inspectors in Brown's Division for the duration of the campaign were Colonel Josiah Snelling, Major Azor Orne, and Major Nathan Hall. N.A., RG 98, vol. 406/290. The use of grey cloth traditionally marks the origins of the West Point uniforms.

26. Reliance on N.A., RG 94, Entry 125, Box 134, *ibid.,* ends here.

27. Samuel White, *A History of American Troops. Under Generals Gaines, Brown, Scott, and Porter* (Baltimore: The Author, 1830, repr. 1896, George P. Humphrey, Rochester, New York), p. 19.

28. N.A., RG 94, Entry 407, Box 47, John G. Camp, voucher 14, June; N.A., M221, Jacob Brown, Letter to the Secretary of War 22 June 1814.

29. Peter B. Porter, Letter to Governor D. D. Tompkins July 1814, Il, p. 26, Narrative of W.L. Stone 26 May 1840, II, p. 358, in E.A. Cruikshank (ed.), *Documentary History of the Campaign Upon the Niagara Frontier* 9 vols. (Welland, Ont.: 1907).

Chapter 3

1. G. Auchinleck, *A History of the War Between Great Britain and the United States of America During the Years 1812, 1813, and 1814* (London: Arms and Armor Press, 1972, repr. 1855 ed.), pp. 312-313; William Ketchum, *Authentic and Comprehensive History of Buffalo* (Buffalo: Rockwell, Baker and Hill, 1865), p.416 (Brown's Order).

2. Allen Johnson, ed., *Dictionary of American Biography,...,* VI: 621-622. After the war, Ripley was voted Congress' thanks for his services, but resigned in 1820 to practice law and politics in Louisiana. From 1835 to his death in 1839, he served in the U.S. Congress.

3. Auchinleck, *ibid.,* p. 313; Eleazer W. Ripley, *Facts Relative to the Campaign on the Niagara in 1814* (Boston: Patriot Office, 1815), p. 5 (statement by Major Darby Noon).

4. Ketchum, *ibid.,* p. 416; Library of Congress (LC), Jesup Papers, Box 11.

5. Ketchum, *ibid.,* pp. 416-417; LC, Jesup Papers, Box 11; Joseph E. Walker, "A Soldier's Diary for 1814," *Pennsylvania History* 12 (1945): 299;

Henry Adams, *The War of 1812* H.A. DeWeerd, ed. (Washington: Infantry Journal, 1944), pp. 174-175; Robert D. Bradford, *Historic Forts of Ontario* (Belleville, Ont.: Mika Publ. Co., 1988), p. 47; E.A. Cruikshank, *Documentary History of the Campaign Upon the Niagara Frontier* 9 vols. (Welland, Ont.: 1907), II: 38 (Hereafter "Cruikshank,"). The wounded men, all from the 25th Infantry, were Corporal Joseph Knapp and Privates Francis Hernandez, Jesse Thurston, and Jeptha Lee. They all were sent to the hospital at Williamsville.

6. J. Mackey Hitsman, *The Incredible War of 1812: A Military History* (Toronto: University of Toronto Press, 1965), p. 195; Auchinleck, *ibid.*, pp 314-315, quotes 6 July letter of Riall to Drummond; LC, Jesup Papers, Box 11; Carl F. Klink and James J. Talman, eds., *The Journal of Major John Norton*, 1816 (Toronto: The Champlain Society, 1970): pp. cxxii, 348.

7. Adams, *ibid.*, p. 175; Bradford, *ibid.*, p. 47; James Hannay, *A History of the War of 1812* (Toronto: Morang And Co., Ltd., 1905), p. 262.

8. Klink and Talman, *ibid.*, p. 349; John K. Mahon, *The War of 1812* (Gainesville: University of Florida Press, 1972), p. 267.

9. Cruikshank, *DH ibid.*, II: 373, Pvt. McMullen Memoir; James L. Babcock, ed. "The Campaign of 1814 on the Niagara Frontier," *Niagara Frontier* 10, No. 4 (1963): 124.

10. Cruikshank, *DH ibid.*, II: 358-359, Letter P. B. Porter to W. J. Stone, 26 May 1840; Cruikshank, *DR ibid.*, p. 49; Joseph E. Walker, "A Soldier's Diary for 1814," *Pennsylvania History* 12 (1945): 299.

11. Jeffrey Kimball, "The Battle of Chippawa: Infantry Tactics in the War of 1812," *Military Affairs* xxxii (1968): 178; Hitsman, *ibid.*, p. 175; Klink and Talman, *ibid.*, p. 349.

12. Klink and Talman, *ibid.*, p. 349; John Brannan, ed., *Official Letters of the Military and Naval Officers of the U.S. During the War With Great Britain* (Washington: 1823): p. 368, Jacob Brown Letter to Secretary of War, 7 July 1814.

13. Cruikshank, *DH ibid.*, II: 360, P.B. Porter Letter to W.J. Stone, 26 May 1840; John K. Mahon, *The War of 1812* (Gainesville: University of Florida Press, 1972): p. 268.

14. Mahon, *ibid.*, p. 269; Frank H. Severance, "General Brown at Chippawa, July 1815," *Proceedings of New York State Historical Assoc.* vol. VIII (Albany: J.B. Lyon Co., 1909): p. 35; LC, Jesup Papers, Box 11; Kimball, *ibid.*, pp. 179, 184; Lewis Einstein, ed., "Recollection of the War of 1812 by George Hay, Eighth Marquis of Tweeddale," *American Historical Review* XXXII (1926-27): p. 73.

15. Kimball, *ibid.*, p. 185; Brannan, *ibid.*, pp. 368-370; Einstein, *ibid.*, p. 73; Klink and Talman, *ibid.*, p. 350.

16. Kimball, *ibid.*, p. 186; Cruikshank, *DH ibid* II: 38, Jacob Brown,

Letter to Secretary of War, 6 July 1814; II: 109, Philadelphia *Democratic Press* 29 July 1814; Celwyn E. Hampton, *The Twenty-Firsts Trophy of Niagara* (Fort Logan, 1909): p. 63.

17. LC, Jesup Papers, Box 11 Klink and Talman, *ibid.*, p. 352; Hitsman, *ibid.*, p. 196.

18. N.A., Microfilm M221, Jacob Brown, Letter to Secretary of War, 11 July 1814; George A. Seibel, *The Niagara Portage Road: 200 Years 1790-1990* (Niagara Falls, Ont.: City of Niagara Falls, 1990), p. 262.

19. N.A., RG 94, Entry 125, Box 134, General Orders, 11, 12, and 16, July 1814.

20. Klink and Talman, *ibid.*, pp. cxxiii, 352-353; Cruikshank, *DH ibid.*, II: 368; William L. Stone, *The Life and Times of Red Jacket* (New York: Wiley, Putnam, 1841), p. 265.

21. Cruikshank, *DH ibid.*, II: p. 64; Hitsman, *ibid.*, p. 197.

22. Kimball, *ibid.*, p. 177; Cruikshank, *DH ibid.*, II: p. 86.

23. Hugh Hastings, ed., *Public Papers of Daniel D. Tompkins, Governor of New York, 1807-1817 3* vols. (New York and Albany: Wynkoop, Hallenbeck, Crawford Co., 1898), III: 560, 632; Cruikshank, *DH ibid.*, II: 68.

24. Mahon, *ibid.*, p. 272; Klink and Talman, *ibid.*, p. 353; Cruikshank, *DH, ibid.*, II: 64, 86; N.A., RG 94, Entry 125, Box 134, Misc. Documents. The strengths of some of the U.S. regiments were specified on 19 July so the issue of one wagon per 100 men could be made: 9th Infantry—323, 21st Infantry—683, 22d Infantry—376, 25th Infantry—330.

25. Klink and Talman, *ibid.*, pp. 355-356; Hitsman, *ibid.*, p. 197.

26. N.A., RG 94, *ibid.*, General Order 18 July.

27. N.A., RG 94, *ibid.*, General Orders, 22 and 23 July.

28. Hitsman, *ibid.*, pp. 197-198; Mahon, *ibid.*, p. 272.

29. Mahon, *ibid.*, p. 274.

30. Klink and Talman, *ibid.*, p. 357; Hitsman, *ibid.*, p. 198.

31. LC, Jesup Papers, Box 11.

32. Mahon, *ibid.*, p. 274; Brannan, *ibid.*, pp. 380-383, Jacob Brown, Report to Secretary of War, August 1814.

33. LC, Amasa Troubridge Papers; Chester Kieffer, *Maligned General: The Biography of Thomas Sidney Jesup* (San Rafael, CA: Presidio Press, 1979), p. 38; Percy M. Ashburn, "American Army Hospitals of the Revolution and War of 1812," *Bulletin of Johns Hopkins Hospital* 46 (1930): 54; National Archives of Canada, (NAC) Unsigned Description of Battle 25 July 1814, MG 19/A39/File.

34. Cruikshank, *DH ibid.*, II: 480, Narrative of T. S. Jesup; Hitsman, *ibid.*, p. 200.

35. Eleazer W. Ripley, *Facts Relative to the Campaign on the Niagara in 1814* (Boston: Patriot Office, 1815), pp. 24, 31, 34, 42.

Chapter 4

1. Henry Adams, *The War of 1812* H. A. DeWeerd, ed., (Washington: Infantry Journal, 1946): p.191; Carl F. Klink and James J. Talman, eds., *The Journal of Major John Norton, 1816* (Toronto: The Champlain Society, 1970): pp. 358-359.

2. Klink and Talman, *ibid.*, p. 359; Cruikshank, *DH* I: 115, Letter, Drummond to Prevost, 31 July, 1814.

3. Eleazer W. Ripley, *Facts Relative to the Campaign on the Niagara In 1814* (Boston: Patriot Office, 1815): pp. 39-40.

4. Ernest Cruikshank, "The Siege of Fort Erie, August 1st-September 23d 1814," *Lundy's Lane Historical Society Publications* (Welland: Tribune Office, 1905): p. 17.

5. Klink and Talman, *ibid.*, p. 36.

6. G.W. Cullum, ed., *Campaigns of the War of 1812* (New York: James Miller, Publ., 1879), p. 272; David B. Douglass, "An Original Narrative of the Niagara Campaign of 1814," ed., John T. Horton, *Niagara Frontier* II, No. 1 (1964): 23-25.

7. National Archives of Canada (Hereafter "NAC") RG 8 I, vol 685, p. 31, Orders, Harvey to Conran, 2 August 1814.

8. NAC, RG 8 I, vol 685, p. 34, Tucker to Conran, 4 August 1814; John Brannan, ed., *Official Letters of the Military and Naval Officers of the U.S. During the War With Great Britain* (Washington: 1823): p. 383.

9. Klink and Talman, *ibid.*, p. 360; Cruikshank, *DH*, II: 33.

10. John D. P. Morton, "The Regiment DeWatteville: Its Settlement and Service in Upper Canada," *Ontario History* vol. LXII (1960): 17-20.

11. David B. Douglass, *The American Voyager The Journal of David Bates Douglass,* Sidney W. Jackman and John F. Freeman, eds. (Marquette, Ml: Northern Michigan University Press, 1969), p. 25.

12. NA, RG 92, Entry 225, Col. John B. Hogan Consolidated Correspondence File; NA, RG 94, Entry 407, Box 88, Letter Directives Aug- Sep 1814; Ernest Cruikshank, "The Siege of Fort Erie," *ibid.*, p. 31; "Biographical Sketch of Major Thomas Biddle," *Hazard's Register of Pennsylvania* X, No. 8 (August 25, 1832): 125.

13. C. Edward Skeen, *John Armstrong, Jr., 1758-1843, A Biography* (Syracuse: Syracuse University Press, 1981): p. 181; NA, RG 98, vol. 406/290, Letter DQMG to Major Hogan 1 August 1814. Boats on hand: 1 large gunboat, 2 Durham boats, 4 large bateaux, 2 keel boats, 1 small express boat, 2 bateaux, 1 open sail boat.

14. N.A., RG 94, Entry 95, Certificates of Disability; LC Amasa Troubridge Papers, *ibid.*; Cruikshank, *DH* II: 136; John C. Fredriksen, ed.,

"Chronicle of Valor: The Journal of a Pennsylvania Officer in the War of 1812," *Western Pennsylvania Historical Magazine* 67 (3) (1984): 283.

15. LC, Amasa Troubridge Papers, *ibid.*; Cruikshank, *DH ibid.*, Mann's Medical History, II: 452; N.A., Envy 95, Certificates of Disability.

16. The Army ration officially consisted of the following: 1-1/4 lb. beef or 3/4 lb. pork; 18 oz. bread or flour; 1 gill rum, whiskey, or brandy per man. Two qts. salt, 4 qts. vinegar, 4 lbs. soap, 1/2 lb. candles per 100 men. (NA, RG 98, Volume 273, Pentland's Co. Book.) Five thousand men required 200,000 lbs. of bread and meat monthly. A two-horse wagon could haul about 1500 lbs., a pack horse 250 lbs.

17. N.A., RG 94, Entry 125, Box 134, General Order 3 May.

18. N.A., RG 94, Entry 125, Box 134, War Department General Order 18 July; N.A., RG 94, Entry 407, Box 87, Hogan Vouchers. Items procured for the hospitals included potatoes, turnips, apples, vinegar, Indian meal, milk, butter, cheese, bread, mutton, black pepper, tea, whiskey, brandy, and "nails for coffins."

19. N.A., RG 94, Entry 407, Box 90, Statement of Rufus Wright, AQM, 16 October 1814, to Major Hogan.

20. N.A., RG 94, Entry 407, Box 90, Letter from E. P. Gaines 25 August 1814 to Major Hogan; David B. Douglass, *ibid.*, p. 31.

21. LC, Amasa Troubridge Papers, *ibid.*

22. Robert W. Bingham, "The History of Williamsville," *Niagara Frontier Miscellany* xxxv, (Buffalo Historical Society, 1947): pp. 100-101; Carolyn Shrauger, et al., *Williamsville New York: Where the Past is Present* (Village of Williamsville Historical Society, 1985): p. 14.

23. N.A., RG 94, Entry 407, Box 90, Hogan Vouchers.

24. N.A., RG 94, Entry 125, Box 134, Vouchers; Percy M. Ashburn, "American Army Hospitals of the Revolution and the War of 1812," *Bulletin of Johns Hopkins Hospital* 46 (1930), p. 32.

25. Percy M. Ashburn, *History of the Medical Department of the United States Army* (Boston: Houghton, Mifflin, 1929), pp. 33-34; Severance, *ibid.*, p. 247; Another burying ground was identified at Park Meadow, near Scott's old Flint Hill encampment (RG 98, Entry 407, Box 88).

26. See Annex K; N.A., RG 94, Entry 125, Box 134; N.A., RG 94, Entry 225, Box 651, Medical Department, Francis LeBaron letter 14 November 1814 to Callendar Irvine.

27. Klink and Talman, *ibid.*, p. 360; George Phillpotts Diary, Public Records Office, London, War Office 55, Vol 860: 135-144, (Hereafter Phillpotts Diary).

28. Phillpotts Diary, *ibid.*

29. LC, MS Div, Papers of Jacob Brown, Letter E. P. Gaines to John Armstrong 20 July; Allen Johnson, ed., *Dictionary of American Biography*

11 vols. (New York: Charles Scribner's Sons, 1927-64), IV: 92-93, Gaines remained in the Army after the war, a contentious individualist and bitter enemy of Winfield Scott. He died at New Orleans in 1849.

30. Klink and Talman, *ibid.*, p. 361; Societe Jersial, Jersey, *Journal of Lt. John Le Couteur 104th Regt.*, (Hereafter LeCouteur); Phillpotts Diary; Celwyn E. Hampton, *The Twenty First's Trophy of Niagara* (Ft. Logan: 1909), p. 81; Cruikshank, *DH ibid.*, II: 109, 122-3; 134-5; Louis L. Babcock, *The Siege of Fort Erie, An Episode of the War of 1812* (Buffalo: Peter Paul Book Co., 1890), pp. 30-31.

31. Babcock, *ibid.*, p. 31; William Dunlop, *Tiger Dunlop's Upper Canada...* (Toronto: McClelland and Stewart, 1907), pp. 64, 66.

32. Theodore Roosevelt, *The Naval War of 1812* (Annapolis, MD: Naval Institute Press, 1987, repr. 1882 ed.), pp. 336-337; John K. Mahon, *The War of 1812* (Gainesville: University of Florida Press, 1972), p. 177.

33. Ernest Cruikshank, "The Siege of Fort Erie, August 1st-September 23d 1814," *Lundy's Lane Historical Society Publications* (Welland: Tribune Office 1905), p. 8; Carl Guelzo, "Fort Erie: High Point of a Low War," *Military Review, 38, No. 10, (January 1959): 9;* J. Mackay Hitsman, *The Incredible War of 1812: A Military History* (Toronto: University of Toronto Press, 1965), p. 200. The ships on station off the mouth of the Niagara were *Jefferson, Sylph*, and *Oneida*.

34 NAC, RG 8 I, vol 685: 83, Arrangement for the Attack on Fort Erie, 14 August 1814.

35 NAC, *ibid.*, p. 90, Instructions to Lieutenant Colonel Fischer, Commanding Right Column....

36. N.A., RG 94, Entry 407, Box 144, Ration Vouchers, 15 August 1814; Cruikshank, *DH, ibid.*, II: 432.

37. L.L. Babcock, "The Siege of Fort Erie," *Proceedings of the New York State Historical Association* VII (1909): 34,42.

38. Cruikshank, *DH ibid.*, p. 157, Letter 17 August to E. Gaines; G.W. Cullum, ed., *Campaigns of the War of 1812* (New York: James Miller, Publ., 1879), pp. 130-131.

Chapter 5

1. Phillpotts Diary, *ibid.*; Cruikshank, *DH ibid.*, I: 152, Letter Gaines to Armstrong, 23 August 1814.

2. Eleazer W. Ripley, *Facts Relative to the Campaign on the Niagara in 1814* (Boston: Patriot Office, 1815), pp. 40-41.

3 NAC, Ms Gp 24, L 8, Jacques Viger Papers, Letters of Joseph D. Mermet, Adj. DeWatteville's; John D. Martin, "The Regiment DeWatteville:

Its Settlement and Services in Upper Canada," *Ontario Historical Society papers and Records*, LXII (1960), p. 22.

4. NAC, Ms Gp 24, L 8, *ibid.*; John D. Martin, *ibid.*, p. 23; Cruikshank, *DH ibid.*, p. 157; James L. Babcock, ed., "Campaign of 1814 on the Niagara Frontier," *Niagara Frontier* 10, No. 4 (1963): 168, 171.

5. NAC, RG 8 I, Vol. 685, p. 86, Fischer to Harvey, 15 August 1814; Benjamin Ropes, "Benjamin Ropes' Autobiography," *Essex Institute Historical Collections, 91* (January 1955): 123; John Brannan, ed., *Official Letters of the Military and Naval Officers of the U.S. During the War With Great Britain* (Washington, 1823), pp. 399-400, Gaines to Armstrong, 26 August 1814.

6. [David B. Douglas], "An Original Narrative of the Niagara Campaign of 1814," ed. by John T. Horton, *Niagara Frontier II*, No. I (1964): p. 27, "Go back to your post you infamous cowardly poltroons! Go back this instant or we'll fire on you"; Ripley, *ibid.*, p. 41.

7. Cruikshank, Siege... *ibid.*, p. 156; N.A., RG 94, Entry 407, QM Accounts and Returns, Box 144 passim.

8. "Assault on Fort Erie, or, Two Ways of Telling a Story," *Littells Museum of Foreign Literature*, 43 (1834): p. 431.

9. Cruikshank, Siege..., *ibid.*, p. 157; Benson J. Lossing, *Pictorial Field Book of the War of 1812* (New York: Harper, 1869), p. 834.

10. Douglass, *ibid.*, p. 29. 11. Brannan, *ibid.*, p. 399, (quote); Carl F. Klink and James J. Talman, eds., *The Journal of Major John Norton, 1816* (Toronto: Champlain Society, 1970), p. 362; N.A., RG 94, Entry 53, Bombardiers Muster Roll, May-August 1814, Private Michael Carroll of the U.S. engineers was killed by falling debris from the explosion.

12. L.L. Babcock, "The Siege of Fort Erie," *Proceedings of the New York State Historical Society* VII (1909): 44; Cruikshank, *DH ibid.*, II: 164; NAC, RG 8 I, Vol. 685, p. 101, Drummond to Prevost, 16 August 1814.

13. LC, Amasa Troubridge Papers; N.A., RG 94, Entry 407, Box 93, Hogan Voucher File.

14. Troubridge, *ibid.*; Douglass, *ibid.*, p. 29; Cruikshank, *DH ibid.*, II: 109, N.N. Hall, AIG Report 15 Aug 1814,; L.L. Babcock, *ibid.*, p. 44.

15. Lossing, *ibid.*, p. 846.

16. Cruikshank, *DH ibid.*, II: 435, *Buffalo Gazette* 16 Aug 1814.

17. N.A., RG 94, Entry 407, Box 93, Hogan Voucher File; Box 90, John G. Camp, Pay Vouchers to Mary Anna Cole 1 Sep-1 Dec 1814; Box 13, Contractor's Accounts-William D. Cheever; Article 95, Army Regulations 1813.

18. N.A., RG 94, Entry 407, Box 13, Cheever, *ibid.*; Entry 53, Box 124, Paymaster P. L. Hogeboom, case of Pvt. William Duffy.

19. N.A., RG 94, Entry 407, Box 93, Militia Hospital-Hogan Voucher

Files; Allen J. Ferguson, "Militia Medicine in New York, 1812," *Military Collector and Historian* 35, No. 4 (1983): 167.

20. NAC, RG 8 I, Vol 685: 123, Drummond to Prevost, 21 August 1814; Cruikshank, *DH ibid.*, I: 180; William Dunlop, *Recollections of the War of 1812* (Toronto: Historical Publ. Co., 1908), pp. 58-59.

21. PRO, Phillpotts Diary; William Dunlop, *ibid.*, p. 67.

22. PRO, Phillpotts Diary; NAC, RG 8 I Vol. 685: 123, Drummond to Prevost, 30 August 1814.

23. PRO, Phillpotts Diary; NAC, RG 8 I, Vol. 685: 104, Drummond to Prevost, 2 September 1814.

24. Lossing, *ibid.*, p. 836; Louis Babcock, *ibid.*, p. 57.

Chapter 6

1. Cruikshank, *DH ibid.*, II: 103-104, Jacob Brown Letter to Gov. Tompkins 1 Aug 1814; II: 438-439, *Buffalo Gazette* 30 Aug 1814; II: 447, P.B. Porter organizational order; Cruikshank, *DR, ibid.*, pp. 67-68.

2. N.A., RG 94, Entry 407, Box 89, Hogan-receipts; RG 94, Entry 19, Daniel D. Tompkins Letters 21 Aug, 3 Sept. & 20 Sept. to Col. Yates; RG 156, Entry 3, Box 4, Letters Received.

3. NA, RG 94, Entry 407, Box 93, LCol. Wm. MacRee order 7 Sept. 1814 to Maj. Hogan; RG 156, Entry 3, Ord. Dept. Letterbook No. 2, 1814-15, Letter Decius Wadsworth 21 July 1814 to Capt. James Dalliba.

4. N.A., RG 94, Entry 407, Box 16, Contractor's Accounts-William D. Cheever; Box 52, Hogan Contracts.

5. NA, RG 98, Vol. 406/290, IG Order, Letter Book; NA, RG 92, Entry 225, Jacob Brown Letter to Callender Irvine 2 Nov 1814.

6. NAC, RG 8 I, Vol. 685: 179, Drummond to Prevost, 8 September 1814; John K. Mahon, *The War of 1812* (Gainesville: University of Florida Press, 1972), p. 282; Lloyd Graham, *Niagara Country* (New York: Duell, Sloan, and Pierce, 1949), p. 107; NAC, Ms Gp 24, L8, Jacques Viger, Viger Papers, Vols. 4 and 5, microf. M 8; Ernest Cruikshank, "The Siege of Fort Erie...," *Lundy's Lane Historical Society of Publications* (Welland: Tribune Office, 1905), p. 35.

7. John Brannan, ed., *Official Letters of the Military and Naval Officers of the U.S. During the War With Great Britain* (Washington: 1823), p. 400; Carl F. Klink and James J. Talman, eds., *The Journal of Major John Norton, 1816* (Toronto: The Champlain Society, 1970), p. 363.

8. Cruikshank, *DH* II: 194; II: 445; PRO, Phillpotts Diary, NAC, LeCouter, 4 September.

9. PRO, Phillpotts Diary; Cruikshank, *ibid.*, II: 195; Louis L. Babcock, *The Siege of Fort Erie, An Episode of the War of 1812* (Buffalo: Peter Paul Book Co., 1899), pp. 52-54.

10. NAC, RG 8 I, Vol. 685: 192, Drummond to Prevost, 11 Sept. 1814; RG 8 I, Vol. 685: 197, Drummond to Prevost, 14 Sept. 1814; PRO, Phillpotts Diary; NAC, Ms Gp 24, F 96 DeWatteville Papers.

11. C. Edward Skeen, *John Armstrong, Jr., 1758-1843. A Biography* (Syracuse: Syracuse University Press, 1981), pp. 182-185.

12. Cruikshank, *DH* II: 480, Jesup Narrative.

13. Benjamin Ropes, "Benjamin Ropes' Autobiography," *Essex Institute Historical Collections* 91 (January 1955): 120; Cruikshank, *DH ibid.*, II: 207, Brown letter to Governor Tompkins; II: 480, Jesup Narrative; N.A. RG 94, Entry 407, Box 90-Hogan; Louis L. Babcock, *ibid.*, p. 215.

14. N.A., RG 94, Entry 407, Box 90-Hogan; NAC, Ms Gp 24, F 96, DeWatteville Papers.

15. Cruikshank, *DH ibid.*, II: 198-199.

16. Cruikshank, *DH ibid.*, II: 482; Cruikshank, *DH ibid.*, p. 91; George W. Holley, "The Sortie From Fort Erie, *"The Magazine of American History* VI (1881): p. 407.

17. John Brannan, *ibid.*, p. 442, Brown to Secretary of War, 29 September 1814.

18. George W. Holley, *ibid.*, p. 408; Cruikshank, *DH ibid.*, p. 91.

19. John Brannan, *ibid.*, pp. 435-436, Porter's Report, 22 September 1814; pp. 441-442, Brown's Report, 29 September 1814.

20. Cruikshank, *DH ibid.*, p. 91; Cruikshank, *DH ibid.*, II: 215, Brown Letter to Secretary of War, 1 October 1814; II: 480, Jesup Narrative.

21. Cruikshank, *DH ibid.*, II: 482; *ibid.*, II: 215; John Brannan, *ibid.*, pp. 436-439, Porter's Report, 22 September 1814.

22. George W. Holley, *ibid.*, p. 410; Cruikshank, *ibid.*, II: 215; John Brannan, *ibid.*, pp. 442-445, Brown's Report, 29 September 1814.

23. LeCouteur *Journal*; Henry Hall, *The Story of Auburn* (Auburn: Dennis Brother's Co., 1869), pp. 114-115; Auburn, New York, *Cayuga Patriot* Vol. I, No. 5 (16 November 1814), p. 37; Elliot Starke, *History of Cayuga Co. New York* (Syracuse: D. Mason and Co., 1879), p. 143.

24. John Brannan, *ibid.*, p. 438, Porter's Report, 22 September 1814; William Dunlop, *Recollections of the War of 1812* Toronto: Historical Publ. Co., 1908), pp. 75-76.

25. John Brannan, *ibid.*, pp. 442-443, Brown's Report, 29 September 1814.

26. N.A., M 221, Brown Letter to Secretary of War, 10 October 1814;

Auburn, New York, *Cayuga Patriot* Vol. I No. 3 (2 Nov. 1814), p. 23; Vol. I, No. 26 (12 April 1815), p. 202; N.A., RG 94, Entry 407, Hogan Accounts.

Chapter 7

1. Societe Jersiase, John LeCouteur, *Journal*, 20 Sept. 1814; NAC RG 8 I, Vol. 685: 216, Drummond to Prevost, 19 Sept. 1814.

2. NAC RG 8 I, Vol. 685: 266; Drummond to Prevost, 21 Sept. 1814.

3. NAC, MG 24, F 96, DeWatteville Papers, *Journal*; Carl F. Klink and James J. Talman, eds., *The Journal of Major John Norton 1816* (Toronto: The Champlain Society), p. 365; LeCouteur, *Journal* 23 Sept. 1814; Benjamin Ropes, "Benjamin Ropes, A Biography," *Essex Institute Historical Collections* 91 (January 1955): 124 (quote); LeCouteur, *Journal* 23 Sept.

4. DeWatteville Papers, *Journal*; Klink and Talman, *ibid.*, p. 365; Cruikshank, *DH* II: 211, Drummond to Prevost, 24 Sept. 1814.

5. Ernest Cruikshank, "The Siege of Fort Erie...," *Lundy's Lane Historical Society Publications* (Welland: Tribune Office, 1905), p. 34; James L. Babcock, ed., "Campaign of 1814 on the Niagara Frontier,"*Niagara Frontier* 10, No. 4 (1963): 172, Letter Brown to Izard, 10 Sept. 1814.

6. Allen Johnson, ed. *Dictionary of American Biography* 11 vols. (New York: Charles Scribner's Sons, 1927-64); V: 523-524; N.A., M 222, Secretary of War Letters Received (LR), Izard to Armstrong, 19 July. Criticized for his Niagara performance, Izard resigned and lived the life of a scholar until appointed governor of Arkansas Territory in 1825. He died there in 1828.

7. N.A., M 222, LR, Izard to Armstrong, 20, 23 August 1814; C. Edward Skeen *John Armstrong, Jr., 1758-1843, A Biography* (Syracuse: Syracuse University Press, 1981), p. 186.

8. Allen S. Everest, *The War of 1812 in the Champlain Valley* (Syracuse: Syracuse University Press, 1981), pp. 158-159; Henry Adams, The War of 1812, H.A. DeWeerd, ed. (Washington: Infantry Journal, 1944), p. 212.

9. N.A., M 222, LR, Izard to Secretary of War, 9 Sept. 1814; Benson J. Lossing *Pictorial Field Book of the War of 1812* (New York: Harper, 1869), p. 844. Izards Division contained the 4th, 5th, 10th, 12th, 13th, 14th, 15th, 16th, and 45th infantry regiments.

10. Cruikshank, *DH* II: 233, Izard to Secretary of War, 28 Sept., 7 Oct. 1814.

11. LeCouteur, *Journal*, 6, 9 Oct. 1814.

12. Cruikshank, *DH* II: 254, Izard to Secretary of War, 16 Oct. 1814; N.A., RG 98, Entry 52, Box 144, Casualties 15 Oct.

13. LeCouteur, *Journal*, 15 Oct. 1814, (quote); DeWatteville Papers, Journal; J. Mackay Hitsman, *The Incredible War of 1812: A Military History* (Toronto: University of Toronto Press, 1965), p. 230.

14. Cruikshank, *DH*, p. 270, Bissell to Izard, 20 Oct. 1814; LeCouteur, *Journal* 20 Oct. 1814; John Brannan, *Official Letters of the Military and Naval Officers of the U.S. During the War With Great Britain* (Washington: 1823), pp. 450-451, C.K. Gardner, G.O., 23 Oct. 1814.

15. LeCouteur, *Journal* 19, 20 Oct.; Lewis Einstein, ed., "Recollections of the War by George Hay, Eighth Marquis of Tweeddale," *American Historical Review*, xxxii (1926-1927): p. 74; NAC, RG 8 I, 636: 34, Drummond to Prevost, 18 Oct. 1814.

16. Lewis Einstein, *ibid.*, p. 75; Brannan, *ibid.*, pp. 450-451, C.K. Gardner, G.O., 23 Oct. 1814.

17. Benjamin Ropes, *ibid.*, p. 125; N.A., RG 98, Entry 52, Box 144, Casualties 19 Oct., 1814.

18. Klink and Talman, *ibid.*, p. 366; NAC R 8 I, Vol. 686: 85, Drummond to Prevost, 23 Oct. 1814.

19. Cruikshank, *DH* II: 275, Izard to Secretary of War, 23 Oct. 1814.

20. N.A., M 222, Letters Received by Secretary of War Office (LR), Brown to Secretary of War, 31 Oct. 1814; NAC RG 8 I, Vol. 686: 85, Drummond to Prevost, 23 Oct. 1814.

21. Cruikshank, *DH* II: 458, *Boston Centinel*, quoting 25 Oct. letter; Auburn, New York, *Cayuga Patriot* (Vol. I, No. 6, 23 Nov. 1814): 46 (They would be paid the following Feb. and March *(Cayuga Patriot, March 1815: p. 143)*; N.A., M 221, LR, 15 Nov. 1814; Benjamin Ropes, *ibid.*, p. 125.

22. N.A., RG 98, Entry 40, Div. G.O., 19 Oct. 1814; N.A., RG 94, Entry 40, Box 134, Captain S.B. Archer statement 26 Oct. 1814; N.A., M 221, Jacob Brown Letters to Secretary of War (LS), 31 Oct., 15 Nov. 1814.

23. N.A., RG 94, *ibid.*; RG 98, Vol. 22/509, Northern Army, AGO, 3 Nov 1814.

24. Cruikshank, *DH* II: 282, Major Totten to General Izard, 1 November 1814; II: 286, Izard to Secretary of War, 2 November 1814; II: 290, Drummond to Prevost, 5 November 1814; II: 298, Izard to Secretary of War, 8 November, 1814.

25. Cruikshank, *DH* II: 298, *ibid.*; N.A., RG 94, Entry 125, Box 134-Contract, Captain James Dalliba; RG 94, Entry 407, Box 51, Camp Vouchers 51; Epstein, *ibid.*, p. 75; Lossing, *ibid.*, p. 845.

26. George H. Seibel, *The Niagara Portage Road: 200 Years, 1790-1990* (Niagara Falls, Ontario: City of Niagara Falls, 1990), p. 262; Robert D. Bradford, *Historic Forts of Ontario* (Belleville, Ontario: Mika Publ. Co., 1988), p. 50.

27. LC, Jesup Papers, Box 11.

INDEX

Alexander, Hugh 9, 33, 92
Armstrong, John x, 15–16, 17, 18, 48, 84, 85, 90
Army training, US 20–22

Bath, NY., National Cemetery 96
Bisshopp, Cecil 8, 10
Black Rock 3, 5, 7, 8, 9, 11, 47, 49, 53, 59, 86
Brock, Isaac 2, 5, 7
Brown, Jacob 2, 14, 15–16, 69 (sortie)
Buffalo, British burning of 11

Camp, John G. 23, 89
Canadian Volunteers 10, 34, 75–76
Chapin, Cyrenius 10, 11
Chauncey, Isaac 16–17, 34, 55, 85
Chippawa, Battle of xi, 2, 30–32
Cooks Mills (Lyon's Creek), Battle of 86–88

Declaration of War 5
DeWatteville, Louis 48, 76, 78, 83
Douglass, David B. 42, 48, 56, 61, 63, 65
Drummond, Gordon 10–11, wounded, 37

Elliot, Jesse D. 5, 6

Fenton, James 23
Fort Erie, origins 3
Fort George, US attack, 1813 2, 9
Fort Niagara 3, 5, 11, 18, 19, 33, 84, 85

Gaines, Edmund P. 16, 34, 54, 59, 62, 69

Hall, Amos 11, 25, 69
Hogan, John B. 48, 49, 50

Inspectors General, US 20, 21, 70–75, 79, 87

Izard, George 15, 84–85, 88, 90

Jesup, Thomas 20, 28, 31, 36, 77, 79, 92

Lundys Lane, Battle of xi, 2, 36–37

Madison, James x, 1, 17
McClure, George 10, 11
McDonough, Patrick 29, 42, 61
MacRee, William 28, 48, 56, 70, 78
Medical conditions 49, 50, 75
Medical staff 35, 37, 63, 64
Medical supplies 21, 64
Medical system 50–53, 62–63, 64, 89, 90
Military Districts x, 15
Militia x, 7, 25, 33, 64, 69–70, 77
Morgan, Lodowick 47, 54, 63

Navy, US 2, 16–17, 18, 33, 34, 55, 64, 75, 86, 91
Niagara area ix, x, 2, 3, 5, 10, 19
Norton, John 5, 8, 9, 30, 31–32, 33, 35, 41, 47, 54, 62, 81, 83, 84

Old Fort Erie, Historic Park xi, 96

Phillpotts, George 53, 65
Plattsburgh, Battle of 85
Port Dover 19
Port Talbot 19
Porter, Peter B. 8, 10, 25, 30, 31, 32, 34, 56, 64, 69, 77, 78–80, 89
Prevost, Sir George x, 11, 18, 83, 85

Queenston Heights, Battle of 2, 7

Rations 50, 70
Regiments, British Infantry
   1st (Royal Scots) 11, 18, 19, 29, 31, 32, 35, 80
   6th 11, 33, 65, 80

8th (Kings) 10, 19, 29, 30, 32, 34, 55, 60, 80, 83
41st 19, 35, 47, 48, 56, 61
42d 11
49th 7, 8
82d 11, 33, 64, 80, 87
89th 33, 35, 36, 42, 47, 55, 60, 64, 80
90th 11, 33
100th 19, 29, 31, 55, 60, 87
103d 19, 33, 35, 37, 55, 56, 61, 64
104th 33, 37, 47, 55, 56, 87
Dewatteville 48, 55, 60, 62, 80, 83
Glengarry 19, 34, 42, 75, 80, 81, 83, 87
Lincoln Militia 9, 10, 19, 33, 34, 55
Upper Canada Incorp. Militia 33
Regiments, US Infantry
   1st 79
   1st Rifles 17, 47, 54, 56
   4th Rifles 56, 60, 61, 79, 87
   5th 87
   5th PA Vol. 23–25, 27, 30, 31, 33, 56
   9th 9, 21, 22, 31, 35, 36, 37, 56, 79
   11th 21, 31, 32, 35, 36, 37, 56, 61, 79
   14th 87
   15th 8, 79
   16th 87
   17th 56, 61, 79, 86
   19th 56, 61, 79
   21st 27, 36, 56, 60, 75, 79, 81, 88
   22d 22, 31, 36, 56, 61
   23d 36, 37, 56, 60, 61, 64, 75, 79

25th 20, 21, 28, 31, 36, 77,
   79
Riall, Phineas 11, 19, 29, 30, 31,
   32, 34, 36, 52, 76
Ripley, Eleazer 22, 27–28, 36, 37,
   38, 42, 54, 59, 78–79, 81, 90

Sandytown 49, 52, 63
Scajaquada Creek 3, 5, 9, 10, 11,
   47 (battle), 52, 54
Scott, Winfield 7, 9, 16, 18, 20–22,
   23, 28, 31–32, 33, 36, 67, 50,
   52
Second War of Independence ix
Sheaffe, Roger H. 3, 7
Smyth, Alexander 7–8, 20, 22, 50
Snelling, Josiah 70–75
"Somers" and "Porcupine"
   incident 55
Supply system 34, 70
Swift, John 34

Tompkins, Daniel D. 25, 69
Towson, Nathan 5, 31, 42, 56, 60,
   86

Van Rensselaer, Stephen 5, 7

War of 1812, causes 1–2, influence
   of ix, 2
Washington, burning of ix, x
Watts, Thomas 5
Willcocks, Joseph 10, 75–76
Williamsville Hospital 50–52, 63
Winder, William 7–8, 89
Wood, Eleazer D. 28, 34, 56, 78–
   80